From the Petition to the Strike

American University Studies

Series IX
History

Vol. 67

PETER LANG
New York · San Francisco · Bern
Frankfurt am Main · Paris · London

Richard W. Reichard

From the Petition to the Strike

A History of Strikes in Germany, 1869-1914

PETER LANG
New York · San Francisco · Bern
Frankfurt am Main · Paris · London

Library of Congress Cataloging-in-Publication Data

Reichard, Richard W.
From the petition to the strike : a history of strikes in Germany, 1869-1914 / Richard W. Reichard.
p. cm. — (American university studies. Series IX, History ; vol. 67)
Includes bibliographical references and index.
1. Strikes and lockouts—Germany—History. 2. Trade-unions—Germany—History. 3. Labor movement—Germany—History. I. Title. II. Series.
HD5378.R45 1991 331.89'2943—dc20 90-46469
ISBN 0-8204-0905-7 CIP
ISSN 0740-0462

Printed in the United States of America.

CONTENTS

LIST OF ILLUSTRATIONS

1

WALDENBURG

In the 1860s the Prussian government undertook a partial modernization of its society and thus restraints were removed from the mining industry. The matter was of consequence, for Germany possessed some of the world's largest known coal deposits, and coal was to be the chief source of energy for the coming industrial era. As usual, other German states followed Prussia in economic matters.

Prussian inspectors who once had had more influence on conditions in the mines than did the owners now fell to a position of inconsequence. Emphasis was shifted to production. Pay may have gone up, but shifts were extended beyond the traditional 8 hours, and safety rules were relaxed. Men coming from the East could go straight to work without training. A quarter of the miners in Essen protested the new situation in a statement to the King of Prussia,[1] but their views were brushed aside. That was in 1867 and the following year owner Gustav Stinnes announced a prolongation of the working day at two Ruhr pits.[2] His management would not meet with a miners' delegation and so on September 14, without announcing a strike (which would have been illegal), the men commenced staying at home. Their goal was the traditional 8 hour shift, counted from mine entrance to exit. Upset by the scandal of having a *de facto* strike in their locality, authorities put pressure on the Stinnes family who, after a 9 day walkout, granted an 8¼ hour day. Some of the leaders of the outbreak were fined, and some jailed.

Waldenburg (now Walbrzych) lies 30 miles south of the old Breslau in the heart of Central Europe. The town partook of a Silesian standard of living, notoriously below the national in economic terms and in culture. In parts of the province mothers lost up to 70 percent of their infants,[3] and there is probably no more telling index of social backwardness. Miners' shifts were longer than elsewhere and pay was lower. Both on and off the job, there was more violence.

There were Silesian traditions of resistance. When Waldenburg miners had lost their free Saturday afternoons in 1853, they had at first refused to return to the pits. In the 1860s they had launched their own *Kassen*. Then what tinder lay in the area in 1869 was lit by Dr. Hirsch, a Berlin liberal who was no partisan of the class struggle, but rather a politician seeking support among workingmen.[4] Hirsch and his friends had just been dropped by the Bebel-Liebknecht wing of social democracy, and his Silesian campaign was partly an effort to recover a position all but lost elsewhere. Hirsch had been impressed by the "friendly societies" of English workingmen;[5] they offered more benefits than the *Kassen*. Further, he believed in arbitration of labor disputes, for he held that this method would give the men more control over their own lives, while tending to restrain them from strikes. Some of his ideas were to give birth to the minuscule liberal Hirsch-Duncker unions. However, the irony of history was to bring it about that this conciliator would provoke an epic class struggle, while doctrinaire believers in such struggles were not allowed to command a platform!

On July 10, 1869, under the sky, Hirsch addressed several thousand miners.[6] That such an open gathering, forbidden since 1848, should take place, testified to the extent of local support for the men. They in turn must have been impressed that a man with an academic title, who appeared to be the captain of a great party, should repair to their obscure corner of the land. Under his inspiration they formed a *Gewerkverein* (Works Association), which was to provide them with protection from illness, death and invalidism.[7] With or without Hirsch's approval a provision, for strike benefits was added to the constitution, though it was said that strikes could only take place when sufficient funds were on hand. This new *Gewerkverein* was to mean much to the miners; hundreds of them were to sacrifice both home and livelihood in its defense.

The miners proceeded to frame demands on their employers, in first place recognition of their *Gewerkverein*. Second, they asked for humane handling. A management spokesman who wrote a history of the affair, and who was so conservative that he believed paying by the hour instead of by weight was communist, admitted that two foremen beat miners.[8] If this was the unusual admission, then there were probably many more such cases. Further, the miners wanted the two automatic demands of all strikers: increased pay and shorter hours, in this instance the 8 hour day. (The machinists' union, destined to become the Empire's largest, stated simply in the first issue of its weekly, published in 1883, that what the members wanted was more money and shorter hours.)[9] In fact, workingmen have not ordinarily, like Aristotle, occupied themselves with the nature of the state, nor like St. Thomas and Luther with the place of the earthly king in the divine order. The social contract, whether according to Hobbes, Locke or Rousseau, is a mystery to them. The ideas of Marx and of Bebel might inspire German workingmen to dream of a better society, but not as early as the 1860s, nor in this benighted piece of Central Europe. A laboring man's existence is that of a poorly paid drudge, not very well nourished, insufficiently housed and without modern medical care. The schools he has attended, the quarter of town in which he resides, and the experiences he has on the job all conspire to teach him that he is forever confined to a lowly position, where political philosophy is superfluous. What he believes in therefore is simple: wages and hours.

The twin demands had different significance in different industries. First as to coal wages: in early industrial society about 80 percent of the force went down below, a percentage that was to decline as products other than coal began to be produced. Those under ground were very appropriately described as being *unter Tage,* i.e., under the day. The minority hauled up the black diamond from below, washed it and sorted it, or were "pen miners" in the office. *Unter Tage* mostly were *Hauer* or hackers, who cut the coal from the seams after dynamiting. *Schlepper* were those who dragged the stuff through the long, low tunnels, with their uncertain footing and their uneven ceilings, to the lift. (Pit-horses helped somewhat.) Everyone toiled bent over, in cramped spaces, with poor light, and often lying on their backs. A small number saw to the bracing of the galleries. For each 80-100 men underground there was a *Steiger* or overseer, who assigned places, checked progress, fixed individual rates and generally supervised. No other personnel were underground. When the men went *unter Tage,* they had to wrestle with death without either medical or sanitation aid.

Hauer and *Schlepper* normally worked in gangs of 4. Among them hackers were best rewarded, and draggers received about a quarter less. Apprentices could advance rapidly after a very slow start. In this study emphasis will be upon the long term swings in pay, for these movements, rather than the levels of pay, are what tended to bring on the great clashes of man and master.

As a general rule, the further east one went from the Ruhr, the less the owners paid. (The rule functioned even beyond the borders of Germany.) Thus at this time Ruhr coalies were more prosperous than all others save miners in the state-owned Saar establishments. Silesian wages usually came to about 70 percent of those in the west, but living was cheaper in the east, which lacked the Rhineland's expensive urban allures. Silesian diggers who wanted to better themselves moved to the Ruhr. In 1869 Waldenburgers were making about two *thalers* a day. Management claimed that wages had risen by a third or more during the previous decade and this may have been true.[10] However, unrest in the coal fields could as well be the product of a large spread between the men's pay and the price of the ton, as of that price itself.

How many hours men should toil, away from the sun, in desperate conditions amid danger to their lives is a question that yet awaits an answer. In nineteenth century Germany few attempted to think it through since it was only by the sacrifice of thousands of overworked miners' lives that German industrial success was to be achieved. Save in the mine fields, hours of labor were everywhere in decline, and continued to be so for decades. Yet when the coal mine owners wished to extend the day in the belief that it would bring greater production, no law, no economic force, no association of men and no principle of human behavior existed to prevent the prolongation of the day *unter Tage.* Statisticians may have known that the long day was not productive, but acting as if it was convenient to the ideas of management and in accord with ideas of Prussian discipline. Silesian mine owners in particular appear to have had an affection for the 12 hour day. They preserved it into the twentieth century.[11]

An individual who served a mine half the day could do naught the other half but walk to the pit, eat and sleep. With luck he could raise a stein or two on Saturday or Sunday. Yet worse was the double grind. The twenty-4 hour shift would be announced in the morning, when no one could turn back. Young men liked the challenge of the extra hours and the money it brought. Family men, whose dependents were not told when their men would be gone 24 hours and who always feared injury and death, knew the double shift ate up life's energy.

The Waldenburgers' fight for the 8 hour day was a cause quite in the spirit of the 1860s, in company with Lasalle's cooperatives, Marx's internationalism and the publication of *Capital*. Historians of French strikes find a coincidence between major outbreaks and political crises;[12] in Germany there was no crisis, though there was some rebelliousness showing in the working class. The Silesian miners were too innocent to take advantage of the current atmosphere and, worse, had not correctly judged the determination of their opponents. The men did have one immense psychological advantage, for the Reichstag had just a few months before made strikes semi-legal. When this fact was put together with the appearance of Dr. Hirsch, these thousands, utterly unacquainted with the realities of politics, may well have imagined that a substantial part of German public opinion would rally to their cause.

If it took the miners time to screw up their courage, such was not the case with the owners. Their role in life was to give orders, and they reacted instinctively against giving up any of their powers. They saw themselves as *Arbeitgeber,* i.e., providers of labor, a term found ubiquitously in propertied class literature and occasionally slipping into social democratic journalism as well. The term *Arbeitgeber* made workingmen into mere recipients of generosity.

Though they were quite conscious of their own authority, the Waldenburg mine owners understood that they had to address some words to what political public existed. In their declaration they regretted that the legislature had recently permitted strikes;[13] they hoped that that decision would be reversed. They warned against the union, whose only purpose could be promoting social disruption. There was no need for a strike, they alleged, for they paid excellent wages and the miners received free coal, as well as tuition payments for elementary schooling for their children. The owners avoided answering the most serious charge against them, that of excessive hours.[14]

In private the *Arbeitgeber* saw to the punishment of those who opposed them. Miners who spoke publicly were identified, as were those who signed published letters; all these were declared to be *Rädelsführer,* or ringleaders. All of them were dismissed. Strikers were ordered to vacate their homes on January 1. The right to a secure home was much treasured in Germany, and no action of the owners was as much criticized as this.[15] Yet they gained the cooperation of their colleagues, and no man released at Waldenburg could expect to be taken on elsewhere as long as the conflict persisted.

With their leaders fired, and with mid-winter evictions hanging over their heads, the miners made one last appeal. Their document was unique in German history, for laboring men were speaking from their hearts before either union, or social democratic ideology, had penetrated their minds. After noting their bosses' failure to respond to them directly, they protested their fundamental innocence:

> We have already for a long time through both word and deed shown that our efforts have *nothing to do with demagogic agitation and empty opposition* against existing [social] relationships. Rather our earnest desire is for a *just compromise and for a reconciliation* which will be satisfying to both parties. We hope very much that the following requests will not go unregarded.[16]

Implicit in these words was the Silesians' complete acceptance of their lowly position. Like the proverbial Russian peasant with his faith in the goodwill of the Tsar, the miners went on to suggest that their superiors might not know how badly they were treated. But if their hours were cut, and their pay increased, they would then be able to demonstrate their real loyalty. "We pledge ourselves to continue to serve our *Arbeitgeber* with all our strength as true and honest laborers, thereby showing ourselves worthy of our *Gewerkverein.*" (By mid-November the companies were saying that peace could not come until the *Gewerkverein* was dissolved.)

Economics out of the way, the miners candidly unburdened themselves. They were almost embarrassed by their rebellion:

> It is a most painful feeling for us when, in the present strained situation, we have to go about our daily labors while being looked upon by many as rebels and agitators.[17]

Such consciousness of the inferior moral position of striking men was probably characteristic of most who rebelled against their bosses in this century, but the sentiment was rarely expressed. However that consciousness did bring it about that the annual total of Germans who had the temerity to walk off their jobs was far below the comparable figure in even such lightly industrialized lands as

Italy and Austria.[18]

Neither this supplicating letter, which surely falls under the heading of a petition, nor Hirsch's efforts at compromise (the owners would not see him) achieved the slightest progress. The miners had either to strike or submit. Being men of determination, they commenced staying away from the pits on December 1. The younger were urged to go elsewhere. A delegation was sent to Prussian King Wilhelm I. Meanwhile 1,000 continued to work. Hirsch's Progressives, in their season of national collapse, did their bit to help. The party collected 26,000 thalers, about the equivalent of pay for two shifts. Here was tangible support from the upper classes. The Breslau unit publicly sided with the strikers. The Progressives' Berlin paper *Zukunft* was wary, however, of giving the strike too much attention.[19]

The newborn Bebel-Liebknecht wing of social democracy, the Eisenachers, also offered assistance. Silesia was next to their home base in Saxony, and they were anxious to penetrate Prussia. But the Waldenburgers were traditionalists. They had been told that the social democrats were irreligious (only partly true) and that they had joined the First International. And for such reasons they would not hear the alleged rabble rouser August Bebel, already one of the major orators of the land. Undaunted, Liebknecht's *Volksstaat,* with more than the usual social democratic enthusiasm for walkouts, proclaimed the justice of the struggle.[20] A collection was begun, but the money raising powers of the journal were not very great.

Lacking money, the miners were thrown back upon their own resources. Here they excelled. They not only cut back sharply on expenses, as was the way with strikers in other lands, they contracted debts which, ordinarily, German proletarians did not do. Their leaders had scrip printed as a substitute for non-existent money, and some local merchants accepted it. Yet altogether it was hard to hold out, and by the end of December a further 1,000 had gone back.

State and local officials sided with the owners, and the nearby border with Austria-Hungary, across which there might have been temporary jobs, was closed to strikers. The meetings of the *Gewerkverein* were at first harassed and then outright blocked. Pickets were arrested, as was allowed under the new strike legislation. The delegation to the Prussian king returned empty-handed after an interview with the Crown Prince.

To keep going the strikers had to reduce what they ate. There was probably more fasting here than in any other major walkout. During the First World War fat-loving Germans were to have their daily ration cut to 1200 calories; Waldenburgers probably reached that level in their first fight for the *Gewerkverein* and the 8 hour day.

Early in January 1870, there was talk of a break, probably induced among the men by a growing sense of helplessness. But the owners were never for a moment inclined to yield, and every day they had less reason than before to do so, for more men than ever were returning to work. The *Gewerkverein* was by now out of funds, and the miners could find no alternative labor. By mid-January half of them were back in the pits. Others had already discovered that they were not to be rehired. Uncertainty over rehiring drove yet more men back.

In the second half of the month the defeat became a rout. *Gewerkverein* chiefs, all of whom had lost their jobs, finally called it off. This had been the largest walkout in national history, with more than 150,000 labor days lost, and it had ended in capitulation. Almost 1,100 men were denied further employment in Silesia, the greatest number blacklisted in any strike down to 1914.[21] Despite the miners' humble posture, this had been a class struggle, especially because of its length. The owners preferred both the longer hours and the sense of complete control. The men cherished the easier and healthier 8 hour day and a bit of sense of independence. The stronger had prevailed.

The protracted battle in Waldenburg had long term effects on Silesia. Miners' pay set the standard for other trades. When the miners' effort was broken, the wages and conditions of hundreds of thousands of other Silesian proletarians were condemned to remain substantially below what they might otherwise have been. Such was the case even though many Silesian pits were more productive than those in the Ruhr[22] and benefitted as well from the cheap rail rates which the state granted coal. Silesia was to remain the home of the 10-12 hour day *unter Tage,* with its early invalidism and shortened life. Unions got no foothold, and the Hirsch-Dunckers remained statistically trivial. Strikes might now be legal in Germany, but they could still be crushed, with effects lasting over a generation.

It was only two years before German miners let themselves be heard from again, this time in the Ruhr. This celebrated valley, hardly a thousand square miles, and soon to be the premier coal producing region of the continent, was, in the 1870s, about halfway from its pastoral heritage to it smog-laden metropolitan future. Money was at hand for exploitation of the coal veins. The amount invested between 1870 and 1874 was more than two times as much as all the capital which had been brought into play in all Ruhr history, as well as almost double what was to be invested in the depression which soon followed.[23] The Second Reich was not a poor land, men had only been awaiting opportunities, and one of the most important was in that coal which heated the cities and fueled the new industries.

As a commodity coal has a very peculiar nature, for it is not greatly subject to loss. Tomatoes and oranges rot, and moths eat wool. Wheat often does not reach the silo, shrinks enroute to the market, and at all times is eaten by rats. Cloth is woven, then goes out of fashion. So also automobiles. No similar hazards attend the black diamond in its passage from seam to furnace. Proletarian children were sent to steal it at yards, and off railway cars, but they hardly took a substantial amount.[24] Essentially a ton mined was a ton for sale. Coal was even cheap to store, and could be kept in out of the way places without the slightest cover. Prussian railroads transported it at specially low rates.[25] The indestructible character of coal was to be of great advantage to mine owners in their future battles with the miners.

However, the near permanent character of coal provided aid to miners as well. For coal lent itself to simple mathematics. Each man knew, of course, what his gang was getting for a ton. The price of the ton related to the hope of increased pay. Likewise he was aware of the publicly quoted price for the ton, for that figure was posted everywhere in the Ruhr and, having much to do with everybody's well-being, was well-remembered. In this work the difference between the advertised price of coal, and what the miners received for it, is called the "spread." From it must be subtracted the costs of loading and washing, and those of the office. The rest of the "spread" belonged to the owners, and could be distributed as dividends, or turned into capital. For the men the difference between coal and other industries lay in the ease with which the "spread" could be calculated, and the familiarity which everyone in the mines had toward it.[26]

The matter is illustrated by the history of Ruhr mining. 1867 was a bad year, and no one would have gone out on a strike, had it been legal. In 1871, however, the price of the black diamond began to rise very smartly. Everyone who went *unter Tage* knew that the spread had widened, and the men grew restive. They would labor with at least some contentment when their share in the declared price was around 50 percent, but when their share sank into the forties, they began to bestir themselves.[27] None of them had learned about wages and profits from Marx's *Capital,* in fact it may be doubted whether a single coalie read *Capital* through before 1914. When social democrats came, belatedly, to the Ruhr, they did not teach the doctrine of surplus value. But in the late 1860s the miners were beginning to discuss serious money matters among themselves, and the work below gave them more freedom of discussion than other laboring men had. An experienced hand could explain the "spread" to a novice from the East in 10 minutes. By contrast, in the traditional social democratic trades, it would take an economist to calculate how much a master painter, plumber or carpenter was making from the labor of his men.

Coal prices rose in the 1850s, then crashed with the economy in 1857.[28] In the next decade production grew to 10,000,000 tons, while the price ranged between 5-7 marks per ton. Then the market firmed and in 1870 the price began to rise. There followed three years of almost unbelievable prosperity for German business, not to be equalled until the 1950s. In 1871 the black diamond rose to 9, and reached 11.50 the following year. Coal was to top out at 15 marks in 1873, a level not to be reached again in peacetime.

In his miners' history Hue maintained that while coal prices were going up 40 percent between 1870 and 1872, pay increased by only about 20 percent.[29] The Catholic union leader Imbusch had wages moving from 2.75 a shift in 1870 to 4 marks in 1872.[30] These figures are averages, for pay varied from pit to pit, and from one district to another, the veins being varied in quality and the attitudes of management not all in harmony with each other. Further, in the hectic early 1870s, the price of coal might change every day. But the figures of Hue and Imbusch are similar to those in Bry's recent academic study.[31] In sum, in the months before the crash of 1873, the percentage of final sales price which the men were receiving was sinking toward a third, while the companies were making extraordinary (and an-nounced) profits. A strike lurked behind this situation.

Next to the spread, no circumstance was as important to Ruhr working class life as that two antagonistic cultures, with little record of cooperation, competed in the valley.[32] Catholics tended to predominate in the west and were based on Essen, while Protestants, many of whom had abandoned religion, lived in the east, with Dortmund as their chief center of strength. The unification of Germany by Bismarck had had a Protestant coloration, with Catholics deprived of their traditional supports: Austria, France and an independent Bavaria. They recognized that dominating positions in the political and economic life of the new state would likely fall to Protestants. They were more on the defensive than ever. At some of the Ruhr miner rallies the familiar patriotic "I am a Prussian," was defiantly sung as "I am a Catholic."

In May, 1872 the coalies began their meetings, sometimes in the open, and sometimes through representatives.[33] In these years a few tens of thousands of German workers were organized in unions, but almost none of these were miners. The men of the Catholic Ruhr settled on demanding a 25 percent raise, which was more than in any subsequent walkout. But in 1872 money seemed to be growing on bushes. Like the Waldenburgers, they wanted the 8 hour day from portal to portal. The issue of penalty for partially loaded carts was broached, but not pressed. Those in charge had learned from the firings at the Stinnes pits, and sent the list of demands anonymously.

In what became the usual way, the owners refused to talk. They preferred absolute control, and while they had but minimal organization among themselves, they could count on support from the Berlin government. When in mid-June the men learned that they could expect nothing from the companies, those in Essen left the pits. On Monday, June 17, more than 12,000 were out. Three matters were to determine the outcome of this strike. First, the miners were formidable only if united. Recognizing this, Essen sent emissaries to the rest of the Ruhr.[34] The response from the east was to go out for a shift or two, as if to sample the situation, before returning, with the *Steiger's* blessing. The notion of a strike was, after all, recent to the area, and hostility between Catholic and non-Catholic greater in the 1870s than before. Thus Protestants had reason to show where they stood, yet leave Blacks in the lurch.

Second, the strike turned upon what support there would be from the supportive minority of Catholics. Lasalle had once sought aid from Bishop Ketteler of Mainz, one of the forerunners of socially conscious Pope Leo XIII. Already in the Ruhr there was talk of a Catholic miners' union. Thus if Essen miners felt they were rebelling against one set of authorities, they had at least partial support from others. Most of this support, however, was moral in nature, and the miners' committee received only 900 marks in donations,[35] hardly enough to care for medical emergencies during the outbreak.

Nor was there substantial aid from the small workingmen's groups. The Saxon social democrats looked the other way, and the 1870 convention of the Bebel-Liebknecht wing had come down hard on strikes.[36] More consequential, since they were Prussians, was the failure of the Lassalleans to offer assistance. In 1872 their pro-strike President, Schweitzer, had just resigned.[37] When it became clear that the Esseners were going out, the association's *Neuer Social Demokrat* carried its first 1872 leader on strikes. It made the point that walkouts can often be avoided,[38] a prudent view likely to appeal to many of the skilled workers in small shops who favored social democracy.[39] It was not until the struggle had extended well into July that *Neuer Social Demokrat* printed a fund appeal. This was accompanied by comments from Hasenclever, Schweitzer's successor and a man who never strayed from established party doctrine:

> In general the Essen miners appear to be well organized. It is not possible to support such a large number through collections. However the time is favorable, for the miners can tend to their fields, or help with crops and thus have income. Furthermore, the need for coal will soon bring the mining companies...severe losses.[40]

Things were harder for the miners than the complacent and condescending Hasenclever believed. For while they were divided there was no hint that the owners were. Their spokesman, Dr. Friedrich Hammacher, declared that the men were already well paid, and denounced them for being under the influence of social democrats, and for being "unGerman," the latter being a contemporary way of referring to Catholics.

In mid-July, when they had been out for a month, the 12,000 began drifting back, and on July 29 the walkout was called off. The miners absorbed some loss of jobs, but the judicial system treated them mildly. About 300,000 workdays had been lost, making this the largest conflict yet. Once they were back they achieved some of the same gains which they had sought through the walkout. Imbusch claimed that wages reached 5 marks in 1873, which would have been the high point for the century. Pay might well have risen without a strike, but probably not by as much. Then also the action of the Esseners prompted their colleagues in the Ruhr to be more active promoters of unions.

Waldenburg had been too small and too remote to contribute to the building of a national union tradition. Not so the "Jesuit" strike of 1872, which took place in the heart of the country's industrial region. Miners of the future were able to build upon the memory of what had been done in 1872 by 12,000.

Between poor years for the economy and the moderately repressive atmosphere sponsored by Bismarck, the 1870s were a discouraging time both for unions and strikes. Bismarck's Exceptional Law of 1878, passed in response to two alleged attempts on the emperor's life, added very greatly to the usual hostile atmosphere in which strikes took place. When it was passed in 1878, the 50,000 workers who belonged to unions found their organizations dissolved, and they were never to recover their funds. That this year and the next were the very worst of the 12 year depression did not help. Steglich, a historian who has tabulated the walkouts of this period, lists the following strikes for 1879:

> Porcelain workers of Schmiedefeld/Suhl
> Horse trolley drivers of Kassel
> Droshky operators of Stettin.[41]

These were hardly rebellions to shake the nation's security. They may have been strikes of but an hour's duration.

One collision of the period 1878-1889, coming in the coal fields, is worth a word because of its type. In 1883, a year when workingmen had some inclination to militancy as a result of prosperity, the management of the *Germania* pit announced just before a noon shift came on that the workday was to be lengthened by an hour. For the men the loss of 6 hours of their meager weekly store of disposable time was most serious. The usual delegation of three was chosen at once, and the men refused to go down until the threat of the increased hours was removed. While the trio were conferring with management, gendarmes appeared. One of them, Hussmann, had a bad name; he began by pointing a sword at the crowd. The miners were enraged by Hussmann's conduct and fell back on the centuries old revenge of the poor and distressed. They attacked a mine building and a manager's home. There was much damage to property and none to human beings. The company sent for more police, and those miners not clever enough to run were presently sent to jail. The company found it wise to say that the extra hour would be postponed for some months. By then the *Rädelsführer* would be in prison, the discontented would have changed pits, and the rest would acquiesce.

In the 1880s, when German-based social democratic publications could not appear, the party showed hostility to actions like that at *Germania*. A "worker" - thus not a miner - sent a report on that strike action to the party's *Sozialdemokrat,* published in Zurich. He summarized his account with the familiar party query: "Will they ever learn to organize?"[42] That same summer 200 Stuttgart carpenters walked off their jobs. The scale of this walkout, the skilled occupation involved and the men's quiet conduct all appealed to social democratic tastes. Clearly this one would not get out of hand. *Sozialdemokrat* requested donations for the carpenters and warned journeymen from the city.[43]

Of 32 arrested at *Germania,* 17 were imprisoned, the longest sentence being 9 months. Historians have long theorized that the hanging of Lenin's brother turned his sibling into a revolutionary. German patriarchal justice, however, instinctively shied from creating martyrs. The miners received only small punishments for their riot. The court did not intend favoritism thereby. That was reserved for men from the propertied classes. *Germania's* director had denied under oath that he supplied the names of rowdy hands to other mines. When a copy of his black list nevertheless surfaced, he was not indicted for perjury. That failure of justice was long remembered in the Ruhr, for *Germania* was the major incident of the 1880s in the valley.

* * * * *

In the 1930s George Orwell went *unter Tage* and sampled conditions which were not much different from those in the Ruhr in the nineteenth century. Here is his description of the trip from cable car to pitface and back:

> At the start to walk stooping is rather a joke, but it is a joke that soon wears off...when the roof falls to four feet or less it is a tough job for anyone except a dwarf or a child. You have not only got to bend double, you have also got to keep your head up all the while so as to see the beams and girders and dodge them when they come. You have, therefore, a constant crick in the neck, but this is nothing compared to the pain in your knees and thighs. After a while it becomes...an unbearable agony. You begin to wonder whether you will ever get to the end - still more, how on earth you are going to get back. Your pace grows slower and slower. You come to a stretch of a couple of hundred yards where it is all exceptionally low and you have to work yourself along in a squatting position. Then suddenly the roof opens out to a mysterious height -the scene of an old fall of rock, probably - and for twenty whole yards you can stand upright. The relief is overwhelming.
>
> But after this there is another low stretch of a hundred yards and then a succession of beams which you have to crawl under. You go down on all four; even this is a relief after the squatting business. But when you come to the

end of the beams and try to get up again, you find your knees have temporarily struck work and refuse to lift you. You rest for a minute or two. Your guide (a miner) is sympathetic. He knows that your muscles are not the same as his: 'Only another four hundred yards,' he says encouragingly; you feel that he might as well say another four hundred face. You have gone a mile and taken the best part of an hour; having got there, you have to sprawl in the coal dust and get your strength back for several minutes before you can watch the work...

Coming back is worse than going, not only because you are already tired out, but because the journey back to the shaft is slightly uphill. You get through the low places at the speed of a tortoise, and you have no shame now about calling a halt when your knees give way.

NOTES

1. Klaus Tenfelde, *Sozialgeschichte der Bergarbeiterschaft an der Ruhr im 19 Jahrhundert* (Bonn-Bad Godesberg: 1977), 192.

2. Ibid. 448-51.

3. Georg Schmidt, *Lohnformen und Arbeitsverhältnisse in der Landwirtschaft* (Berlin: 1913), 22-23. Schmidt is here quoting an academic source.

4. On the earlier tradition of such non-class conflict societies see Toni Offermann, *Arbeiterbewegung und liberales Bürgertum in Deutschland, 1850-1863*, Bonn: 1979.

5. For Hirsch's ideas see *Die hauptsächlichen Streitfragen der Arbeiterbewegung* (Berlin: 1886).

6. *Historischer Bericht über den am 1. Dez. 1869 begonnene 8 wöchentliche allgemeine Arbeits-Einstellung der Waldenburger Bergleute* (Schweidnitz: n.d. [1870]) 3.

7. Otto Hue, *Die Bergarbeiter: Darstellung der Bergarbeiter-Verhältnisse von der ältesten Zeit in die neueste Zeit*, 2 vols. (Stuttgart: 1910-1913), 2, 289-290.

8. *Historicher Bericht*, 7.

9. Quoted from the December 15, 1883 issue of the machinists' weekly in Otto Hommer, *Die Entwicklung und Tätigkeit des deutschen Metallarbeiter-Verbandes* (Berlin: 1912), 7.

10. *Historischer Bericht*, 4.

11. Lawrence Schofer, *The Formation of a Modern Labor Force: Upper Silesia, 1865-1914* (Berkeley: 1975), 113.

12. Edmund Shorter and Charles Tilley, *Strikes in France, 1830-1968*, (London: 1974), ch. 5.

13. *Historischer Bericht*, 40.

14. Ibid., 9-11.

15. Ibid., 9.

16. The text of the letter had been reprinted in Heinrich Imbusch, *Arbeitsverhältnis und Arbeiterbewegung im deutschen Bergbau* (Essen: 1908), 215-16.

17. Idem.

18. In the 1890s when Carl Legien, then the most powerful trade union politician, was in charge of the *Correspondenzblatt der Generalkommission der Gewerkschaften Deutschlands*, henceforth *Corrblatt*, central organ of those unions, that weekly frequently supplied information on the occurrence of strikes in other Western European lands. Whether he intended to make that point or not, each one of these articles demonstrated that German workers went on strike much less often than proletarians in other lands. Examples of such articles are: "Die französischen Streiks im Jahre 1893," *Corrblatt*, Nov. 5, 1894; "Streiks in Österreich," idem., "Streiks und Lockouts in den Vereinigten Staaten in den Jahren 1881-1894," Aug. 31, 1896; "Streiks und Ausperrungen in Frankreich 1895," ibid.; "Streiks, Lockouts und *probi viri* in Italien 1886-1895," May 10, 1897; "Die Streiks in Italien von 1879-1896," November 14, 1898; "Die Streiks in England in Jahr 1898," January 23, 1898.

The practice was continued in later years, e.g., "Die Streiks in England," September 30 & October 6, 1906.

19. *Zukunft* did not report on Waldenburg, as if suffering political embarrassment by the participation of certain liberals in the conflict.

20. *Volksstaat*, December 18, 1869.

21. Imbusch, *Arbeitsverhältnis*, 218, specifies that 1,118 were not re-employed. It was the kind of question on which Catholics focused their attention.

22. See the table in ibid., 111.

23. See Jürgen Kuczynski, *Geschichte der Lage der arbeiter Klassen unter dem Kapitalismus*, [hereafter *GdL*] (Berlin: 1961 and after), 3, 11.

24. Ludwig Turek, *Ein Proletarier erzählt* (Cologne: 1972), 11.

25. Tenfelde notes that the rate for transporting coal was finally reduced to 1.25 Pfennigs per ton per kilometer, with favorable effect on the development of the industry "scarcely to be overestimated." *Sozialgeschichte*, 201.

26. Scholars normally speak of the exploitation of workingmen in the first and even second generations of industrial capitalism and then go lightly on the subject. Such should probably not be the practice in a work on strikes.

27. Hue, for instance, several times played with the question of surplus value, then dropped it. *Bergarbeiter,* 2, 181 & 582. Most social democratic writers on economic subjects simply do not bring it up; they were satisfied with a society which practiced wage labor.

28. From the Essen bourse prices as listed in Helmut Lüthgen, *Das Rheinisch-Westfälische Kohlensyndikat in der Vorkriegs, Kriegs, und Nachkriegszeit und seine Hauptprobleme,* (Leipzig: 1926), 3.

29. Hue, *Bergarbeiter,* 2, 304ff.

30. Imbusch, *Arbeitsverhältnis,* 104. His figures come from owners' sources.

31. See Gerhard Bry, *Wages in Germany, 1871-1945* (Princeton: 1960), 60.

32. Tenfelde has suggestive figures covering the whole century on Catholic-Evangelical splits in the different parts of the Ruhr. *Sozialgeschichte,* 51-52.

33. On the 1872 walkout see ibid., 470-486, also Imbusch, *Arbeitsverhältnis,* 236-245.

34. On the failed emissaries: Tenfelde, *Sozialgeschichte,* 476-77. A recent work treating the strike is Knut Hartmann, *Der Weg zur gewerkschaftlichen Organisation: Bergarbeiterbewegung und Kapitalistischer Bergbau im Ruhrgebiet, 1851-1889* (Munich: 1977), 37-44.

35. August Bebel, *Aus meinem Leben,* 3 vols. (Berlin: 1953), 40.

36. Tenfelde, *Sozialgeschichte,* 478.

37. Hue entitled one section of his work "The Jesuit Strike," (*Bergarbeiter,* 2, 304ff.), and other social democrats identified it the same way.

38. *SPD Protocol 1870* (Leipzig: 1870), 40.

39. See below, Chapter 3, for a fuller exposition of the social democratic attitude toward strikes.

40. *Neuer Social-Demokrat,* May 31, 1872.

41. Walter Steglich, "Eine Streiktabelle für Deutschland, 1864 bis 1880," *Jahrbuch für Wirtschaftsgeschichte,* 1960, 281.

42. *Sozialdemokrat,* August 2, 1883.

43. *Sozialdemokrat,* July 12 & August 9, 1883.

2

THE RUHR TEACHES GERMANY TO STRIKE

Though few of them would have known it, 1889 had a significance for European workingmen such as no year since 1848 had. All Western Europe was caught up by a spirit of militant action. The London dock strike projected unions into prominence in England for decades to come. On the continent those divergent views over a Second International which had been plaguing planners since 1871 melted away. A new organization, which was to educate not only the proletariat but other classes as well, was born. In Germany, even before miners left their pits, there had been a Rhineland strike wave, followed by a walkout of Berlin construction workers in which a million days were lost.[1]

The moods of individuals ebb and flow, and such alterations are baffling even to the most expert. How much more this is the case when moods come to nations, to social strata, or to geographical areas, composed as they usually are of disparate millions. Before 1765 the 13 colonies seemed quiet, yet in short years after 1770 a substantial minority was readying itself for war. In the 1840s the abolitionists were isolated in their condemnation of slavery, yet 10 years later the North girded itself for war, in great part over that issue. Who can say why and when such waves of feeling, with men and women prepared to sacrifice their lives for a belief, will wash over a land or a social class?

When a new emotion afflicts an area, the different social strata are affected in different ways. Those which dominate a land take it as their bounden duty to preserve and improve their positions. They endeavor to turn a new situation to their advantage. The unpropertied, the powerless and the disadvantaged, hardly aware of what has happened, and habituated to a subservient position, will only put their limited strength and their wobbly sense of self-confidence into play spasmodically and unpredictably. For those who come after, there is many a trap in grasping why one moment was chosen for a revolt and not another.

A massive Ruhr walkout could, for instance, have come in 1883, the year of the *Germania* outbreak, but the spark from the old-fashioned outbreak did not catch. It was then but 11 years since the "Jesuit strike", and the depressing influence from that loss lingered. The voice of those who had been defeated still predominated below. By 1889 a younger generation was preparing to assert itself. A baby at the breast during the 1872 walkout would now be laboring as a *Schlepper*, that errand boy of the mines; he would be hopeful of advancing to being a better paid hacker, and not too willing to listen to the defeatism of the old-timers. Year by year the men were assembling that proper combination of hope, courage, determination, bravado, depression and despair which was needed to carry on a great strike. Trained all their lives to obedience, the men had to be ready to defy the bosses' authority. They had to be prepared to break with the all too well established habit of going to work every day save Sunday. They had to suppress their fear of being jobless.

Before 1889 there were no encouraging examples of what miners had won through strikes. The strikers of 1872 had instead exhausted their native stocks of hope and courage, while running their families into debt. Subsequently they would relapse into characteristic working class fatalism, reinforced at this time by an economic depression. Early Ruhr history suggests that it took until the generation defeated in a strike fell into numerical inferiority to those who had never been crushed before a new effort would be launched.

An additional factor may have been involved. Men who toil *unter Tage* see the god of the Incas but rarely. That minority who drank themselves unconscious on Saturday night might go several months without a glimpse of the life-giving sun. Though in 1889 the Ruhr had not yet reached its smog-laden maturity, the sun was often hard to see. But it made its appeal in May, 1889. Gardens then needed more attention than men who worked 60 hours a week could give them. Then too, both walking in the countryside and lying in the fields were recreations much beloved of miners. Half of them, after all, had been born peasants. Autobiographer Hans Marchwitza wrote of going back into the pits after an interval of freedom in the countryside: "It surely was not easy to exchange the brightness of the sun for the dark of the pits. Once again to crawl on one's belly and knees and to chew dust."[2]

New rulers bring hope to monarchical lands. A first 1888 change of emperor had only produced a man sick unto death. The second change elevated an appealing young man against whom nothing was known. His very youth was a hint that the Iron Chancellor, of whom all were now weary, might finally have to depart. Encouraging also to working people was the expected demise of the Exceptional Law, directed as it was almost exclusively against them. Events of 1888 were making their contribution to the optimism and intensity of 1889.

Thus there were political, economic, and emotional reasons making for excitement in 1889. Meetings in the Ruhr had already begun in 1888, and the editor of the Saxon miners' *Glückauf* was invited to the valley.[3] *Kassen*, the miners' pension societies, were also becoming more active, for the miners maintained that in depression years certain owners, hungry for capital, had seized some of their pension funds.[4] Aggrieved men brought cases and sometimes they won. Such victories demonstrated that action brought results, and suggested the vulnerability of the companies. The *Kassen* meetings began to take up less technical questions. A gathering of January 13, 1889, with representatives from various pits, came close to discussing the major matters which were on everyone's mind. Instead that assembly voted to convene delegates on March 10.[5] As yet there was no police interference with the meetings, though the *Kassen* were slowly transforming themselves into union locals.

At the March meeting pit representatives began talking about wages.[6] In attendance were exclusively men who worked in the mines; they were anonymous souls for the most part, as this was before the day of union bureaucrats. Once they began discussing money, every other issue became insignificant. They scheduled a further assembly for April 7, and by this time the whole Ruhr was participating in their discussions. Meetings were being held in the individual pits, and those who were delegates felt pressure for action.

It is sometimes argued that while working men and women have a public list of demands, what they really intend is something else, not stated by them, but discernible to social historians. Considering 1889, this is a difficult argument to sustain. Normally strikes have to do with wages and hours, the obvious primary interests of the participants. When companies make

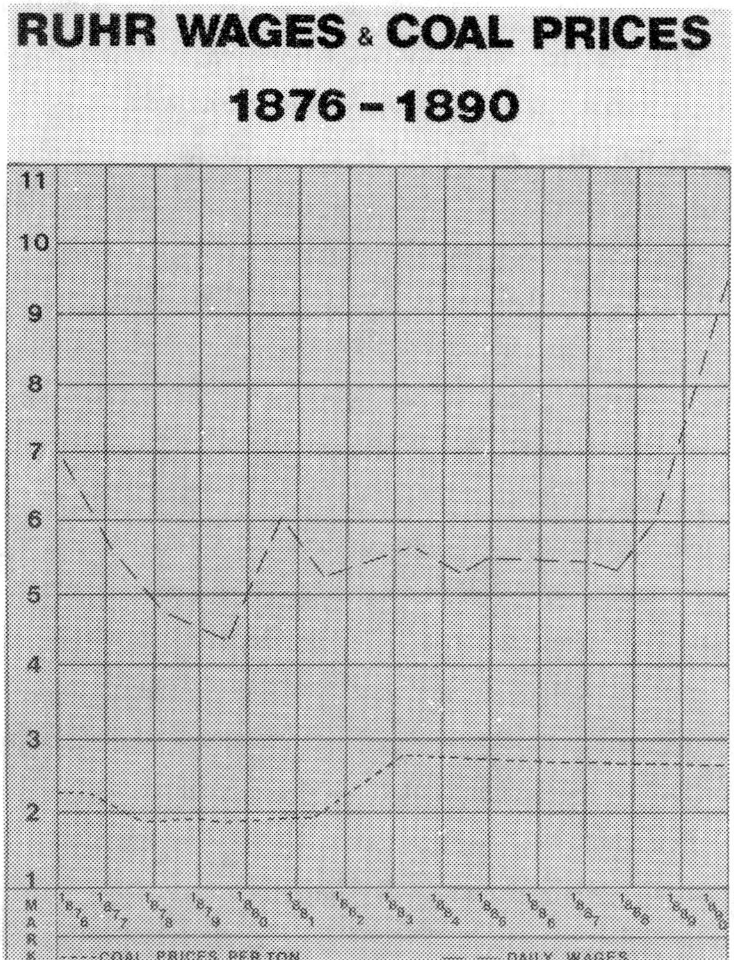
RUHR WAGES & COAL PRICES
1876 - 1890
11
10
9
8
7
6
5
4
3
2
1
MARKS
----COAL PRICES PER TON
— — DAILY WAGES

concessions on these points strikes come to an end, while if wages and hours remain unchanged, no matter what other concessions are made, the conflict is likely to continue, if the workers maintain their strength. All evidence on the great walkout of 1889 suggests that it raised questions of wages and hours, and such was to be the case with the struggles which followed.

Pit representatives reached no decisions at the March meeting, save that they would meet once more April 7. All that month the Ruhr talked about pay. Where permitted, meetings were held at the pits. The valley was heating up. Leaders were expected to provide some action. They met once again, drew up a list of grievances, and mailed it to the Mine Association. They left the statement unsigned, however, in hope that at least a few of their jobs would be preserved (over the years various of them had already been blacklisted and/or fired for proto-union activity). Aggressive as this action was by the German standards of the nineteenth century, it took place only because of pressure from the 100,000 dirty-faced diggers who now expected results, in terms of improved wages and hours. The new leaders made their demands in words, but let it go at that. It was in no way their intention to make threats, nor in any way to influence the men to leave the mines. Ludwig Schröder, who had been one of the more significant, if unofficial, miners' chiefs since the early 1870s was often quoted for saying: "Whoever advises the men to go out on strike is no friend of the miners."[7] Hoping that they could keep a grip on their constituents, yet not wishing to contribute to the prevalent excitement, the men who were trying to direct the miners announced that they would not meet again until June 2, a very distant date considering the rapidity with which events were unfolding. The Saxon sheet *Glückauf*, the miners' only means of public statement, commented on the extreme significance of the upcoming June assembly.[8]

These prestrike meetings were producing the men of the future. Ludwig Schröder had first become well-known when the state church had refused to baptize his child "Lassalle." He did his daily share of heavy physical toil, his job ever endangered by his agitation. He used his nights to overcome those deficiencies in education which the Second Empire forced upon its working class children. He struggled to become an orator, a writer and even a parliamentarian. Daniel Eckhardt, his counterpart among Catholic miners, led a similar existence. This first generation of fighters for unionism made possible the comfortable and unaspiring desk types who led the unions in the future. But that the Schröders had to fight each day for their existence and their freedom did not by any means drive them into rebellion. Quite in the predominant nineteenth century way of the German working class, they were opposed to disorder and rebellion. These were, they believed, with all their conservative fellow subjects of the Second Empire, the probable consequences of a strike. A contemporary writer remarked that one of Schröder's greatest talents was in persuading men to stay on the job.[9] They had that same fear of disrupting social processes which he had. August Bebel too will presently be seen as pacifier in the class struggle. But in spring, 1889, rushes of feeling more powerful than men like Schröder and Bebel had had to deal with were blowing throughout Western Europe.

The prime demand of the miners was for money. It had been on their minds for a decade. The Essen Chamber of Commerce had declared in 1877: "The wages which the men are getting are the wages of hunger," and went on to state that many received less than 40 marks a month.[10] Otto Hue quoted his subjects in that same desperate year: "When the price of coal rises, we want our share."[11] Imbusch's statistics, collected for the later Catholic union, showed miners' pay bouncing around a lowly three marks a day for many years, and even going lower in some.[12] Many of the coalies had left homes in the East for what they believed was the best pay in the land (actually at this time the Saar still outdid the Ruhr)[13] but had never received it. Between the low point of 1879 and the pre-1889 high of 1883, pay had gone up around 18 percent.[14] In the 1880s, as at other times, pay varied with demand for the product. But there was a socio-economic by-product in this situation, for when the owners raised pay, they were teaching the men to expect the same and more when the market improved.

Among the companies the small and middling had had the greater voice, for the day of domination by giant corporations lay in the future. Large and small companies had been having difficulties over the past 16 years. Total coal production had been increasing, but competition was pressing them all, and the price of the black diamond rarely exceeded 6 marks a ton. Capital was increasing but slowly, and dividends were hard to come by.

In late 1888 began the swift reversal of fortunes for those who owned mines in the Ruhr. By December Dr. Natorp, spokesman for the industry group known as the Mining Association of Dortmund, was able to tell his principals that "prices have reached a very satisfactory condition for the first time in years."[15] That cheering advance was to continue into 1889; in fact, in the boom months of 1889-1890 coal went up an unprecedented 20 pfennigs a week. As the quotas for coal became more promising, owners and public began bidding up the shares. But what happened on the stock market was not done in secret. Already at this time, informed miners were aware of stock prices. Their chief source of information, the Saxon miners' *Glückauf*, reported in its special May supplement, that *Dortmund Union* had already gone up from 65 to 102 marks a share, and *Hibernia* from 88 to 159.[16] Great expectations were born in more than one strata of the population.

Not without a touch of arrogance, the owners described themselves as *Arbeitgeber* (work-givers), and thereby apparently committed themselves to benevolence. Germany did have a medieval tradition of patriarchalism. Yet in 1889 when the price of coal began to move up, the owners did not raise wages. There was little reason to do so, since every day trains arrived from the East with willing hands. For too many years the owner had had bad times, and the temptation was to store up cash for dividends and capital. The impulse to play the patriarch grew less intense each year, and, desiring to keep their gains from the boom, the companies believed that they could count upon the well known docility of the men. History was on their side. There was no sign of militancy from the Ruhr in the years 1872-1889, the *Germania* incident excepted, nor yet from Saar, Silesia or Saxony.

Might the companies have averted the great rebellion, and all which it brought in its wake, with a timely raise of 25 or even 50 pfennig a day? Such a boon would have had to be granted before March, when strike talk began in earnest. The men were inexperienced and ill-organized, and fearful of being sacked for union activity; their leaders preferred calm above all. Had the owners made the necessary concession, they would still have the best profits since 1873, and could have easily satisfied their shareholders. As it was, each week they were saving themselves, reckoning on an advance of 25 pfennig a shift, 2,000,000 marks.

More likely the great rebellion could not have been headed off by a timely, modest raise. The men felt that they had suffered for a decade and a half and were not in the mood to be bought off. All their days were spent bent over in cramped and dangerous quarters. They fought with masses of intractable material which could maim, crush or kill at any moment. They did their labor while sweating so formidably from the heat that they frequently had to strip off their clothes and wring them out.[17] Altogether, this was a labor more arduous than almost any other in Wilhelmine Germany, as was recognized by all classes. They felt it themselves. Sociologist Levenstein queried 2,100 miners on how long they would like to labor. His respondents replied as follows:

144	(8.3%)	after the 4th hour
449	(26.1%)	after the 5th hour
238	(14.0%)	after the 6th hour
267	(15.5%)	after the 7th hour
518	(30.0%)	after the 8th hour
93	(5.4%)	after the 9th hour
11	(.6%)	after the 10th hour

1720[18]		

Thus only 11 claimed to be unwearied after 10 hours. Clearly in the 1880s, with a 10 hour day the minimum, men were toiling longer than they felt they should. Thirty-four percent had to work 6 days a week, twice as long as they felt reasonable. Fewer than one percent could easily tolerate what was only the minimum, and which was often exceeded. In the matter of hours there was clearly tinder which could make a fire.

In the 1880s overtime became frequent, for it was always easier to keep certain men on the job rather than to hire new ones. In the morning a placard would announce that the day's shift would be extended until "x" hour. The men had no choice. If one of them tried to leave at the normal hour, the cable car would not be there. If individuals protested, they risked the overseer's wrath. Extra hours did push pay above the usual three marks, but sometimes overtime was not recorded, and thus not paid. Again it was wisest not to engage in futile protest. The same was true when an individual was given the occasional Sunday shift.

Beyond wages and hours, the miners had a variety of what could be called underdeveloped grievances. In his sympathetic analysis of the strike, Lensing, editor of the Catholic paper *Tremonia*, linked overtime with invalidism.[19] A tabulation of age groups which was made in 1880 in a Hannover pit confirmed his opinion that mining crippled the men:

AGE OF MINERS	NUMBER	PERCENT
14-25	420	25
25-35	657	40
35-45	428	25
45-55	122	7
55-65	37	2
over 65	5	.5[20]

Evidently only those with the most solid constitutions could survive the 40's below and go on working. A generation later, after the digging day had been forced down by the 1889 strike and its successors, the social democratic Mine Workers Association still maintained that a career *unter Tage* cost a miner as much as 11 years of his life.[21] In 1889, however, longevity was not yet a direct issue.

Further, the miners were concerned with *Nullen*, which meant the cancellation by foremen of payment for badly loaded carts. They asked also for more humane handling and for washrooms, then totally lacking. Since there was no formal union, the question of recognition was not raised. But all these were secondary issues: what moved the men in 1889 were only the classic matters of wages and hours.

Well over 90 percent of those who took up the fight this year were Germans. More than half of them came from the surrounding area, i.e., the larger Rhine-Westphalian region, while the rest were from Silesia or other parts of the East. Nearly all the non-Germans who mined the Ruhr were Poles born inside the Second Reich. The Ruhr had not yet become a magnet for proletarians of the entire continent. Poles, the largest minority of the Second Empire, came to the Ruhr expecting higher wages than they could obtain anywhere else, but in return had to perform brute labor and to submit to discriminatory circumstances. Marchwitza quotes Poles in Silesia, but the same would have been true in the Ruhr: "We are illiterate, and people pay us whatever they wish."[22] The way that Polish miners lived was not the way their German colleagues lived, and the latter looked down upon the Slavs. It was not only an ethnic conflict, but also the antagonism between those who lived on a slightly higher standard of living and those who were a step below. (The Germans drew better wages, had better housing and better opportunities and, slightly more modern, had fewer children.) Otto Hue, the usually intelligent and reasonably unprejudiced historian of the miners, all but calls his fellow proletarians "dirty Poles" in several passages.[23] The sons of Kosciusko were considered pay-cutters, not a happy appellation at any time, and particularly not in depressed years. As of 1889 Poles in the Ruhr were almost entirely males, and thus less respectable and thought to be prone to violence. Although they were inclined very strongly to social clubs,[24] they were as yet too few to have churches or newspapers of consequence.

Such were the 100,000 miners now surging into battle. In a generous moment the owners' mouthpiece Dr. Natorp was to concede that "the miners were only trying to benefit from the good times."[25] An example had been given them from what was then called the "highest quarter." Young Emperor Wilhelm II, already among the two or three richest men in the land, had just wrested a pay raise from the Prussian legislature.[26] His plea had been that prices were rising and cutting his standard of living.

A corollary of the idea that strikes occur when the old generation has passed is that when the new effort is made, youth leads the way. Already on April 25 in Bochum, no answer having been received from the owners, some of the younger men had left the pits. Being without families, they could afford the loss of pay, and would have no one to criticize them for it. Being footloose, they could more easily find substitute employment. Meanwhile the miners' leaders were urging men to sign a petition to the owners, but by now emotions were running too strong for such tame expedients.[27] In a few cases the threat of going out won the men immediate 20 pfennig increases.[28] The number of those on strike kept increasing, and on May 1 the important Essen area stopped working. The *Rheinisch-Westfälische Zeitung*, the paper closest to the owners, was incredulous at the way the rebellion was growing.[29]

Men not only quit the mines, but exhibited signs of revolt. In the German proletariat it was a brave and bold deed to fly the red flag, and this was especially not done in the conservative Ruhr.[30] Ordinarily they were stashed away in trunks like wedding dresses. This spring the blood red pennants were blowing in the wind,[31] while the names of Marx and Lassalle served for graffiti. Here were bits of news to make the masters of the coal fields anxious.

Though the strikers held meetings, their legal right to do so remained in doubt. Throughout the Wilhelmine period social democrats had to beg police permission to meet, and then had to tolerate a uniformed officer on stage during the meeting. He had the power to call it off. The danger which hung over union assemblies was of being declared political and unannounced in advance, and therefore ripe for suspension. This spring, however, police backed off from the newly found assertiveness of the miners, who won a small right of assembly. There is no doubt that the miners, this time around, were the recipients of some sympathy from officials and members of the upper class; the provincial governor, for instance, was to lose his post for having handled the situation too leniently.[32] For the most part the men seem to have assembled in woods, ravines, and in every other open place, and only secondarily in taverns. The flood of possible discussion which had been stopped up through the 1880s was now let loose. Siegel, one of the new leaders, reported:

> Those of us who were in charge of things had rest neither day nor night. Often I came home at twelve midnight, and went out again at five in the morning. Frequently I had to go on foot, to get to the meeting on time. In those assemblies the anger which had been piling up for fifteen years finally found expression.[33]

With more men out every day, with meetings on all sides, the situation seemed ever more menacing to the owners. Repeatedly they called for troops to protect their property. The area's commanding general wailed to Chief of Staff von Waldersee:

> Nearly every ten minutes I get a telegram in which the fall of the universe is threatened if military aid is not dispatched at once. And nothing at all has happened, there has been hardly any damage to property...I can't promise quiet to every district and to every mine owner. It would take more than a company before every bedroom door.[34]

Many another general agreed that the Prussian army should not sully its reputation by intervening.

In her autobiography the talented daughter of General von Kretschmeyer reconstructed contemporary salon gossip on precisely this point.[35] The morning headlines had read: "Rebellion in the Coal Regions." All the officers who were her dancing partners had been put on alert. Her father, who later had to abandon his club after his daughter became known as a "Red," did not believe that the army of Frederick II and von Moltke should be used against fellow Prussians. He was not alone in this opinion. He thought that a few kicks administered to the "moneybags" would get them to pay their men better. A count referred to the miners' demands as modest; he also found the historic 8 hour day for work underneath the ground quite reasonable. A baron regretted the passing of state supervision over the mines (in the 1860s), while a prince began to dispute whether the miners were really poor. Another visitor to the imaginary conversation found it understandable if workingmen should take advantage of rising prices to improve their lots. All these aristocrats were envious of the mine owners, whom they called "men with rubber-wheeled carriages." Only the *beau de jour* of this General's daughter brought in the irrational note, alleging that social democrats were behind the strike. He was a member of the bureaucracy.

In the first days of the rebellion miners went out of the pits gradually, and also freely.[36] But a tension presently developed between those who wanted to stay on the job and those who did not. At Gelsenkirchen the young miners were characteristically the first out. They gathered on May 5 to dissuade those still appearing for the shift. Police came to the aid of the non-strikers. Stones were thrown at the uniforms, and police opened fire. That was what had happened at *Germania*, was to occur among Polish miners at Herne, and must have taken place in other instances now lost.

Violence was everyday to the miners, who did some of the world's most muscular labor. Unlike that of the peasant, it was endlessly repetitious while containing no possibility of being satisfying. In every way mining seemed to encourage physical expression. The men brawled in taverns more than did other German workers; they practiced the general custom of beating wives and children. Overseers, some of whom carried guns, abused the men physically. The feeling of guilt at going on strike, and the worry over not getting one's job back after the strike accentuated the tendency among the young men to be physical. Leaders warned the men to remain calm - this admonition was customary from the first in the German working class movement - but such warnings could come only at the occasional assemblies. These were not trained social democrats of several decades standing, but men who had only just undertaken some kind of action. Personal confrontation between strikers and non-strikers occurred all the time. At the normal change-of-shift hour men came to the pit to see who was going to work, and what else was happening. Once a crowd had come together, it was a rare strikebreaker who got through with only hard words. Even when they made it to the gate, they were not safe. Back in the villages, those who entered the pits could well have their windows thrown in.

Troops were sent the night of the first disturbances at Gelsenkirchen. The country had become uneasy and there were many calls for action. Neither officials nor those who influenced public opinion were really able to take reports of stone-throwing calmly. When the soldiers did appear, the miners were further angered at this, the first official answer to their request for better pay from rising prices.

The soldiers had been told that the strikers were rebels, and were untrained for the situations they faced. Whatever some generals might have thought, the officers on the scene saw disorder before their eyes, and it was they who gave the order to fire. Bloodshed in defense of the strike was a natural consequence. Hue complained that the officers were too young and inexperienced,[37] but this probably misses the point. It was very natural for the army to fire on the lower classes, just as the army did in other lands. The miners, however, continued to assemble undaunted at each change of shift. They did not always disperse rapidly on command. Multiple killings occurred at the *Moltke* and *Schleswig* pits, while elsewhere there were individual mortalities. *Sozialdemokrat* counted a total of 15 deaths, among whom were both women and children.[38]

Put in perspective, the number of the dead was quite small. Each European nation has a different history of military violence against its citizenry. Peterloo has often been featured by historians, for English troops almost never fired on their countrymen. The same slaughter would have been unnoticed in Russia. France, famous for its armies, was a state which killed, as in the massacres of working people in June 1848, and May 1871.

As a state whose chief resource was its army, Prussia would seem to belong naturally among the killers. The Nazis' war on other Germans makes this thesis yet more likely. But the land of the Hohenzollerns preferred to treat its subjects, of whom there were never too many, as children. Children who err are reproved, and even beaten - but they are not often slaughtered. In the nineteenth century there is no example of the Prussian state gunning down strikers on a large scale, and in 1848 the army was gentle compared to the French, the Russian or the Austrian. German social democracy built itself into one of the world's greatest political machines without benefit of a single honest martyr. (In his history of the Berlin party Bernstein tries to convert three workingmen who fell through the ice while returning from an illegal meeting into such, but this was not reasonable.) Essentially German authorities, down to 1918, did not kill or torture political enemies.

It was not in open political struggle then, but in the hidden precincts of factory, farm and mine that proletarian lives were being lost, unknown to the world. Had the 100,000 men who were out in May, 1889 gone down into the pits, about 30 would have died. The class struggle was evidently safer than daily toil. The strike gave the men another benefit. One reason they died young was that they never had proper respites from labor. A three week vacation in May surely lengthened many a life. The same was true of the miserable horses who worked *unter Tage* and who were now ridden through the miners' villages to frighten families that the cavalry was on hand.[39]

Neither soldiers nor shootings drove the men back to the mines. Nor did the efforts of their leaders. On May 5 delegates from the *Kassen* and from the pits, few of whom could have been chosen in regular fashion, met at Essen; they called upon the men to remain calm and to continue working. Their words were quite without effect. In hope of diversion, *Glückauf* absurdly devoted its first strike issue to German investments in Samoa.[40]

In the first days of May there was much uncertainty among the men. It was most difficult for them to break the rhythm of their lives, which sent them to work 6 days a week, and even more to defy the authority of their bosses. The conflict with themselves which German proletarians faced when they struck is well pictured by non-miner Anna Altmann:

> We had decided to toil no more! We were all still babes-in-arms and one could not really speak of an organization, or of a movement in L...On the next Monday we stopped our machines, and wanted to leave the factory. Everything would have gone well, if we had not chanced on the owner. When the women saw the

> "master," and when he opened up on them with such expressions of affection as "tramps," "trollops," most of them lost their bravery. With much more rapidity than that with which they had originally left the place, they hurried back to their machines...Only we three remained outside. We were considered the *Rädelsführer* (troublemakers).[41]

Tens of thousands had the courage to enter the cable car and descend into the dark, but few could exchange antagonistic words with the boss without trembling. Both miner-writers Marchwitza and Siegel record tense and unnerving clashes with the boss at the entrances to a mine. Fear of such encounters held men back.

The mine owners were now far stronger than they had been at the time of the Essen strike of 1872. Some of their lesser colleagues had fallen away during the long depression, and the remaining ones were growing used to dealing with each other. They possessed fine seams in the nation which then produced a tenth of the world's coal. Not only were they wealthy (the 'rubber-wheeled carriages') but they had better political connections than in 1872.

Strong and self-willed as they were, the owners recognized that they had to make a case before public opinion, if not to the men. Their press release[42] (May 10) stated first that the strike was illegal because the miners had broken their contracts.[43] According to this theory Hans Gerst, wishing in his heart of hearts to be a miner, came to the Gelsenkirchen firm and made an individual arrangement with its manager, Emil Kirdorf. Their mutually satisfactory pact between equals provided that Gerst was to give all his strength to Kirdorf for unspecified hours, and to follow all Kirdorf's rules, in return for which the great manager would reward Gerst as he saw fit. Each side was to give two weeks' notice of termination. In truth Gerst arrived at the mine without a pfennig, needed the job, and hated the work. However, Wilhelmine society believed in being law-abiding and the men were wounded by the illegality charge. Their temperate reply was that their large meetings took the place of notice. The private and more radical response was that the bosses continually altered the terms of the contract, giving the men the right to do as much.

Second, the owners, speaking through the Dortmund Mining Association, asserted that wages averaged 1,000 marks a year, higher than other fields. In fact, they were the best on the continent. Then as always management preferred to inquire: why do the Junkers' field hands always come to us? Only an overworked handful of miners would have earned 1,000 marks in 1888, and more likely in the Saar than in the Ruhr. However in general the owners' argument rang true. The 100,000 strikers were better off than nearly all German proletarians.

The owners alleged further that their hours were more reasonable than those in other trades, but here their argument lost force, as if they were conceding that the miners had a case. They concluded by asserting that as soon as the men returned, pay would go up.

As they themselves recognized, this hard announcement granting nothing won the owners no support.[44] Propertied classes thought them quite rich already, while working people knew the miners "earned a bitter bread." Then by conceding that they would raise wages, the owners seemed to admit that they had been tardy in doing so. Kirdorf, Stinnes, Krupp, Haniel, the men of the future in one of the world's great industries, did not find support in press, pulpit, Reichstag, or cabinet.[45] Their statement even brought more miners out of the shafts. Yet if they were isolated and under attack, they were yet almost invulnerable. It was what occurred next that proved costly to them.

The first appeal of the miners had been modern: from its tone they might all have been union veterans of 20 years. When that maneuver failed, they fell back upon a more medieval way of proceeding.

In 1889 belief in the young emperor as a good father was quite strong. Everywhere he was pictured as a charming and agreeable ruler, who was accessible to his people. The idea of approaching the emperor during a strike had been used two decades before, during the long and desperate Waldenburg engagement. Since early in the Ruhr strike a tavern owner in the old Hanseatic town of Dorst, a man who was in sympathy with the miners like many of his trade, had been suggesting that if the emperor understood the plight of the miners he would aid them. The old legend about the good monarchy was being played once again.[46] On May 9 a miners' meeting commenced discussing the ancient myth which was now to prove true. Those who were assembled in Dorst agreed that the owners were not going to act, and everyone believed that it would be most difficult for 100,000 men to hold out for weeks. The idea of the populist monarch, dispensing justice from under a tree, had its appeal for the men less politically experienced than, and separate from, their fellow proletarians elsewhere. Once they approved the notion, it was easily decided that the usual trio should go. Likewise it was simple to agree upon Ludwig Schröder, indefatigable veteran of the class struggle, and on Bunte and Siegel, who had made names for themselves in *Kassen* meetings. All three were known to be social democrats, yet Catholics felt sufficient solidarity not to protest. As soon as the three were selected, they wired to request an imperial audience. It was said that the 161 marks for fares was collected in an hour.[47]

By lending themselves to this petitioning trip social democrats were, like their sponsors, sanctioning the monarchy. Actually the party's republicanism was purely formal, a leftover from 1848 and a way of proving that they were a genuine opposition party. Only a few months before the peerless Bebel himself had told the Reichstag, amid catcalls, that the Second Empire might one day have a social democratic emperor,[48] his own version of the myth of the good ruler. Subsequent working class literature makes no criticism of the 1889 delegation to the emperor.

Chancellor Bismarck and Emperor Wilhelm II each had reasons to welcome the miners' delegation. The Iron Chancellor, who was not hostile to the idea of nationalizing the coal fields,[49] was seeking internal crises which might give him the opportunity for a *coup d'etat*.[50] The emperor wanted to come out of the shadows and become a political figure in his own right.

Schröder, Bunte and Siegel were summoned to the palace on the 14th. The majority of strikers had then been out 10 days, and the owners' rejection of the miners' demands was three days old. In trying to put the case for the 100,000, Schröder and his friends had an awesome responsibility. To the people of the Second Reich the emperor was a demi-god. Criticism of him, which for a decade extended only to a small educated minority, would only begin in the 1890s. Crowds would stand for hours to glimpse Wilhelm II in passing. When they were lucky they remembered the occasion forever. Nothing that these three men had ever done, or had received by way of education or experience, qualified them for interchange of opinion in the august presence amid the glitter and opulence of the court. Only if the social democrats had been republicans, and had seen Wilhelm II as simply another man, however flawed, would they have been able to come up to their task. But they were men of duty, and their duty that day was to overcome the intimidatory effects of the imperial surroundings and to present, as best they could, the case of their thousands of aggrieved colleagues. Upon arrival they were informed that the emperor could spare them but a few minutes. They would not be able to present their case thoroughly, and there would surely be no dialogue.

Schröder was selected as spokesman. He was the most experienced of the three, yet all German proletarians found it specially hard to face authority. Carl Severing, the Weimar politician, went in his youth with two "greybeards" to discuss wages and hours with the boss.[51] The older men turned dumb on arrival in his office. Schröder was never to maintain that he spoke well this day in Berlin. He mumbled a few words about wanting to return to the 8 hour day, then lapsed into the loyal subject's plea that the monarch "dry the tears of his people."[52]

Schröder's syllables were succeeded by 400 imperial words. In his 30 year reign this was Wilhelm's most direct contact with the men who did the labor of his land. They represented, to boot, one of Germany's great industries. The emperor was not, at that moment, in a very strong position. Ruhr output was minimal and on the tenth day of the walkout many Silesian miners had begun going out. Theirs was the country's second most important field. On the thirteenth the small Aachen region quit work, leaving only militant Saxony and the state mines in the Saar on the job. Germany was now close to a general strike in coal, and had no alternative energy source. If then the emperor was edgy, that was not only because such was his habit, and because he faced individuals of an alien social class, but because there was sound economic reason to be anxious. Yet the picture was not entirely negative, for he had opportunity to win popularity and a place in history.

Wilhelm II commenced with words borrowed from the owners, alleging that the men had broken contract, and that they were preventing others from working. To the best of their ability, in spite of the power of police and military, such indeed were the intentions of the miners. He went on, in 27 words, to remark that his regime would examine the complaints of the men. This hint of state action heartened the strikers, incensed the owners, and was taken everywhere to mean that Berlin would intervene directly to resolve the conflict. These necessaries out of the way, the last of the Hohenzollerns let loose in that frenzy of oratory he favored. Prominent in his words were threats. Having before him three important social democrats, he denounced individuals of this persuasion as "enemies of the Fatherland." If miners were to fall under the party's influence, he declared, he would have them shot. The printed versions of the emperor's speech did not include these last bellicose remarks, but Schröder reported them, knowing he risked jail if he put phrases in the mouth of Wilhelm II. Likewise, Hue recounted the 'shooting' reference, and no judicial action was taken against him.[53]

The miners out of the way, the emperor summoned representatives of the owners. They too sent a trio, of whom Dr. Friedrich Hammacher, non-owner, was the spokesman. After Hammacher explained his case, the emperor proceeded to tax the companies with their sins. The duty of capitalists, he argued, included knowing the mentality of their men. Complaints should have been anticipated. He went so far as to take up what is described in this volume as the "spread":

> It is quite natural and human for every man to wish to have the best possible standard of living. Working people read the newspapers and know what the relation is between their pay and the profits of the companies. It is quite easy to understand that they want to have a share in [those profits]. So I would like to

> request you to examine the situation with the greatest seriousness and, where possible, to seek to avoid the same sort of occurrence in the future.[54]

Wilhelm II was criticizing the coal owners for having offended against principles of a paternalistic state. One of these was that it was the responsibility of the parents in the social order (the capitalists) to grasp the moods of the children (miners) and to apply proper remedies. The owners' idea of economics was more modern: if new hands arrived every day from the East, why care about the wage rate?

Schröder, Bunte and Siegel lingered in Berlin. Basking in imperial favor helped their cause, but wages had not yet been raised even 10 pfennigs the shift. The three had carefully avoided consulting with any of the 11 social democratic deputies, but they did come in contact with Dr. Hammacher. He was later to say that chance had led him to the miners, to which Bismarck responded that chance had also made him head of state.

Hammacher and the trio of miners constructed an agreement bringing about the one more or less negotiated end to a major Wilhelmine strike.[55] They had the advantage that a vague raise in pay had been promised, so they could pass over that. They had the disadvantage of complete inexperience in arranging a contract. The first article of their joint statement began with the well-nigh revolutionary clause:

> 1. The administration of the Dortmund hard coal mining district obligates itself in the future to have their personnel work no more than the normal eight hour shift....[56]

This statement the 4 hit upon was a great victory for the miners and its life-prolonging effect was gradually to extend to nearly all Germans who worked with their hands. Hammacher, Schröder, Bunte and Siegel further agreed that extra shifts, that bane of depression years, would take place only in exceptional circumstances. Miners' representatives would have to assent to them, giving the men a foot in the door of mine management.

Perhaps because the word "work" in the first article made for confusion, or because Hammacher thought to slow the onrush of miners' gains, this clause, productive of doubt and dispute, was added:

> 5. The trip into the mine, and the trip out of the mine shall not be reckoned into the normal eight hour shift. The trip in and the trip out shall as a rule not exceed half an hour. [They] are to be counted so that the miner does not remain underground more than eight hours.

Hammacher himself was to confess that the first item and the fifth were not in consonance.[57] The parties may have been weary, or Hammacher, with a thought to his principals, may have wanted to muddy the waters. Toward the end of the negotiations they tackled minor points, the most significant being the unreal stipulation that no one was to be punished for striking.

In hardly 10 days the men appeared to have won an amazing victory, with the raise, an 8 hour day and no firings. The boldness of the 100,000, the intervention by the monarchy, and the unpopularity of the owners had all contributed. Feeling that all was won, some miners started back to the pits on the 16th. They deceived themselves, for it was not to be so easy to gain the 8 hour day. Their strength was in part illusory, for they were not united and had no solid organization. The emperor had made a fine theatrical gesture and he had answered their petition when their strike seemed lost. But he lacked consistency, as the years were to prove. By contrast the owners were few, wealthy, powerful, united and most determined. They could make sizeable concessions without really losing anything. Much of the final decision was thus to lie with them.

When Hammacher returned to the Ruhr his chiefs were in no mood to accept all the concessions which he had made. They rejected further talks with the miners. In short order they announced what the real settlement terms would be. Wages were to rise, but by an unspecified amount and by decision of the individual mines. As to hours, they were adamant, and corrected what had become known as the "Berlin protocol" of Hammacher, Schröder *et al.* These are their words:

> 1. The normal length of the underground shift is eight hours...neither the entering [of the mine], nor the return [from the mine] shall be included in the normal eight hour day.

Stinnes, Kirdorf, Krupp and the other coal barons gained this point, yet they had surrendered this day in May much more than they could have imagined.

Almost painlessly the miners had gained an unprecedented triumph for themselves and, although no one realized it, for all German working people as well. The miners were hardly even short of cash as yet. Their free time had been vastly expanded, they had had a life-giving vacation, more money had been promised. Yet the fact that they had, for a moment, had a clear 8 hour day and then lost it, rankled. Mine delegates met Sunday, May 12, in Bochum. These men, the most respected among their fellows, knew that their deliberations were being watched throughout the land. They also realized that their own jobs were at stake. Yet they were divided about whether to suspend the walkout, and their debate was long and furious. Much had been won, but the true 8 hour day eluded them yet. The Ruhr was aware by now that returnees were being rudely handled by their foremen and they knew what that meant. However these disadvantages were not enough to make them want to continue a strike which most of them had not originally approved. The resolution which they passed was to accept the situation as it was, and a reference was made to the economic well-being of the *Vaterland*. They vowed to recommence the strike should the owners break the agreements, which were no longer such, since they had already been violated.[58]

In telling the men at the beginning of May to stay on the job, and then to go back at the first reasonable opportunity, the leaders were quite in accord with social democratic thinking. The party was made uneasy by the stoppage. Then on May 18, with the end in sight, Bismarck told the Reichstag that social democrats were revolutionaries, enemies of the Fatherland, etc.[59] This was the regular litany of the Right. Actually the party was on its best behavior, making sure that the hated Exceptional Law would actually lapse in 1890. Actions by the working class which could be described, no matter how dishonestly, as revolutionary, were the last thing desired. Rising after Bismarck, Bebel replied that his party was interested neither in strikes nor in revolution.[60] He went yet further. In a public letter to the *Rheinisch-Westfälische Zeitung*, generally regarded as the mouthpiece of the mine operators, copies of which were mailed to *Sozialdemokrat* and *Glückauf*, he made his point as emphatically as possible:

> Social democracy...was just as much surprised as the rest of the world by the outbreak of the miners' strike. We do not deceive ourselves as to its probable result. [i.e., defeat] A few days after the outbreak of the strike, a [*Kassen*] trustee at the *Hibernia* pit, a man until then completely unknown to me personally, or by name, wrote me...to ask what prospects the striking miners might have for support from their colleagues abroad. I replied that there were no such prospects...Furthermore, I added that in view of the great number of the strikers, and because the walkout had spread into nearly all districts, support from *German* workers was also not to be expected in sufficient quantity. I advised them to accept a suitable compromise with their employers, and to postpone the rest of their demands, which I recognized as just and moderate, until another time.[61]

No man understood the German working class better than August Bebel.[62] It is most unlikely that the strike surprised him: it was only better to say that it did, by way of distancing himself from it. He could well have believed that the miners would be defeated, since no major strike had ever been won. His notion that the success of strikes depended upon money and not on the determination of the participants is orthodox party doctrine. What is notable is that no single action in German history (1848-1914) did as much as this miners' strike to elevate the working class standard of living, yet the great hero of that class advised that it be broken off.

In 1872 social democrats stood aside while Catholics struck. This time Catholics did not stand aside, but they did not try for leadership. Their Daniel Eckhardt commented: "Here are only miners, no others. They are not social democrats, nor ultramontanists, nor Christian Socialists, but only miners who are pursuing their own affairs."[63] Catholic representatives attended all the meetings where key decisions were taken. Possibly they were less anxious to end the walkout than their more experienced colleagues.

The 100,000 had been counselled by their emerging captains. It remained for them to decide, as they had done at the beginning. They had had 4 possible courses of action then, but now they had fewer. Most of them had rejected the historic way, which was to submit to their employers, come what may. Their ancestors had been peasants and serfs who also, a burned hayrick or two notwithstanding, had found it difficult to stand up to their lords. This May, in the Ruhr, Saxony, Silesia and the Saar, tens of thousands had remained *unter Tage* during the crucial days. And, as the owners and the emperor had alleged, many more would have done so had it not been that their windows would have been broken back in the villages. The men felt they ate better if they had the boss's favor. This line of thinking was more popular in Germany than in other industrialized lands.

Second, the 100,000 could have petitioned the emperor and the boss and let it go at that. When strikes were only quasi-legal, this method had great appeal. It was advocated by the leaders. Plaintive missives to Berlin cost little money and few jobs; they were not disturbing either to signer oraddressee, and were quite in accord with the ways of a patriarchal society. The single difficulty with this method of procedure was that it generally produced nothing.

A third way of going about the struggle added more force to the demands. The Barmen-Elberfeld dyers of 1855 framed a statement, stayed away from their plants - all 800 of them - did a bit of damage and then returned.[64] This was not a strike, as historians from both Germanies now regularly maintain,[65] but these textile workers were putting some determination behind their expression of grievance. Two years later they went out again, this time for three days,[66] and without vandalism. They were in an intermediary stage toward becoming strikers. They carried within themselves the threat of initiating a genuine walkout.

Essentially the 1889 strike was a petition with some force added. The first communication was sent to the Mining Association and the largest group left the pits while awaiting an answer. Then came the overlapping delegation to the emperor. When the results of both appeals were known, 20,000 returned to work. They were hardly acting as unionists, they were not even in accord with their colleagues. They were simply responding to their economic and political chiefs. "What will you do for us?" they asked. "Not very much, if that," was the answer. "Very well, we accept that." When their leaders, the *Kassen* heads, swallowed this thin soup, 35,000 more returned to the pits. They were acting out a stronger version of petition plus force, a form of action transitional to the strike.

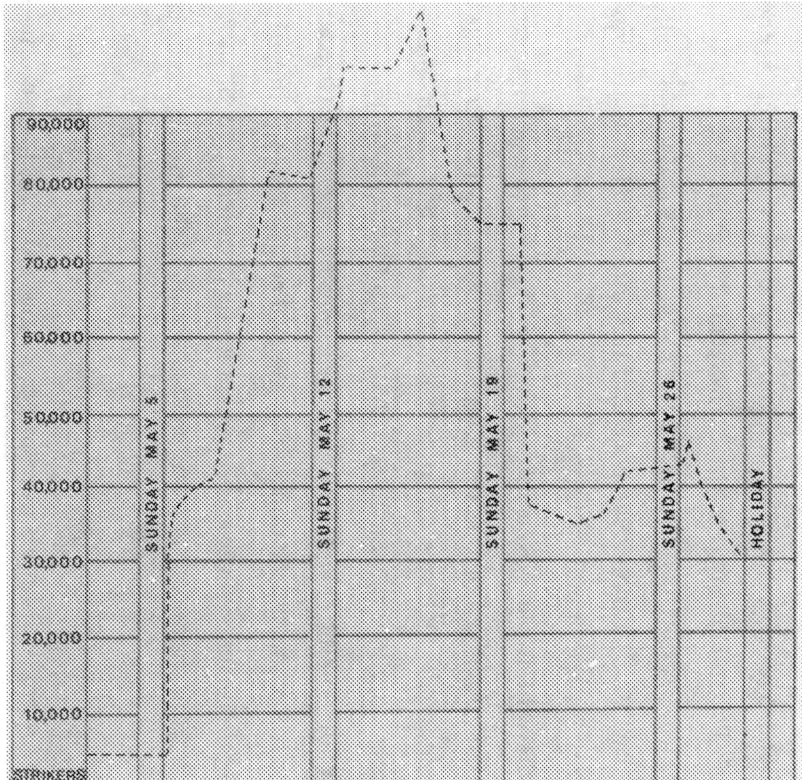

1889

MEN
ON
STRIKE

About 30-35,000 stayed out even after their chiefs had agreed to the uncertain terms offered (no pay increase specified). This last group wanted a true 8 hour day, and to know what the promised raise would be. This was the fourth option of 1889, which was to fight out the class struggle until victory should come. Or defeat. This was what the Waldenburgers had tried for in the largest and most intense class conflict Germany had ever experienced. This later strike took place in 1889, a year of proletarian self-confidence. There had already been one sign, from Hammacher, that owners might grant the true 8 hour day. The militant minority set a May 23rd meeting and issued a call for renewed strike. Some few thousands more came back out of the shafts. Hue was to growl that Catholics were behind this effort.[67] But there was clearly no majority for continued strike.

Further, the Berlin government, which was hostile to a genuine strike, had by now had enough. For one thing, the mine owners, who were beginning to have their good measure of political influence, had been pressing the government to get the men back. Also, if public opinion had once been predominantly on the side of the miners, this was no longer the case when they continued the conflict. The danger of a general coal strike, and there had been such for two to three days, was now ended by the defection of other fields. These being the circumstances, and the Ruhr miners themselves being split, the moment was ripe for government intervention. Every man who spoke for continuing found himself arrested. House searches for suspicious material became frequent. By June 1 everyone who still had a job had returned to the shafts. The effort of the militants who wanted to strike, and who were not more than 30 percent of all, had been broken.

Back on the job, more of the day belonged to the miners. Sunday shifts and overtime were dead. The regular 6 day 8½ hour shift soon began to be shaved as well. Wages went up, and the Ruhr presently led all the fields in pay. Its miners became some of Germany's most prosperous workers. In a few years pay in most industries was to commence rising and this was much the result of the Ruhr miners' efforts. Likewise they were responsible for the first real surge of trade unionism which began in the mid nineties. They had demonstrated the value of action.

One other gain, not easy to measure, was achieved. The miners cast off some of the subservience that had come down to them over the centuries. A contemporary pamphleteer remarked:

> The miners had [now] *become conscious of their own power.* They had likewise become aware of their *dignity as human beings*, as became noticeable in dealings between officials and workers. Crudities and insults *were no longer absorbed in silence*, and the rough types among the officials, who always reached for the stick, had gradually to accustom themselves to look *no longer* on the workers as cattle or as slaves....[68]

The "humane handling" for which the miners asked was apparently being won.

Whatever the men had gained, the owners had lost very little. Higher wages were soon recovered as the price of coal rose. The overtime hours and the extra shifts had not been the most productive, so they were not a loss. Above all, they had not demeaned themselves in their own eyes by parlaying openly with the miners. Hammacher, who sinned in this regard, was shortly dismissed, despite decades of service. The appearance of total control over the men, however much violated by the latter's victories, was maintained to the great satisfaction of the coal owners. The lesson which they learned from 1889 was that great unity would give them yet greater power. They could readily apply the notion, being only a few dozen. The miners could not, for there were hundreds of thousands of them and they held to different creeds.

A CONTEMPORARY BRITISH STRIKE

Close to the time of the 1889 Ruhr strike there occurred an outbreak of much greater dimension among the English coalies, who were many times more experienced in such matters than their Teutonic colleagues.

For centuries coal was part of the growth of British industry. Already in the time of Elizabeth the black diamond was shipped beyond local markets. James I visited a Scottish shaft which extended under the sea. It has been argued, in fact, that the problem of keeping underground galleries dry prompted the invention of the steam engine.[69]

The men whose digging was so essential to the oncoming Industrial Revolution were hardly more than slaves. They were kept by force in isolated villages under long term agreement. They could be beaten, for England had nothing of the glorious medieval *Bergmann* tradition. The first great rebellion, whose central issue was the long term contract, came in 1765 in the Newcastle region. After this long stoppage Parliament, doubtless influenced by the freer winds then blowing in the Western world, ended the coalies' contract slavery.

By mid-19th century, with British world position at its peak, miners were making a great contribution to the economy. They did not become Chartists, but in 1848 48,000 of them struck the same fields their forebears had in 1765. They wanted to end one year contracts, and they wanted to reduce underground gas. It was a tense struggle. The men were driven from company homes and had to live with their families in tents. They had no union, and it was too early to expect help from other trades. They held out for 5 months; it was the fight publicized in Engels' *Condition of the Working Class in England*. So early in the Industrial Revolution, a struggle of this size could not have been lost, and this was the largest strike in world history. The contract holding the men on the job for one year soon died.

British coal mining continued to grow, the biggest seams being in Northumberland, Yorkshire and Wales. For half a century each region fought its own class wars, but there was no repeat of the epic 1844 encounter. A miner-autobiographer paid tribute to what was accomplished in the early days:

> As a body and as a class the miners were fed, housed, and treated more like cattle than like human beings 50 years ago, when my life's struggles first began. *All has since changed*, and the result of men's labour and hope is now seen and felt everywhere...The men of '32 and '44 showed us how to suffer and how to fight.[70]

By the 1880s there were miners in Parliament, one of whom, the Scotsman Keir Hardie, was the first to wear street clothes there.

In 1892-93 the price of coal was falling in Britain, then still the chief European energy producer. Owners accordingly wanted to transfer their losses to the coalies, and announced a massive 25 percent cut in pay.[71] They did not realize that European proletarians were a shade different after 1889 than before. When the men were asked to sign papers assenting to the cut, 221 did so, and 143,695 refused. The fight was on.

Through the summer the men held out without difficulty. Two were killed at Featherstone early in the conflict. Shootings were not common during English walkouts, and the tragedy helped solidify the men. Public opinion sided with the miners because of the extraordinary size of the pay cut. The

Gladstone cabinet soon had to become involved, for the economy was beginning to be affected. The owners buckled and in the fall they commenced, one by one, paying the men at the previous rate. Meanwhile miners' families held out as well as they could. The union laid a food tax on returning miners to assist those still striking. By November there was a national contract guaranteeing the pre-strike level of wages. This victory immensely strengthened the miners. All British unions were encouraged by what the miners had done. More than 13,000,000 days work had been lost, a figure unprecedented in European history, and larger than all the work losses in this volume added together.

Along with Holland, England had the best developed European system of popular representation. After the execution of the King in 1649, political power moved gradually to a parliamentary body elected by property owners. Emphasis upon voting by male inhabitants and upon legislative power, and the weakness of the army, created favorable conditions for strikes such as could not be equalled on the continent. For generations are required before industrial workers can acquire the skill, courage and experience to challenge their betters through strikes, isolated instances like Waldenburg excepted. That wearisome and painful education comes easier in a land with a tradition of self-government and relatively open politics. A continental nation, forever seeing itself in a nutcracker between more powerful states, whose rulers feared not the gallows, lacked favorable conditions for successful strikes.

NOTES

1. For the Berlin strike see Eduard Bernstein, *Die Berliner Arbeiterbewegung,* 3 vols., (Berlin: 1907-1910), 2, 278; for the miners' strikes, Karl Oldenburg, "Studien über die rheinisch-westfälische Bergarbeiterbewegung." *Jahrbuch für Gesetzgebung, Verwaltung und Volkswirtschaft im Deutschen Reich* [henceforth Schmollers Jahrbuch] 14 (1890), 923.

2. Hans Marchwitza, *Meine Jugend* (Berlin and Weimar, 1974), 237.

3. Hue described the Saxon influence on the Ruhr. *Bergarbeiter*, 2, 239. Imbusch reports that Ruhr Catholics were suspicious of what came from Saxony. *Arbeitsverhältnis*, 274-75.

4. L. Lensing, *Der grosse Bergarbeiter Streik des Jahres 1889 im Rheinisch-Westfälischen Kohlenrevier* (Dortmund, n.d. [1889], 5ff.

5. Ibid., 15.

6. Max Jürgen Koch, *Die Bergarbeiterbewegung im Ruhrgebiet zur Zeit Zilhelms II (1889-1914)* (Dusseldorf: 1954), 37.

7. Hue, *Bergarbeiter*, 2, 355-356.

8. *Glückauf*, April 20, 1889.

9. Oldenburg, *Schmollers Jahrbuch*, 14, 929.

10. Liebtraut Rothert, *Umwelt und Arbeitsverhältnisse von Ruhrbergleuten in der 2. Hälfte des 19. Jahrhunderts* (Munster: 1978), 33.

11. Hue, *Bergarbeiter*, 2, 315.

12. Imbusch, *Arbeitsverhältnis*, 104ff. He has taken his figures from industry sources.

13. Hue, *Bergarbeiter*, 2, 256-57.

14. Helmut Lüthgen, *Die Rheinisch-Westfälische Kohlensyndikat in der Vorkriegs- Kriegs- und Nachkriegszeit und seine Hauptprobleme* (Leipzip: 1926), 2-3.

15. Imbusch, *Arbeitsverhältnis*, 278-79.

16. *Glückauf Beilage*, May 18, 1889.

17. Men frequently had to wring out their clothes. See the story of Max Lotz, as reported in Adolf Levenstein, *Aus der Tiefe* (Berlin: 1909), 57.

18. Adolf Levenstein, *Die Arbeiterfrage* (Munich: 1912), 161.

19. Lensing, *Der grosse*, 26ff.

20. Rothert, *Umwelt*, 33.

21. The Mine Workers Association later maintained that work in hard coal cut a man's life span from 56 to 45 on the average. See "Bergarbeiter! Aufgewacht und erkennt eure macht!", Bochum, 1911.

22. For instance, Hue, *Bergarbeiter*, 2, 116ff.

23. Krystyna Muryzynsky, *Polskie wychodzstwo zarobkowe w Zagtebiu Ruhry, 1880-1914* (Warsaw: 1972), ch. 2.

24. Marchwitza, *Meine Jugend*, 132.

25. Gustav Natorp, *Der Ausstand der Bergarbeiter im Niederrheinisch-Westfälischen Industriebezirk* (Essen: 1889), 73.

26. *Sozialdemokrat*, February 10, 1889.

27. *Glückauf*, April 27, 1889.

28. Rothert, *Umwelt*, 50, provides an example.

29. *Rheinisch-Westfälische Zeitung*, May 8, 1899.

30. Oldenburg, *Schmollers Jahrbuch*, 14, 934.

31. Natorp, *Der Ausstand*, 11.

32. Hans Georg Kirchoff, *Die staatliche Sozialpolitik im Ruhrbergbau, 1871-1914* (Cologne: 1958), 60-61.

33. August Siegel's account, "Ruhrbergarbeiterstreik 1889" has been reprinted in Wolfgang Emmerich, edit., *Proletarische Lebensläufe: Autobiographische Dokumente zur Entstehung der Zweiten Kultur in Deutschland, Vol. 1, Anfänge bis 1914,* (Reinbek bei Hamburg: 1974), 228-230.

34. Quoted in Dieter Fricke, *Bismarcks Prätorianer: Die Berliner politische Polizei im Kampf gegen die deutsche Arbeiterbewegung (1871-1918)* (Berlin: 1962), 271, fn. 545.

35. Lily Braun, *Memoiren einer Sozialistin*, 2 vols. (Munich: 1909-1911), 1, 393.

36. Compare the table in Koch, *Bergarbeiterbewegung*, 142, table 6.

37. Hue, *Bergarbeiter*, 2, 357.

38. *Sozialdemokrat*, May 18, 1889.

39. Siegel in *Proletarische Lebensläufe*, 229-230.

40. *Glückauf*, May 4, 1889.

41. Anna Altmann, "Jugendgeschichte einer Fabrikarbeiterin," in *Proletarische Lebensläufe*, 129.

42. Hue, *Bergarbeiter*, 2, 360-61.

43. Natorp, *Der Ausstand*, 54.

44. Gustav Seeber and Walter Wittwer, "Friedrich Hammachers Aufzeichnungen über den Bergarbeiterstreik von 1889," *Jahrbuch für Geschichte*, 16 (1977), 424-25.

45. The house of Krupp, for one, recognized that no organ of public opinion sided with the coal magnates. Rothert, *Umwelt*, 57.

46. Koch, *Die Arbeiterbewegung*, 37.

47. Oldenburg, *Schmollers Jahrbuch*, 14, 933.

48. Speech of August Bebel, February 17, 1888, *Reichstags Verhandlungen*, (henceforth RV), 7 Leg. Per., 2 Sess., vol. 2, 957.

49. Paul Grebe, "Bismarcks Sturz und der Bergarbeiterstreik von Mai 1889: ein Beitrag aus den Akten des Staatsministerium," *Historische Zeitschrift*, 157 (1938), 92.

50. Pöls, Werner, *Sozialistenfrage und Revolutionsfurcht in ihrem Zusammenhang mit dem angeblichen staatsstreichplänen Bismarcks*, Lubeck, 1966.

51. Carl Severing, *Mein Lebensweg*, 2 vols., (Cologne, 1950), 1, 44-45.

52. Hue, *Bergarbeiter*, 2, 365.

53. Ibid., 2, 366.

54. Ibid., 2, 367.

55. Seeber/Witwer, *JfG*, 16, 441.

56. Hue, *Bergarbeiter*, 2, 370-71.

57. Seeber/Witwer, *JfG*, 16, 433.

58. Hue, *Bergarbeiter*, 2, 371.

59. *RV*, 7 Leg. Per., 4 Sess., vol. 2, 1832.

60. *RV*, 7 Leg. Per., 4 Sess., vol. 2, 1845.

61. *Sozialdemokrat*, June 1, 1889.

62. William Harvey Maehl, *August Bebel: Shadow Emperor of the German Workers* (Philadelphia: 1980) composed an encyclopedic study of the man, though its value was reduced by the annual approach to events. He does not analyze the symbiotic relation between Bebel and the German working class.

63. Quoted in Tenfelde, *Sozialgeschichte*, 583, fn. 14.

64. Wolfgang Köllmann, *Wuppertaler Färbergesellen-Innung und Färbergesellen-Streiks, 1848-1957* (Wiesbaden: 1962), 11-13.

65. That it was usual in this period to go out briefly and then return quickly to the plant may be seen in Elizabeth Todt, *Die gewerkschaftliche Betätigung in Deutschland, 1850-1859*, (Berlin: 1950), 118.

66. Köllmann, *Wuppertaler Färbergesellen*, 11-13.

67. Hue, *Bergarbeiter*, 2, 373.

68. Anton Bredenbock, *1889: Die erste Erhebung der Bergarbeiter* (Dortmund: 1909), 24.

69. R. Page Arnot, *A History of the Miners Federation of Great Britain, 1889-1910* (London: 1949), ch. 1.

70. Rymer's autobiography, *The Martyrdom of the Mine*, from which this excerpt has been taken, was reprinted in *History Workshop*, 2 (1976), 27.

71. The strike is described in Arnot, *Miners Federation*, 2, ch. 8.

3

THE PARTY AND THE UNIONS

From its birth in the 1860s until the First World War, the social democratic movement was the repository of the hopes of millions within Germany and without. In its first half century the party was under the influence of the 1848 Revolution, in which Germans attempted to resolve political problems, but did rather less towards economic betterment. As the needs of German capital development impeded the growth of unions,[1] social democracy was until 1900 the chief shield of laboring people against the propertied classes, but it continued to concentrate exclusively on politics.

The first continuous development of workingmen's groups dates from the late 1840s. Then in the spring of 1848, after the other major nations had had revolts, the Rhineland, of all Germany closest to Paris, broke out, followed by more economically developed Saxony and finally monarchical Berlin. Conditions of that year provided a favorable atmosphere for workingmen's societies. They were led by proto-social democrat and compositor Stephan Born,[2] whose childhood in Posen made him a son of the lost Ashkenazim. A chat or two with Engels had persuaded him to call himself a "communist," as many did that exciting year. His *Verbrüderung* (Brotherhood) was the forerunner of the giant social democratic newspaper empire.[3] Born also briefly became a strike leader as his colleagues, who were among the best paid of all workingmen, moved for a taler a day more pay and a 10 hour day.[4] They made their demands and then left the shops, which was quite illegal, save that this was 1848. The Prussian government was in no position to resist; young Born was called in at once to see Minister Pieper. A compromise was quickly arranged, as happened rarely in walkouts. Such was the major strike of the year of revolution. Born himself later fled Prussia and ended his days as a Swiss professor.[5]

Post-1848 emigration hurt the working class movement, not quite alive as it was, as promising people left the homeland. The old notion that whenever the common people raise their heads they are defeated was reinforced. Men reverted to the humbler ways of yore. Friedrich Lessner reported on comparatively free Thuringia:

> Here I attempted to agitate, but the people were too intimidated, and froze up at the mere mention of the word "Communist." They all seemed to be like children who had been beaten and were afraid of the master...[6]

In the 1860s different winds began blowing. Serfs were "liberated" in Russia and slaves in the United States, and on the continent national and popular movements took heart. Around 1859 the first German workers' discussion groups began meeting.[7] Feeling their inadequacy in framing a program, they hunted among the various would-be champions of their affairs,[8] and hit upon Ferdinand Lassalle. Between 1862 and 1864, in those months when he was not vacationing in the Alps, Lassalle barnstormed through laboring men's centers. He did found a movement but it seemed slow work:

> Then about a thousand members in our whole Association! These then are the fruits of our victory? For this I have written down my fingers and worn out my

> lungs! Is it not true, dear Vahlteich, that this apathy of the masses is enough to drive one to despair?[9]

Weary of politics, Lassalle pursued a teenage lady he hardly knew, and died painfully in a duel about her.[10]

The laboring men of Hamburg, Saxony and the Rhineland who had been groping their way toward politics before Lassalle continued to do so after his brief stay among them. A down-on-his-luck Frankfurt patrician, Johann Baptist von Schweitzer, who had once been involved in an incident in a park with a young boy, was their next chief. This second outsider, who wrote well, and who knew how to lead, had yet a further weakness, as his biographer, Gustav Mayer, later confessed:

> many years after Bebel's death I discovered in the archives a document which showed that Schweitzer had actually received modest aid from the regime.[11]

Bebel had long maintained that Schweitzer was in Prussian pay.[12] He rode to the Reichstag in a carriage with 4 white horses, and his newspaper was not self-supporting; likely he received more than one modest payment.[13] That same awe in the face of their betters which handicapped strikers gave early social democracy such dubious captains as these. The movement prospered better the moment it began to draw leaders from its own ranks.

The Lassalleans were Prussian-oriented, and their founder had confided in Bismarck. The so-called Eisenachers, led by Bebel and Wilhelm Liebknecht rose to counter them with a party drawn from the rest of Germany; they had their greatest strength in Saxony, Thuringia and Brunswick. Here the heads of the organization were cut of the same cloth as the followers: honest, realistic, patient, hard-working and looking for advancement in the world. The two branches now commenced the glacial progression of skilled Protestant workingmen into that fraternity-party known as social democracy.

The culture of earlier generations of workingmen had been formed by religion. Social democracy had the unparalleled good fortune to grow to maturity in the half century interval between the nadir of religious conviction and the rise of mass amusements. This period was characterized by optimism, was without wars, and experienced only distant genocide, while enjoying a rising standard of living. The high degree of literacy among German proletarians aided the leaders of social democracy who, until 1914, believed with John Stuart Mill that it was better to be Socrates dissatisfied than a pig satisfied. Party members were fed Marx, Darwin and even Goethe. "Do you read Dostoevsky, or are you only reading junk?" Marchwitza's political mentor asked him.[14] Recent scholarship indicates that the workworn proletarian audiences may not have relished their evening lectures,[15] yet men remained hungry for that education which was expected to elevate them. Much of this educational aspect of social democracy perished on that Western Front which the party was not able to close down.

In the radical year 1869 the Eisenachers made their then much condemned tie to the First International, which was a natural one since German workingmen had been tramping through Mediterranean lands[16] or laboring in shops in London or Paris for centuries. Before the Industrial Revolution they were not intensely nationalist; the Breslau general strike of 1792, which ended in massacre, had been provoked by an injury to a Magyar colleague.[17] Yet when the Eisenachers declared themselves internationalists, they were set upon as never before. Actually they were also expressing small state patriotism, that emotion which made Bebel and Liebknecht abstain from voting credits for the Franco-Prussian War. Though they became members of the First

International, they did not undertake activity on its behalf, and doubtless their hearts did not cease to be warmed by the many regimental bands of the German Empire,[18] nor were they less inclined to believe that the French were oversexed, the Poles dirty, and the Russians barbaric.

Social democracy was much shaped by Bismarck. In his new Empire he allowed the princes, the *latifundia* owners and the police to retain their old powers, while the influence of the Prussian Army was greatly increased by its achievements. The owners of coal and steel industries rose up to take their share of power through indirect means. What was left to the lower classes by way of power and influence was slight indeed, and was largely a censored voice of protest. The Reichstag ballot went to males at the then advanced age of 25, 10 or more years after most proletarians had begun holding a full time job. The Reichstag lacked control over army, foreign affairs and police, and could not overturn a cabinet.

Four years after the Second Empire was formed the social democrats took the logical step of combining Prussian and non-Prussian wings (1875). The united party received nearly half a million votes in 1877. Then came the Exceptional Law (1878),[19] based on the premise that social democrats had tried to kill the emperor.[20] But late nineteenth century Europe lacked the viciousness of the twentieth; it was not thought desirable to apply to workingmen's movements such means as might have destroyed them. The party was restricted in its public meetings and in its publications, yet by 1884 it gained 44 percent more votes than in 1877. A small outburst of strikes, the most important of which was at the *Germania* pit in the Ruhr, showed that working people had not lost their courage. Then despite Bismarck's renewed and false argument that the nation was in danger, social democratic votes went up 38 percent in 1887. The Protestant working class continued to mobilize around what it felt was its own party. The Reichstag refused to follow the Iron Chancellor and the hated Exceptional Law was allowed to lapse in 1890. Worker-writer August Winnig related how men greeted this event in his small town:

> As the strokes [of midnight] rang out, everyone rose. A wonderful feeling of joy came over all of us, and great deep shouts echoed back and forth. Round the table men reached out their hands to one another. Many embraced, and all eyes glistened.[21]

They deceived themselves that workingmen could now act freely in the political world, but it was nonetheless a great occasion.

Thus at the start of the 1890s social democracy seemed favorably situated in an improving economy. People did not believe Bismarck would last much longer, and the new emperor was expected, according to the ancient illusion, to be less repressive. Germany's subjects might yet become citizens.

In February, 1890 social democracy attained 1,427,298 votes, triple its pre-Exceptional Law total. It was a great triumph, for statistics and the myth of the future society were what substituted among social democrats for power. The party claimed 35 seats; the Catholics had three times as many deputies with fewer votes, for districts were rigged to favor the conservative countryside.

Party leaders met in 1891 to replace the 1875 program. Those who govern Germany foregather in Berlin, Munich or the Rhineland; men of good will, excluded from power, gather in more liberal Thuringia. The preamble of the party's new Erfurt program argued the inevitable fall of capitalism, and there followed proposals for social legislation and civil liberties. The first part of the Erfurt program was the dream, the second the proposals for legislation. Sharp-witted Austrian Friedrich Stampfer recalled conversing with comrades about this schizophrenic split:

> That the revolution...would come one day was an incontestable article of belief in Leipzig. But since its coming was "an act of natural necessity" no one had to do anything in the meantime but wait it out. Everything would be postponed until then.
>
> One day I was sitting in a circle of functionaries whom I was amusing with my naive questions. The encounter came to a peak with this one: You Saxons have the "Red Kingdom," and you have the majority of the Reichstag seats...If some unforeseen circumstances should suddenly bring you to power, would you be prepared to rule Saxony at least as successfully, if not better, than it has been ruled so far?
>
> The answer was explosive. Laughter gripped everyone, and voices broke in on one another. "What a thought - Mer is going to be a ruler. You, Kleemann, will be a finance minister!" All doubled over with laughter. "And you, Lipinski, will be Minister of Police! Ha-ha-ha, Lipinski will be Police Minister!" It had been a long time since they had had such fun.[22]

Stampfer concluded that a quarter of a century later Lipinski, hopefully by then better adjusted to the notion that a common man could be a cabinet minister, did indeed evolve into Saxony's Minister of the Interior.

Depression and police measures drove a minority of social democrats into radicalism. These were the *Junge*, mild anarchists whose forte was in revealing the compromises which party leaders made with existing imperial institutions. The *Junge* were not workingmen, not one held a Reichstag seat or headed a city organization, hence they were not a real menace.[23] But their departure from conventional ways alarmed party chiefs. The biggest guns, Bebel himself included, were sent against these mosquitoes, and they made an attack on this minority worthy of the Iron Chancellor.[24] Similarly, in 1880 social democracy, wanting to prove its innocence in the era of the Exceptional Law, had expelled anarchists from the party.[25] A precedent for getting rid of noxious radicals had then been established. It was quite superfluous, for the Second Empire did not really provide growing room for such dissidents.

The nineties brought new statistical gains, starting with 25 percent in the 1893 Reichstag balloting. The party was gradually dispersing itself beyond the traditional Saxony-Hamburg-Berlin-Brunswick base. Each city with a population of 100,000 now had a social democratic paper, usually published daily. Competent captains, well-disciplined rank and file, sufficient funds and enough attention to the wishes of the constituency all combined to build the strength of the movement.

The public voice that social democracy had through newspapers, meetings, and Reichstag speeches gave men who worked with their hands a human dignity they had never before enjoyed. Down until 1914 the party was the only laboring man's association which counted, at least for its own numerous strata. The grandchildren of isolated, illiterate peasants were here transformed into citizens of the world who read papers which contained parliamentary debates and editorials on the latest Italian cabinet crisis. The very best among them, as rank and file could plainly see, advanced to petty bourgeoisie by becoming editors and organizers, and perhaps even went to the Reichstag. From their achievements individuals gained a self confidence their forebears would never have had. It was harder for the boss to lay a stick on a man who belonged to the party with two million votes.

Men alone made these gains. Partly by law of the land, created by males, but much more by convention, when the comrades gathered on that foamy night once a week, their women remained at home with the children.

Social democracy preached parliamentary government, civil liberties and peace, which were Enlightenment concepts not previously popular in the land of the Hohenzollerns. Unlike England, France and the United States, Germany had no historically created ideological barriers against oppressive institutions. Fritz Stern remarks that when political anti-Semitism reared his head, there was no generally recognized principle with which to combat it.[26] Social democracy did much more than liberal parties to erode authoritarian concepts, an effort which was courageous if not sufficient.

To comprehend British politics study of the cabinet is necessary, to understand France the dichotomy brought on by the great revolution, but to have a grasp of Germany the essential is to realize the power of the Right. The owners of large estates and major industries found it outrageous that ordinary workingmen should pretend to a voice in public affairs. A large part of the population, cherishing the ways of the past and honoring great men, agreed with this point of view. These conservatives persuaded themselves, against all evidence, that "Reds" want to "divvy up" property, while favoring "free love" and an end to religion. Perceptive academicians such as Max Weber and Ferdinand Tönnies were already aware that social democracy was a type of liberal-labor party,[27] but the men on the Right preferred their anxieties, which were only increased by the statistical success of the workers' party. Nothing would bring them to reason. Machinists, for instance, pasted memorabilia from "the best years of our lives" (in the army) to their machines,[28] but the Emperor and von Stumm would still refer to them as "enemies of the Fatherland." The emotional force which the Right was able to mobilize against largely imaginary foes was to become a menace not only to its own nation but to the world.

Hardly less remarkable than social democracy's ability to mobilize and educate men was its inability to do anything more. The party's impotence, which was as fateful for the world as the power of the Right, may be conveniently broken down into four parts.

Between its remarkable triumphs of 1870 and its 1918 collapse after struggle with the whole world, the German army was palpably the strongest in existence. Naturally it cast its shadow upon German society, influencing in particular the budget, foreign policy, and heavy industry, hence being also potentially related to strikes. Social democracy did try to get a handle on the army by running stories on the cruelty of drill practice, by publicizing soldier suicides, and other scandals. But the Prussian Army remained untroubled by such petty criticisms and none of its actions, 1862-1914, can be said to have been influenced by social democracy.

The fate of Germany rested also with those who controlled foreign policy. Historians have identified turning points on the road to disaster: Bismarck's Austrian alliance, the venture into colonialism, the dropping of Russia, the building of the fleet and the failure of negotiations with England. Above all, the post-1905 isolation, to be compensated for by the bones of workingmen and peasants. Down to 1912 the party left matters like these, crucial to a nation in the heart of the continent, to its betters. They were not discussed in the party press or by Reichstag deputies.

As Germany became the second industrial state of the world, her economy was characterized by concentration of power. The men who took the decisions among the industrial giants in steel, coal, armaments, and electricity could do so without reference to working people. When Fritz Fischer offered detailed evidence that industrial barons sought French and Belgian resources through war, he found no need to discuss what trade union leaders thought of such plans.[29] Feldman's history of wartime and postwar German economy makes but exiguous comment on the unions.[30] These historians are correct, for the working class movement never attained any influence on the economy. Because workingmen were organized employers may have dealt out raises a bit faster when the economy turned up, and cut back wages slightly less when the cycle went downwards, but that was all. Crucial matters of unemployment, shorter hours, lower prices for food, etc. were beyond the reach of those to whom they mattered the most.

Social democrats affected to believe that all other weaknesses were compensated for by voting strength. "It is the ballot alone which gives us a fatherland," Bebel said in effect (1907).[31] Yet already in the 1890s there began to be losses in this area. Bebel's legions, used to regular 25 percent gains, now found the legislative period extended from 3-5 years, hurting social democrats the most, for they needed the stimulus of frequent campaigns. A second change was yet more painful. Saxony was the "Red" kingdom, the native home of the party,[32] where Lassalle had first campaigned. The comrades were now approaching a majority in the kingdom's lower house. A bloc of all other parties then combined to pass a Prussian-type three tier franchise, permanently excluding the unpropertied from a legislative majority.

Saxon party members put on a major struggle to save one-man, one-vote with Bebel speaking to 40-50,000 in Leipzig, the century's biggest rally. Then 80,000 marched, in the only such display between 1848 and 1906. But the other parties held firm against the disgrace of a social democratic majority. *Vorwärts* wrote, for neither the first nor last time, "whom the gods would destroy, they first make mad,"[33] but divine intervention failed just as did the giant march.

A thoughtful memoirist told how he lost hope when the Saxon franchise was restricted:

> In the twenty years between...the Anti-Socialist Law's going into effect and the ballot loss [his miscount-RWR] the working class had really shown the utter calm and discipline of which it was capable...there was not one political crime in Saxony. Had someone come forward with a plan for one, he would have been laughed down. If indeed at odd moments a red flag would unexpectedly appear on a tower to shock the timid greatly, at bottom this showed nothing but a sound sense of humor...[34]

Exemplary conduct went for nothing; social democrats were deprived even of illusory power. Hamburg (in 1906), Kiel, Lübeck, and even tiny Koburg were to fend off the moment of the Reds' parliamentary majority in the lower house in like fashion. (Lower house decisions could usually be vetoed by upper house, so the matter was largely psychological.) Despite these defeats, party leaders preached on about the future Reichstag majority. "There is one thing an authoritarian welfare subject cannot permit," writes Ralf Dahrendorf, "the development of the subject into the citizen," and this began to be achieved in Wilhelmine Germany by such means as the resistance to the Saxon franchise change.[35]

The social democratic movement had, at birth, a host of sociological, sexual and nationalistic preconceptions which made it difficult to appeal to those with different cultures: Catholic proletarians, agricultural laborers, the tenth of Second Empire population which was not Teutonic, and half which was female. Though social democracy was not ill-supplied with thinkers, neither they nor its political leaders were able to combat these hobbling prejudices, and so no penetration to speak of was made among these numerically significant potential allies.[36]

In the party's heroic days, from 1840 to 1900, because of size and experience, it towered over the unions. In these 6 decades the approach to strikes did not vary.

Engels admired the great English coal walkout of 1844 ("this 19 weeks' strike has torn the miners of the North of England from the intellectual death in which they had hitherto lain...,"[37]), but stopped short of recommending imitation. The *Communist Manifesto* spoke for trade unions, but its thrust was political. In 1848 Born had labored to end a strike, not to cause one. Such mid-century coolness towards unions and their activities accorded with reality, for proletarians were too poor and overworked to form organizations. Lassalle talked down unions and, with a rare bit of wit on this subject, remarked that a strike was "the attempt of a commodity to behave as a man."[38]

The sole party chief condoning work stoppages was Schweitzer. In the summer of 1868, before they were legal, he provoked discussions of strikes and then summoned the Lassalleans to a convention in the activist center Hamburg. As head of the party, it was he who kept the record of the proceedings there.

To the 36 men at this key gathering, he offered a resolution stating that while strikes could not improve wage earners' standards of living, they did help men break out of traditional patterns of subservience.[39] It was a novel idea, taken from Marx, and it was not again proffered in party history. After the fallen aristocrat made his presentation, there were 5 more speakers. Three opposed work stoppages on a variety of grounds. Audorf of Hamburg voiced a mild approval, and one man straddled the issue. This entirely theoretical and somewhat negative endorsement of strikes then passed 3417-2585, each delegate voting his local's membership.[40]

Backing Schweitzer in this vote was Fritzsche, head of the important tobacco workers' union, and the independent-minded Wilhelm Bracke of Brunswick.[41] Schweitzer had the proxies of all clubs too poor to send delegates. These three men, with the votes of strike-approving Hamburg, won the day.

Schweitzer now moved to empower the president (himself) to summon a union convention. A speaker from the floor, in what must have seemed a most visionary utterance, said that it must become possible for 50,000 to leave their jobs "without worrying about a day's pay." This resolution, having to do with practice, failed, 3255-3044. Had a fundamentalist clique of Lassalleans (the Hatzfeldters) not been outside the fold, both resolutions would have lost. It is improbable that these delegates were unsympathetic to strikes because of the difficulties with police which they provoked. But unions, in which any underage youngster could sign up for ten pfennigs a week, must have seemed like an unfortunate comedown from the respectful, ceremonial, traditional gilds, with the greatest prestige going to those who had belonged longest.

Throughout the period under review here social democrats were fond of describing themselves as "fathers of families," responsible for unfailing support for the many mouths at home. In the *de facto* working class marriage contract the question which counted most was not love, but whether the male party was a steady worker. Bringing home the weekly pay was an act of the greatest significance domestically.[42] Workingmen could frequently recall their pay from decades before. Then in later years when there were strikes, the working class press nearly always carried statistical reports on how many "fathers of families" were out, and also exactly how many women and children were affected. In the early years, when Schweitzer's Hamburg convention was held, wives were reported as unanimously opposed to strikes, though this was to change when walkouts were occasionally successful and the unions saw the importance of educating the women about them.

The social psychologist Alexander Mitscherlich has theorized that men bury what is nearest their souls,[43] in this case their unwillingness to contest with employers over hours and wages. It was not only Bebel, but all German workingmen who lacked knowledge of strikes. Although a work stoppage can be conducted in as orderly a fashion as the work itself, what they heard offended against their sense of order and propriety. When the 1848 revolution came to Lübeck, it was that gas lights did not go on in the ordinary way that sickened the elder Buddenbrooks to death. The lower orders had much the same sense of what was decent. Heinrich Fischer's reminiscences prescribed the following traits for book printers: "Obedience, loyalty, respectability, diligence, courtesy, modesty, reliability, and love of order,"[44] hardly what drives a man to the picket line. The miners school at Bochum demanded substantially the same characteristics.[45] A historian of 1889 spoke of how men were torn between what they thought was right, and what would preserve their "good names." The interminable catalogue of proper behaviors prescribed to their employees by many mining and other companies also militated against growth of a spirit of defiance.

Everywhere Teutonic civilization built a reverence for authority from which the owners of business were able to profit. Early nineteenth century memoirist Otto Richter portrayed his father as: "the model of a loyal worker, eager to do his duty, and making no claims on the world. He saw existing class differences as the dispositions of God. Towards those of higher station or toward propertied persons he showed himself anxious and behaved like a subject..."[46] Georg Fischer, the greatest of the proletarian autobiographers, suggested his approach toward authority when as a child he wept at the tribulations of Frederick the Great.[47] The earlier attitudes lingered, especially in those not exposed to politics; thus Otto Buchwitz' mother was ready to eject him from the house if he went on strike.[48] Ministerial student Paul Göhre, working incognito in a factory of the 1890s, commented that many of his workfellows believed that there would always be rich and poor in the world. If the remark of the hated Minister Puttkammer that behind every strike lay the hydra of revolution was long remembered, that may have been because it was believed. Some workingmen always took the bosses' point of view, some part of the time.

Schweitzer lost the vote at the convention, but he was tough and determined. Had he been the miners' chief in 1889, they might have won their eight hour day. In his capacity as Reichstag deputy he summoned a union convention,[49] where he set up one big union for all trades. An unbelievable 140,000 were said to be represented there. This action by the Lassalleans prompted the Eisenachers to call a counter convention, at which an equally ridiculous 100,000 were reported to have sent delegates. Both these somewhat imaginary organizations presently collapsed. Schweitzer lost interest in the movement and turned playwright, and with him the reign of the adventurers among the Prussians passed. Tölcke, first social democrat to make headway in the Ruhr, was enraged to have built a party of 800 only to have it crumble to 20 because of a strike.[50] Lassalleans now returned to the theory of their founder: politics only.

The Eisenachers too, defeated at Waldenburg, became even more cautious toward strikes, laying down two conditions for approving them. First, a stoppage had to be "directly provoked" by capital. In non-coded language this meant that workers had to be defending themselves against a lengthened workday or a cut in pay. Such events occurred normally during a recession, when men would in any case be reluctant to leave their jobs. Second, "sufficient means" had to be on hand, that is to say, there had to be funds to pay each "father of a family" through the duration. Applying the "sufficient support" test to Waldenburg (1869), where 200,000 days were lost, and assuming generously that 300,000 might have brought victory, and that families could subsist on a thaler and a half each day, then 450,000 thalers were needed. It was not remotely possible that the 25-30,000 social democrats could have raised this money, far above a week's pay for each. Only a small, highly paid group of skilled artisans could meet this criterion. An employer could easily, through the police, ascertain the size of the defense fund and plan accordingly. Instances of police providing such information are not wanting, as the weaker party would thus inform the stronger how long to expect resistance. In effect, the Eisenachers were trying to wish all work stoppages out of existence.

Reality soon wiped out these convention decisions. In Chemnitz (Saxony) machinists overrode their leaders and went out for a 10 hour day.[51] The local party leader was Johann Most, the radical of the day, later thought to be mixing too much dynamite with his politics. Even he could only be brought kicking and screaming to back the walkout in formal but insincere terms.

By 1878 healthy starts had been made on union-building by printers, tobacco rollers, construction workers and certain specialized artisans. Miners were beginning to join up in Saxony and the Ruhr. Social democratic related unions, which they called "free," numbered around 50,000 in 1878,[52] which was a low moment for the economy. They were then abolished under the Exceptional Law, though after 1883 they could commence a shadow existence. It was the way of patriarchal Prussia to be less concerned when men wanted to eat than when they wanted to think.

Among charges which "emperor-killer" social democrats had to meet in the 1880s was that of being fomenters of strikes. There were few walkouts then, but Right wing arguments never depended upon evidence. In the legislatures, their only public forum, party chiefs gave fairly uniform answers to this allegation. For example, Wilhelm Meister, "member of the Reichstag from 1884 to his death on April 6, 1907,"[53] representing Hannover, replied thusly to Puttkammer's 'hydra of revolution' metaphor:[54]

> *It has been social democracy* which has explained to the worker his class position, has made clear to him that it is not the *individual employer* who is to be held responsible for economic hardships...It is social democracy which has labored to the greatest possible degree to get rid of *class hatred* and its consequences, particularly in *pay struggles*. Gentlemen, where you do not see a disciplined working class organization...there you will always find that the method of struggle is more dangerous...The actuality is that social democracy always troubles itself to explain to the workers the interconnection of their economic and social relationships, and to hold them back from every overhasty action, in particular from strikes.[55]

Thus what scholars are increasingly recognizing as the passivity of social democracy was here utilized in the service of preventing strikes. In the same vein Liebknecht remarked, in January, 1889, as the first signs of coming Ruhr conflict showed:

> ...We have at all times declared ourselves in principle against strikes, where they are not conditionally required by circumstances. And now I want to mention an expression which was used by a public figure in connection with events in the Rhine-Westphalian coal works. He qualifies as the number one authority there and he spoke to me a couple of weeks ago in the foyer of the Reichstag when I was in the company of a friend. He said: one thing I must remark to you: *if a strike is to be avoided, then we have to thank your friends*, the social democrats. *They are the only reasonable ones.*[56]

Liebknecht was referring, though in error with respect of power, to Hammacher, while also giving the lie to Bebel's denial of knowledge of a coming strike. By way of beating the matter to death, there is Hasenclever's declaration, i.e., of a man twenty years a deputy and onetime Lassallean president, "It is we who are the opponents of strikes...,"[57] while Sabor, two times Frankfurt's deputy in this decade: "Social democracy seeks insofar as possible to prevent strikes."[58] Of course all these statements were made in the presence of some of the dominating figures in German political and economic life, and far out of the earshot of the average dues paying social democrat.

Between 1885 and 1904 major work stoppages took place among men who were heart and soul social democrats. The party was by no means fanatical, and quite conscious of problems of getting and retaining voters. The hopes of tens of thousands could not be sacrificed no matter how often the principle had been iterated. The first such "social democratic" walkout came in Berlin. Lassalle could hardly round up a few score for an oration, but now hundreds of thousands of the capital's subjects counted among the faithful. Bismarck had helped by putting the city under martial law and driving out local leaders.[59] The party had no Goebbels to fire up rank and file, but under the Exceptional Law the "Reds" votes went up from 51,000 to 126,000, and by 1893 5 of 6 Reichstag seats belonged to the party.

Twelve thousand Berlin masons left their jobs in 1885, bringing most building to a stop. Their goal was 50 pfennigs pay an hour for 59 hours toil, which was high for the time, yet their work was seasonal and they were often between jobs. Many of them got their 50 pfennigs.[60] In 1888 they sensed an economic upswing and prepared for another encounter, as did masons in other cities. It is said that in Dortmund miners went to the masons' assemblies and were infected with their militancy. Just one week after Schröder, Bunte, and Siegel had seen the emperor, 20,000 Berlin masons left their jobs to seek 60 pfennigs an hour.[61]

Social democracy could live with this strike, which was not directed at the nation's jugular. There were many contractors, they did not feel a psychological threat to their authority over a few pfennigs, and many would settle, for this was high season. Apprentices could be sent away, and a large sympathetic city could provide support for the "fathers of families." Of course these may only have been the party's rationalizations, as there was little choice, for the building trades likely cast a quarter of its Berlin votes.[62] The strike continued until early July, but by that time many had gained the much prized 9 hour day in this pacesetter city.

Because of the numberless masons who left town, and the varied moments of settlement, lost days cannot be intelligently estimated. The total probably approached that of the Ruhr strike. What distinguished this struggle was its clearcut victory. Social democracy did not join in the celebration, nor draw lessons from what had happened. The attitude of Eduard Bernstein, party intellectual who lived in London during the dock strike of 1889 and the miners' stoppage of 1893, is illustrative. No other thinker puzzled as much how the apparent strength of social democracy might be converted into real power.[63] In his (commissioned) history of the Berlin party, he discussed each election and by-election to the Reichstag and city council, every large meeting and funeral, while reproducing handbills, public statements, pictures of members *ad infinitum*, with 800 pages for the Exceptional Law period alone. This is his grudging, whining, somewhat inaccurate account of one of the greatest strike victories of this era:

> Berlin did not lack for large struggles over pay which required sacrifices...Of these, the one which was particularly prolonged was a strike of masons, who inscribed the nine hour day and sixty pfennigs on their banner. The struggle continued for months and ended with a half success. A portion of the masters granted the demands.[64]

The following year (1890) improvement in the economy, major electoral gains and Bismarck's departure gave the pariah party more breathing room. Better times helped the unions even more. In his autobiography Wilhelm Bock, shoemaker, quoted a Thuringian ditty about three potato meals each day,[65] and, earlier in the century, life had been like that. But after the 1880s few families had to settle for provender of that grade. Each year since 1860, overlooking the worst of the 1870s, there were for families of laboring people a few more marks to spend, and a few more minutes free time for the provider. The money went for improved diet, especially more meat and butter. The more monied workers could now sit down with their colleagues over a stein of beer after a mere 10 hour day (still 6 days a week). In mid-century their predecessors had drunk themselves into oblivion with bad gin or brandy after 14 hours. Proletarians probably require a decent diet before they can form unions or parties, at least in Europe.

Already in 1891 there were nearly 7 times as many union men as in 1878, converts from the time of persecution. Their representatives met in 1891 at Halberstadt to create a national association, led by social democrats. The far less numerous Catholics then moved to set up a union for their people, open to all classes, and not hostile to employers. The social democratic or "free" unions had a small bureaucracy and an informative biweekly, *Correspondenzblatt*. These instruments of potentially large influence fell into the hands of a forceful young man with a clear-headed appreciation of the unions' promising future. This was Carl Legien (1861-1920), like Bebel, a machinist.

Once in office Legien appealed for strike funds. The walkouts of the early 1890s were not on the scale of the United States or England, yet they hinted at a greater militancy than that of the past. For example, 3448 glassworkers, with 3355 children, had had to absorb a pay cut of 7 percent, but bridled when asked to lose a further 25 percent.[66] This occurred in Flensburg, Schleswig Holstein, a province never a center of proletarian action. The glassworkers stayed out an unprecedented 7 months.

Two other walkouts concerned unionists more. Tobacco rollers had long been pathfinders for the movement, second only to book printers in organizing in 1848, then reconstituted by F. W. Fritzsche in 1860. Though not rich or numerous, they had a highly developed sense of fraternity, and were distinguished for their literacy. Franz Bergg pictured the environment in small shops:

> A newspaper was read during work. The men alternated at the reading stand. In addition books of academic character were given a hearing. Comments and exchanges of opinion accompanied the reading...[67]

The rolling of cigars required concentration and was exhausting. Only the indolent took a breath of air during the day. One memoirist commented: "...a capable workingman could with great diligence, only briefly interrupted by a miserable noonday meal at his bench, turn out 1200 pieces, and in some desperate instances even more."[68] That was a pace of nearly 10 a minute. That such cigars were largely consumed by the possessing classes may have intensified class consciousness.

In militant Hamburg, tobacco men went out late in 1890. Their employers had asked 3,000 to sign "yellow dog" contracts, swearing they were not union men. Thus in social democratic eyes, this was a permissible defensive strike.[69] Hamburg had good reasons to back the tobacconists, for they were 5 percent of all the organized, and had excellent political connections. All of 425,000 marks was collected, cash coming from other unions, and from door to door efforts. After the men had stayed out until mid-March, they were forced to return defeated.[70] The loss was to have virtually mortal consequences for their union, and both their significance in working class politics, and their standard of living now declined.

A yet harsher loss was absorbed by the book printers, those heroes of 1848. In the early 1890s they were about 6 percent of the unionized, but their influence upon proletarian politics was much greater than that figure suggested. Better paid than most, in 1891 they went out for a 12½ percent raise and a 9 hour day. Both party and unions leaped to their support and during the three month strike which followed, more than 2,500,000 marks were collected. The 10,000 printers received allowances exceeding the average workingman's pay, so that the argument was heard that strikes meant that richer workingmen were exploiting the poorer.[71] Bosses stood their ground and the printers were hurt by a cyclical downturn. Official statistics put the 1891 jobless rate at 4½ percent (massive for the time), and the next year there were marches of the unemployed in Berlin. Employers had made their calculations well. Previously these printers had ranked with miners, iron, steel, and brewery workers at the top of proletarian pay scales. After the defeat of 1891 they slipped, and were never to participate in the upswing which lay just a few years ahead.[72]

"They [the book printers] would have taken our last pfennig," Bebel lamented privately.[73] In the strike wave of 1889-1891 the party had been forced to back major walkouts for the first time. The cost had been extreme, not only in cash, but in defeats and in the jobs of the faithful which were sacrificed. Social democracy's modest central office had had an income of only 258,000 marks in 1892-1893, a national election year.[74] The printers had soaked up nearly ten times as much. Proletarian funds for elections were precious, but in walkouts they were totally lost. No wonder that when the brief and partial followup strike of 1891 come to the Ruhr, *Vorwärts* wrote: "The Social Democratic Party has done everything in its power, and in the power of human beings, to avoid its outbreak."[75] Bebel took to the road to argue that major gains for proletarians could only come through political means.[76] If party officials dreaded the strikes of 1889-1891, however, a primary reason was financial. Masons, printers, and tobacco rollers were peaceful types in non-crucial trades; their stoppages would never bring the formidable von Stumm to the podium of the Reichstag to denounce. As the figures suggest, the reluctance to spend on the class struggle was an official attitude, and did not extend to rank and file.

Revolutionaries of Tsarist days robbed banks, and other parties have followed their example. Leftwing movements in the United States notoriously run on debt. Few radical movements in the world, in fact, show a moral attitude towards meeting their bills. Not so German social democrats and trade unionists. Both in their public and their private lives, they put a high value on solvency. Already in the Leipzig "treason" trial (1872) Liebknecht had maintained, with good psychological perception, that no one should suspect his party of being revolutionary, for it kept too regular accounts, as well as copies of all letters dispatched.[77] Social democracy always balanced its budget, and then published it to the world, while unions gradually assembled publicly reported millions for pensions. Clearly the accumulation of money was highly prized as a virtue.

Between 1889 and 1892 party and unions collected and paid out millions in strike support. Often the drain did not end with the strike, for those who lost their jobs had to be helped. Nothing unusual in this - in lands where there is the least bit of working class prosperity, support goes to strikers. But in Germany there were particularly high payments, and they were granted in nearly all conflicts. The great British mine strikes of 1844 and 1893 had substantially no allotments. In Germany medieval baggage seems to have been carted into modern times, for the gilds had always taken care of their own. Of course 100,000 miners were never out in medieval times, but when the nineteenth century came the question was not reviewed. Allotments became virtually automatic. Party leaders, preferring no walkout, kept strike payments high, then argued that the costs could not be met. The alternative of modest allotments and sacrifice was not experimented with.

Given social democracy's long standing feeling of superiority toward the unions, and the post-1889 upsurge of the latter, a collision was quite to be expected. The party chose a most favorable moment. In 1891 the economy had turned sour, with unemployment reaching an unprecedented 6 percent. Men left the unions, for they were a job hazard; Göhre reported that they were semi-secret at his factory.[78] Unions had claimed 344,000 members in 1891, but by mid-1892 this figure had shrunk to an official 250,000, which meant a real 200,000.[79] The miners' association was collapsing. Meanwhile social democracy was confidently striding towards two million votes at the next Reichstag election.

Several hundred party chiefs gathered annually for the pleasant proletarian rite of the all-expenses-paid convention, to listen to reports on unceasing progress, and to fight out theoretical matters. In 1893 it was the turn of Cologne, for an effort was being made to penetrate "Black," i.e., Catholic, areas. The sixth item of business was party-union relations, coming just before Anti-Semitism, as the party continued to educate the nation out of barbarisms.

Traditionally historians regarded Dresden (1903) as the key congress, although there the party only squirmed in its impotence, in proof of Fanon's thesis that ghetto residents, unable to attack their real enemies, devour each other. At Cologne the 1868 debate over the utility of unions was continued, amid carping at the dream of the socialist future. Three hundred attended, 7 of them women (apparently, for not every Christian name was listed).[80] The usual reports indicated that 32 newspapers were appearing 6 times a week, 25 three times, others less frequently; members had suffered 37 years in prison for political offenses in the past year, and had been fined 25,000 marks. Etc., etc.

The sixth item, it was soon apparent, was not to be a discussion of unionism, but a pillory of 32 year old Carl Legien. Party executives included Bebel, 53, Liebknecht, 67, Paul Singer, 49, Ignaz Auer, 47, and Richard Fischer, 38, all veterans of both the Reichstag, and the Exceptional Law persecutions. The charges against upstart Legien were that his *Correspondenzblatt* had a disrespectful tone, and that he had consorted with members of the bourgeois at a conference.[81] Actually it was easy for party leaders to be virtuous in this respect, for neither in nor out of the Reichstag would bourgeoisie (one or two individuals excepted) be seen with them. After the personal attack came the resolution. As Muslims believe in but one God, social democracy believed in but one organization. Unions were collapsing in 1893, so why should the party yield? The resolution, backed by the party, and dripping with condescension, expressed "sympathy" with the unions, and recommended that its members labor "tirelessly" and "with all their strength" for their success. A substitute introduced by Arons, a *Dozent* who was to lose his post for associating with the "Reds," urged all party men to join unions. Legien backed the Arons statement.

Legien knew he was outnumbered but would not give way.[82] No man believed more in unions than he, and he hit back at Bebel in a way that his opponents found to be "primitive." He cited reports that the chief, only a little less than a god to most present, had been openly hostile to unions. Without permission, he quoted private correspondence of Bavarian leader Ignaz Auer. He took note of several papers which disliked the very existence of unions. Yet with some of the same artfulness which had marked the majority resolution, he acknowledged that his unions were only preparatory for the more significant political association. More honestly he snapped at his baiters that it was not very difficult for a man to cast a secret ballot once every 5 years, but that an individual put his job on the line when he joined a union.

Auer wrote little, spoke infrequently and jeered almost openly at the socialist future. But when the party had hard negotiations to carry out, or a bit of dirty work, like as not Auer would be selected for the role. Neither unions nor strikes were important in his native Bavaria. In making the official rebuttal to Legien he emphasized that over the years the comrades had been educated to high ideals, and would hardly be taken in by "Gomperism," that is, a few more pfennigs and a few less minutes on the job. Auer denounced Legien for hearsay evidence and misuse of private correspondence. He cited convention proceedings to show that the party had outgrown early negativism on unions. Finally, he had compiled the party's "Book of Martyrs" descriptive of Exceptional Law Days, and he drew Legien's attention to the many comrades who had done something more than cast a furtive ballot.

Though at such congresses men of prominence got the most time, others might have a few words. Rank and filer Reisshaus of Erfurt brought candor to the debate in alleging that in small towns one simply could not ask everyone to join unions - it was too dangerous. Anglophile Wilhelm Liebknecht said that the English example had long ago made him friendly to unions. Yet, he continued, even with the best of fortune, capital could not be worsted on its home grounds and had to be defeated by political means. Schönlank addressed himself to the multifarious handicaps to union organization, especially the prohibition on associations for household and agricultural workers.

Then the great man arose and recalled how he had done the right thing by unions since 1868, speaking countless times before locals. He went on to list the limitations on unions' potential. Bismarck's social legislation had much reduced their normal area of activity. Not only that, but unions were not able to undertake really large struggles:

> We might be as well organized in respect of unions as we could wish, but if capital has once amassed such power as belongs to Krupp, Stumm, and the Dortmund Union in the coal and iron regions of Rhine-Westphalia, then there is no hope for the trade union movement. Then only the political struggle can help.

He repeated this thought in a later brochure on the unions.[83] Understandably these remarks caught the attention of subsequent speakers. The shoemaker Bock suggested that there were regions outside the Ruhr where unions might yet flourish, while Molkenbuhr thought big capital might be attacked during economic upturns. Klara Zetkin iterated the familiar theme of the precedence of politics.

Legien made the first closing,[84] having a response for each criticism, including the one that he was too young to understand. He gave the impression of a vain man - he did curl his moustaches. Legien slid over the matter of Krupp, Stinnes, *et al.*, preferring to deal with Bebel's claim that social security obviated the need for unions.

In summing up Auer was less cutting than before, but showed great self assurance. We in the party had done much for the unions, he averred, and mentioned Legien's safe Reichstag seat. He made plain, however, where the shoe pinched, noting the money lost on strikes, especially the 2,500,000 with the printers. Successful election campaigns, by contrast, cost nowhere near such amounts.

Arons' resolution, backed by Legien, lost 29-169. This tally probably registered the size of the two factions. The resolution of the Executive, which papered over all differences, then passed unanimously. The tone of the entire debate had been petty, and no speaker had undertaken to review how earnestly and persistently German workingmen had been trying for 50 years to establish unions.

At a less quarrelsome moment, Legien had broader views on the possibilities of unions. He wrote of the English miners' struggle of 1893:

> After lasting 14 weeks, the biggest economic battle that has ever taken place has now come to a provisional end in England. We say provisional, for one cannot yet state with certainty that the compromise between the workers and the employers will be achieved through arbitration. And yet even now the workers have already won a brilliant victory. It is a triumph which proves...that the unions are not powerless even in the face of the greatest concentrations of capital...it teaches us that in the case of those large concentrations, strikes are not to be won in fourteen days or four weeks, but that these [huge] struggles constantly raise the number of those taking part and also the duration...The English coal miners' stoppage shows that the power of capital can be limited by the strength of the workers' organization. Furthermore it demonstrates that the point of view which

> says that strikes must be won in fourteen days or, at the outside, in three weeks, if they are to be useful, is completely in error.
>
> ...the strike gives us not only a fine example of the willingness to sacrifice, and of solidarity, but it also fills all those who see in trade unions the true protector of the rights of labor with new courage and hope.[85]

Legien was broaching matters usually considered undiscussable: that sacrifice had a role in strike, that it was necessary to face up to the long struggle, the Krupp and von Stumm might be defeated, and that examples from abroad might be instructive. As the German unions grew large and bureaucratic, such issues never became matters for vital debate.

Social democracy's first, and great, historian, Franz Mehring, writing at the turn of the century, wanted to downplay the notion that unions and party were hostile rivals.[86] It was part of his myth-making. To find evidence he had to go back to Schweitzer in the 1860s. Actually social democracy became great on the argument that only politics matters. Why should they have abandoned one of their most successful ploys? The fight for precedence between party and unions was, of course, never resolved in a formal way. Gradually, however, the activists in the working class movement leaned more and more towards Gomperism, while the great man spoke less and less of the socialist future and, by way of substitute, presently purchased a Swiss villa. As for the degree of power in the hands of Stumm, Kirdorf, Krupp, and the other lords of the mines, no one thought it a part of the socialist future to put restraints upon them.

NOTES

1. Hedwig Wachenheim, *Die deutsche Arbeiterbewegung, 1844 bis 1914* (Oxford and Opladen: 1971), 272ff. It was only after 1850 that accumulation of capital could take place in Germany. Even then it had to be brought together under less favorable circumstances than in England; the German effort at accumulation was further slowed by the long depression, 1873-1889. These difficulties made for holding down the standard of living of the working people, which never reached that of the imperial-nourished British proletariat in the period before 1914.

2. Stephen Born, *Erinnerungen eines Achtundvierzigers*, Leipzig, 1898.

3. See in particular Frolinde Balser, *Social-Demokratie, 1848/49-1863* (Stuttgart: 1962), chs. 3 & 4.

4. The walkout has been described in Francois Martin, *Geschichte der Lohnkämpfe der Buchdrucker von 1848 bis auf die heutigen Tage* (Basle: 1890), 40ff.; also Adolf Wolff, *Darstellung der Berliner Bewegungen im Jahre 1848 nach politischen, sozialen, und literarischen Beziehungen (Berliner Revolutionschronik)* (Berlin: 1849-1852), 153ff.

5. Born, *Erinnerungen*, 125-26.

6. Friedrich Lessner, *Ich brachte das Kommunistische Manifest zum Drucker* [reprint] (Berlin: 1975), 93.

7. See Toni Offermann, *Arbeiterbewegung und liberales Bürgertum in Deutschland, 1850-1863* (Bonn: 1979), 268ff.

8. Most of the liberal politicians spoken of by Dan Simon, *Das Frankreichbild der deutschen Arbeiterbewegung, 1859-1865* (Gerlingen: 1984) are generals without armies, looking to find supporters in the working class.

9. Ferdinand Lassalle to Julius Vahlteich, August 29, 1863, in Bernhard Becker, *Geschichte der Arbeiteragitation Ferdinand Lassalles nach authentischen Aktenstücken* (Brunswick: 1875), 82.

10. Ending his life in this scarcely rational way, Lassalle was never more himself, as his first biographer noted. Hermann Oncken, *Lassalle: eine politische Biographie*, 2nd edit. (Stuttgart and Berlin: 1920), 472.

11. "Scarcely anyone in Germany at that time had a sharper pen," wrote Gustav Mayer, *Erinnerungen: Vom Journalisten zum Historiker der deutschen Arbeiterbewegung* (Zurich and Vienna, 1949), 183.

12. Not only Bebel, who spent almost half a volume of his memoirs accusing Schweitzer of various misdemeanors, but other knowledgeable persons assumed that Schweitzer's heavy spending depended on Prussian funds. Eugen Richter, longtime leader of the liberals in the last quarter of the century, made this assumption. Bismarck had, of course, monies at his disposal for secret purposes. See Robert Noell von der Nahmer, *Bismarcks Reptilenfond: Aus der Geheimakten Preussens und des Deutschen Reiches* (Mainz: 1968), 87-88.

13. Ibid., 186.

14. Marchwitza, *Meine Jugend*, 181.

15. For an analysis of the reading habits of party and union members, devoted as they were to adventure and trash, see Josef Steinberg, *Sozialismus und deutsche Sozialdemokratie: Zur Ideologie der Partei vor dem 1. Weltkrieg* (Hannover: 1976), 129-142.

16. For an example of the jolly adventures of workingmen in pre-industrial Europe, consider Ernst Döbel, *Wanderungen durch einen Theil von Europa, Asien, und Afrika*, Eisenach: 1837.

17. See Waclow Dlugoborski, "Die Klassenkämpfe in Schlesien in den Jahren 1793-1799," *Beiträge zur Geschichte Schlesiens* (Berlin: 1958), 401-442.

18. Paul Göhre, *Drei Monate Fabrikarbeiter und Handwerksbursche* (Leipzig: 1913), 119-121.

19. For the party under the Exceptional Law there is Vernon L. Lidtke, *The Outlawed Party: German Social Democracy, 1878-1890*, Princeton: 1966.

20. Göhre, *Drei Monate*, 127ff. This theological student cites, in shock, a conversation with a worker who suggested that Bismarck was behind the "emperor-killings" of 1878.

21. August Winnig, *Frührot: Die Schulzeit des Maurergesellen* (Magdeburg: 1919), 193.

22. Friedrich Stampfer, *Erfahrungen und Erkenntnisse* (Cologne: 1957), 44-45.

23. The *Junge* assembled lists of social democracy's compromises with the class enemy. These are contained in Hans Müller, *Der Klassenkampf in der deutschen Sozialdemokratie*, Zurich, 1892.

24. These meetings were extensively reported in *Vorwärts*: for instance, the issues of July 18 and 24; August 22; September 3 & 24; October 2 & 27. All are in 1892.

25. At their first Exceptional Law period convention, social democrats took up, as first order of business, the expulsion of anarchists. See *Protokoll des Kongressess der Deutschen Sozialdemokratie*, Zurich, 1892.

26. Fritz Stern, *Gold and Iron: Bismarck, Bleichröder and the Building of the German Empire*, New York, 1977.

27. The sociologist Ferdinand Tönnies remarked in a letter to Friedrich Paulson, April 1, 1897, that "Social democracy is essentially a liberal party..." *Ferdinand Tönnies-Friedrich Paulsen*: Briefwechsel, 1876-1908, edit. Olaf Klees, Eduard Georg Jacoby and Irma Fischer (Jena: 1961), 321.

28. Göhre, *Drei Monate*, 121. Marchwitza wrote of miners who wore their military reserve caps *unter Tage.*

29. Carl Legien, head of the trade unions, and Alexander Schlicke, chief of the key machinists' union, are not in Fritz Fischer's index. The machinists' union included most of the penetration which unions had made into the giant iron and steel firms.

30. Gerald D. Feldman, *Iron and Steel in the German Inflation, 1916-1923*, Princeton: 1977.

31. *Vorwärts*, January 1, 1907.

32. Donald Warren, *The Red Kingdom of Saxony, 1901-1909*, The Hague: 1964.

33. *Vorwärts*, February 11, 1896.

34. Heinrich Lange, *Aus einer alten Handwerks-burschen Mappe* (Leipzig, n.d.), 174-75.

35. Ralf Dahrendorf, *Society and Democracy in Germany* (New York: 1967), 67-78.

36. Those sociological strata unpenetrated by social democrats were noticed by Gerhard A. Ritter (though he passes over women) in his *Die Arbeiterbewegung im Wilhelminischen Reich* (Berlin: 1959), 67-78.

37. Friedrich Engels, *Condition of the Working Class in England* (London: 1845), 258.

38. Quoted in Eduard Bernstein, *Der Streik: Sein Werden und Sein Wirken* (Frankfurt: 1906), 93.

39. *Social-Demokrat*, August 28, 1868.

40. Ibid., September 2, 1868.

41. See Jutta Seidel, *Wilhelm Bracke: Vom Lassalleaner zum Marxisten*, Berlin: 1966.

42. Good examples may be found in the autobiography of Wenzel Holek, *Lebensgang eines Deutsch-tschechischen Handarbeiters*, Jena: 1909.

43. Alexander Mitscherlich, *Thesen zur Stadt* (Frankfurt: 1971), 22-24.

44. Heinrich Fischer, *Buchdruckerleben: aus den Erfahrungen, Betrachtungen und Erlebnissen eines alten Collegen* (Leipzig: n.d. [c. 1857]), 16.

45. Tenfelde, *Bergarbeiterschaft*, 254.

46. Otto Richter, *Lebensfreuden eines Arbeitskinder: Jugenderinnerungen* (Dresden: 1919), 10.

47. Georg Fischer, *Denkwürdigkeiten und Erinnerungen eines Arbeiters*, 2 vols., (Leipzig: 1904), 1, 33-34.

48. Otto Buchwitz, *50 Jahre Funktionär der deutschen Arbeiterbewegung* (Berlin: 1973), 36.

49. Gustav Mayer, *Johann Baptist von Schweitzer und die Sozialdemokratie* (Jena: 1909), discusses the first unions, 248ff. There is now Ulrich Engelhardt's voluminous *"Nur vereinigt sind wir stark": Die Anfänge der deutschen Gewerkschaftsbewegung, 1862/63 bis 1869/70*, 2 vols., Stuttgart: 1977.

50. The first day's discussion at the 1870 convention of the Lassalleans had to do with unions, and it was then that Tölcke made his remarks injurious to them. *Protokoll der Generalversammlung des allgemeinen deutschen Arbeiterverein zu Berlin vom 22. bis 25. Mai 1870* (n.pl. [Berlin], n.d. [1871]).

51. On this major Chemnitz walkout there is Herbert Stöbe, *Der Grosse Streik der Chemnitzer Mettallarbeiter zur Durchsetzung des Zehnstundentages im Jahre 1871*, Karl Marx Stadt [Chemnitz], 1962. Johann Most's bomb articles were published in his New York journal *Freiheit*, January 17 & 24, 1885.

52. Kuczynski, *GdL*, 3, 286.

53. *Die Sozialdemokratie und die Wahlen zum Deutschen Reichstag*, ed. Paul Hirsch and Bruno Borchardt (Berlin: 1907), 137.

54. Puttkammer's entire statement has been reprinted in Auer, *Nach zehn Jahren*, 146-150.

55. *RV*, May 21, 1886, VI Leg. Per., II Sess. 2, 2105.

56. *RV*, Jan. 25, 1889, VII Leg. Per., V Sess. 2, 1245.

57. *RV*, May 21, 1886, VI Leg. Per., II Sess. 3, 2100.

58. *RV*, March 13, 1889, VII Leg. Per., IV Sess. 2, 887.

59. Auer, *Nach zehn Jahren*, 96ff.

60. Fritz Paeplow, *Zur Geschichte der deutschen Bauarbeiterbewegung* (Berlin: n.d. [1932]), 348-49. Also Dieter Fricke, *Bismarcks Prätorianer: Die Berliner politische Polizei in Kampf gegen die deutsche Arbeiter (1871-1898)* (Berlin: 1962), 205-06.

61. Paeplow, *Bauarbeiterbewegung*, 349.

62. Between 1890 and 1914 party locals periodically published lists of members' skills, and which also showed how they looked down upon the rarely listed "laborers" or "factory workers." It is from such tabulations that I have arrived at the rough figure here.

63. In later years he became sympathetic to work stoppages; see especially his *Der Streik*. He even became an advocate of the general strike in the immediate prewar years.

64. Eduard Bernstein, *Die Geschichte der Berliner Arbeiterbewegung*, 3 vols. (Berlin: 1909-10), 2, 278.

65. "Potatoes in the morning, potatoes for soup, we are nothing but wrapped potatoes, it is an eternity of potatoes for us." *Im Dienste der Freiheit, Freud und Leid aus sechs Jarhzehnten Kampf und Aufsteig* (Berlin: 1927), 7.

66. *Corrblatt*, January 11, 1891.

67. From Franz Bergg, *Ein Proletarierleben* in Emmerich, ed., *Proletarische Lebensläufe*, 270-271.

68. From *Die Korber-Chronik: Aus dem Wanderbuch eines Heimatslosen* in ibid., 214.

69. Wilhelmine statistics suffer from the attempt to distinguish between "offensive" and

"defensive" strikes. Both government and trade union statistics made such attempts, which often depended very much upon their opinions.

70. *Corrblatt*, March 22, 1891.

71. The strike article in *Corrblatt*, July 5, 1891, displays a defensive attitude toward the accusation that strikes are a means for richer unions to plunder poorer workingmen.

72. Desai, *Real Wages*, 110-11.

73. August Bebel to Viktor Adler, January 16, 1892 in *Viktor Adler: Briefwechsel mit August Bebel und Karl Kautsky*, ed., Friedrich Adler, (Vienna: 1954), 86.

74. The figures on party income and expenditure were given, as usual, in *SPD Protocol, 1893*, 54ff.

75. *Vorwärts*, April 26, 1891.

76. Ibid., January 22 & 24, 1892.

77. *Der Hochverratsprozess gegen Liebknecht, Bebel, Hepner vor dem Schwurgericht zu Leipzig vom 11. bis 26. März, 1872*, ed. W. Liebknecht (Berlin: 1911), 502.

78. Göhre, *Drei Monate*, 93.

79. *Geschichte der deutschen Arbeiterbewegung: Chronik* [henceforth, *Chronik*] 2 vols., 1 (Berlin: 1965), 165.

80. *SPD Protokoll 1893* lists all those in attendance, 280-85, but ten of these have only family names given.

81. *SPD 1893 Protokoll*, 181ff.

82. Ibid., 201.

83. August Bebel, *Gewerkschafts-Bewegung und Politische Parteien*, Stuttgart: 1900.

84. *SPD Protokoll* 1893, 217.

85. *Corrblatt*, July 16, 1893.

86. Mehring's *Leipziger Volkszeitung* article of June 26, 1902 has been reprinted in his *Gesammelte Schriften*, vol. 4, *Aufsätze zur Geschichte der Arbeiterbewegung* (Berlin: 1963), 397-400. The same idea recurs throughout his history of the party.

4

BREWERY WORKERS, NEEDLEWOMEN AND LONGSHOREMEN

Between 1889 and 1891 Germany made a false start out of the long depression, then the economy sank back again. Capital ceased expanding in 1891 and laboring men grew more cautious. Strike numbers shrank. Only about 31,000 men were out in 1893[1] and there was about the same total the following year.[2] Such minute figures were unusual in Western Europe; Legien's paper reported that in half-agrarian France 170,000 had walked off their jobs in 1894.[3] But Germans did not care to take the risk in bad years.

Likely the social calm gave satisfaction to nearly everyone in society. The world knows the Germans as an orderly folk, given to hard, steady labor and to saving money. No matter how desperate the circumstances, they rarely rebel, or desert in war.[4] They are more upset by inflation and what is called terrorism than are other peoples. Strikes are another unsettling irregularity of modern times. When they declined in numbers and force between 1892 and 1894, commentators began claiming that the "era of strikes" was over. (A look at laboring history would have suggested instead that strikes are cyclical.) In this case the wish was probably father to the thought, whether uttered by bourgeois or workingman. The relative quiet likely accounts for the attention given the Berlin beer boycott both in academic and working class circles.[5] Additionally, there was the well-known affection for the item - proletarians had often rioted over beer price increases over the centuries.[6]

Historically Germany had thousands of breweries, but in the 1890s there was a tendency for the richer companies to swallow the lesser. Leading the way in such expansion was the capital's largest purveyor of malt, Schultheiss. With the large Bohemian Brewing House and five others, these were grouped in what the public called the "Ring." These breweries found an additional source of strength in the trade association which had been founded in 1891.[7]

This was one of the few industries, remarked Ignaz Auer, where bosses were not absolute masters.[8] Earlier in the century men had had to put in as many as 15 hours a day, and would then collapse on rag piles, too weary to go home. By the 1890s they had managed to elevate themselves, chiefly through work stoppages.[9] During conflicts the men had advantages, for their product was seasonal, and subject to spoilage. There was much competition and demand never failed. Boycotts were rather easy to establish.

Social democrats knew all about boycotts, for in the early days of the movement they had had to make use of them against tavern owners who were reluctant to house party meetings, either out of personal conviction or police intimidation. Army officers too might declare a particular watering hole "off limits" if they did not care for the politics of the patrons. Such denial of assembly lasted down through Wilhelmine times in rural areas. The party's response was frequently the boycott. If such an effort was well managed, police and army might threaten as forcefully as they could, but the owner would have to side with the patrons.

Desai indicates that Germans spend about 3 percent of their incomes on beverages.[10] Yet one never reads that a workingman took his mate to the *Hofbräu Haus* or that much went for tea or milk. Most of that 3 percent went for beer, allied in male minds with the few hours of freedom, with conviviality and with politics. These circumstances made a boycott more interesting. Action could be carried on without making a man thirsty - all he had to do was walk on beyond a proscribed drinking spot to the next one, then congratulate himself on his fidelity to the movement. In short, a boycott was as likely a weapon as one could find in that tiny arsenal with which social democracy carried on the class struggle.

Aggressive action from both sides began the Berlin beer boycott. Brewery men were among those who took the militants' holiday on May 1. The "Ring" used this show of independence to lock the men out for a week. A suburban party meeting in Rixdorf, a center of radicalism where there were many breweries, voted to stop drinking "Ring" products.[11] Since unions were so small, it was now up to the party to say yes or no to a boycott. When the party Executive hesitated, the "Ring" fired a fifth of its employees, ridding themselves, it was said, of the older, the better paid, and the activists.

This sharp action angered proletarian Berlin. Perhaps the city had been quiet too long, and it is certain that the "Ring" was hated. *Vorwärts* commented: "If we cannot offer satisfaction to that 20 percent of the brewery workers who have been so badly injured, then solidarity is an empty theory." Party leaders were now compelled to back the boycott, and the party's paper commenced carrying a daily banner: "Party Comrades! Don't drink Boycott Beer!"[12] The 45,000 subscribers and the many who read their copies began to be informed regularly that the men who lost their jobs included 288 married men who had 422 children. The 12,000 marks needed for their support was readily raised, for the boycott was popular and there had been no financial drive for several years. Women were alerted not to pick up groceries where "Ring" merchandise was sold.[13] Meanwhile party members in other towns tried to persuade non-Berlin breweries to take up the slack.

The "Ring" was not at all defenseless. The propertied classes were urged to switch from cognac to beer for the time being. Delivery wagons were specially painted to convince the public that their malt was still being purchased. *Pro forma* declarations were sent to the press saying that "Ring" firms were not being hurt financially. Funds were promised, and in part turned over to weaker companies. Pressure was put on taprooms which served non-Ring beverages. Some employers dispensed free "Ring" brew on the job, making for a great moral dilemma among the comrades.

The many original issues thinned down to three: a jobless 50 who had been released but not rehired; May 1 as a holiday; hiring methods. The last related to whether seniority or company wishes would prevail in rehiring. The battle continued into mid-summer, and then "Ring" representatives began talking to party leaders. Such action was exceptional in German working class history, and is largely to be explained by proletarian control of this particular market. Then too Richard Rösicke was the brewers' spokesman.[14] Bismarck had allotted 6 of 397 Reichstag seats to the capital, and Rösicke possessed the only one of these which had not yet fallen to the "Reds." In meetings with brewery representatives Ignaz Auer and Paul Singer, the popular department store owner, spoke for the workers. At once they cut back on the militant demands, especially that of May 1 as a holiday, while the "Ring" rehired many of the 20 percent who had been fired. Meanwhile the summer doldrums set in. Workingmen drifted back to the neighborhood watering holes as a settlement seemed to be in sight. The party had twin interests in ending the affair, being always inclined to social calm, and being responsible for the remainder of the weekly support money. So Auer and Singer assented to an arrangement which left 33 men without jobs.

This compromise, aired in the fall, provoked such an outcry that negotiations had to be suspended. The 33 were, of course, old-timers not without friends, and had 42 well-publicized children. Everybody realized how simply and cheaply a boycott could be carried on, by contrast to strikes where men lose their employment, and are arrested and jailed. There was no point in concluding it without a triumph. The boycott was now revived as men returned to meetings, pitched in small change, and insisted on victory. *Vorwärts*, more sympathetic than the party leadership, crowed: "A battle of such dimension, carried on with such energy, has never been seen in Germany."[15]

Talks presently recommenced. The owners insisted on their right to fire, and Auer conceded the point. "Ring" negotiators suggested that the jobless workers go on charity.[16] Finally the paper concession was made that these jobless veterans be officially added to the hiring rolls. (Actually the following spring many of them were still being supported by the party.) Essentially the agreement was the same as that of the summer, but the weariness of rank and file was counted upon. The agreement was announced just before Christmas, with ratifying meetings to come after the new year.

Aware that the agreement was provocative, the party sent out its big guns. *Vorwärts* grumbled that there were about 4-5,000 anarchists[17] in all Germany, but that they were centered in Berlin and all went to meetings. The remark was a sign that trouble was to be expected. In some meetings there were motions not to hear the main speakers, elsewhere decisions were postponed. In Rixdorf, where it all began, both Auer and Singer were on hand to awe the opposition,[18] which then bowed to the inevitable. In this month took place in all probability the first social democratic assemblies where those on the platform had to listen to cries of "traitor,"[19] for many wished to fight out this simple battle to the end. However the militants and the anarchists were hampered by lack of prior organization and of major speakers.

Workingmen had won many boycotts, for instance, that same year in Dresden,[20] and almost certainly could have done so in Berlin as well. A victory in the imperial capital on the issue of blacklisting activists would have had an effect on this constant problem. Once it became clear that this was to be a major class conflict, however, party leaders drew back, no matter how cheaply that conflict could be carried on. Social peace was what they desired, as Auer's words make clear:

> A further lesson which working people, in our opinion, ought to draw from the battle just concluded is that it is not enough to lead a struggle with energy and courage...The purpose of the struggle is to bring peace. Certainly not a shameful peace or a peace at any price, but always one which is honorable and respectable...[21]

Both Rösicke and the academic historian of the Berlin boycott were struck with how anxious party leaders were to settle;[22] the idea of a triumph was not part of their vision.

Rank and file appeared to want this particular victory. Yet the usual comrade was not a fanatic, and could be checkmated by maneuvers such as those used here. Auer, and doubtless others, however, saw a difficulty in that the general will might sometimes prevail:

> No institution is less appropriate for evaluating factual and principled questions and for bringing them to decisions than so-called popular meetings. The composition of such gatherings is always accidental, and chance governs their judgments. Where decisions of the greatest tactical and principled importance are to be taken, there accident must not be allowed the final word.[23]

Three times, i.e., in calling for the boycott, in having it prolonged beyond summer, and in attempting to overturn the final settlement, public assemblies with chance makeup had had a large role, and leaders had been defied. They did not care to subject themselves further to the whims of the masses and thought to devise means for self-protection. As to the promising method of carrying on the class struggle through boycotts of consumer products, this was now largely abandoned. At least in part this was done, not because boycotts were likely to be expensive or unsuccessful, both of which eventualities were improbable, but because they often led to victory, which was unsettling to party chiefs. Chimerical gains in elections were sufficient for social democrats.

A conscientious historian might well feel embarrassed to tackle yet once more Lassalle or the revisionist debates.[24] No such embarrassment need be provoked by a description of the neglected German women's movement. For Europe as a whole the appearance of Olympe des Gouges[25] and Mary Wollstonecraft in the time of the French Revolution, and of Theodor Hippel[26] in Germany, dates the beginning of the first interest in a modern public life for women. This first emergence of a sentiment was then crushed by the wave of male aggression emanating from France between 1792 and 1815.

Georges Sand and a few other notables notwithstanding, ideas of women's liberation grew but timidly after Waterloo. It was only in the 1840s that a small revival began, including the work of the well-remembered Luise Otto-Peters, Germany's pioneer female spokesperson. In 1848 there was no organized expression by women, but one unique act of self-assertion is worthy of mention. Domestic servants then lived in annual contract slavery, rising before dawn to set fires, cleaning or making meals during the day, and tending the sick at night. They had no recourse in case of physical or psychological abuse or pregnancy. In Leipzig in 1848 an assembly of such unfortunates made a shattering proposal: they asked for a free Sunday afternoon once a month.[27] (Over the decades it was to come about.)

After the repressive 1850s, the 1860s gave more room to feminine strivings. Two sections of a movement came into being, one for the bourgeois emphasizing voting and professional rights, the other proletarian and allied to the social democrats.

As the instrument of urban, skilled Protestant males, social democracy had the attitude of that stratum. There was neither feminist theory nor a feminist spokesperson to resist that point of view. The men believed that one of their few boons in life was to come home to a well-managed family after a 10-12 hour day. Consequently they wanted to reduce the role of women in factory or shop.[28] They appear never to have asked themselves what women might desire. They could not imagine a home situation other than one managed by a housewife. Birth control was not yet widely known or practiced, and, on the average, females of the poorer classes had to go through three pregnancies to bring two human beings to adulthood (at 16). Further, cleanliness was still very difficult, with the improvement in health which it brought about. The otherwise intelligent Wilhelm Bracke peppered his speeches with stories of a female who unfortunately toiled in a factory; asked on a Sunday to scrub the cabbage, she inquired after soap. This was typical of the woman-as-housewife view, which was also registered in the defeat of Bebel's 1875 proposal at the

Gotha Congress that the party back female suffrage.[29]

The early women's effort in the working class, strongest in central Germany and in particular in Crimmitschau, was intended more to support the party than to be independent. But like its bourgeois sister, it declined in the 1870s in aftermath of war. Yet this is the time of Bebel's noteworthy *Woman and Socialism*, the original edition of which was written in prison.[30] The self-educated sergeant's son's attention went especially to eras when women had more influence, as in fabled matriarchal times, or when they assumed masculine roles after the population losses of the Thirty Years War. In his own century this "Marx of Women"[31] pictured the majority sex as did his colleagues, which was to say as chaste housewives. So he spoke of them also when he returned from jail to the political wars and his volume, no matter how many editions, remained only inspirational, and without practical influence.

In 1883 Madame Guillaume-Schack, daughter of a propertied Silesian family, began lecturing in Berlin on the lives of prostitutes, and showed that she was prepared to go to prison for them.[32] Her efforts are generally taken as the starting point of a modern feminist movement. More proletarian in thrust were the speeches of Emma Ihrer.[33] It was now a generation since the wars of unification, and women had had time to regroup after that explosion of masculinity.

In the prosperous, peaceful and stable 1890s feminism had a better climate in which to grow. Women were now 51 percent of the population,[34] and about 30 percent of the labor force, being significant especially in agriculture. (In the whole of social democratic literature there is hardly any treatment of these lowly women.)[35] One quarter of all employed females were servants, who were paid about 150 marks a year plus room and board. Their hours were still unlimited, save that they now were usually free every other Sunday afternoon. Just under a fifth of employed women were in industry, normally in the lower paid jobs. A differential of a third between their pay and that of men was the minimum. Of all women listed as workers in official statistics, 40 percent were under 20. Thus most women who toiled outside their homes did so before marriage, except in agriculture, where they performed both domestic and remunerated labor all their lives.

Census figures conceal the fact that some women were paid for their labor and others were not. Coal could not be mined, nor textiles spun, nor rye harvested had not women seen to the feeding, health, and cleanliness of the existing labor force and given life to a future crop of workers. Wives and mothers produced their share of the great economic forward thrust of the Second Empire. Diets improved as proletarian housewifery was no longer the desperate effort to do something with potatoes. Childbirth hazards which killed mother or child were yielding to modern medicine. With a higher rate of infant survival, pregnancies did not need to be as frequent. But putting it in terms of human toil, mothers and housewives remained laborers on long term contracts without stated pay or the possibility of breaking those contracts.[36]

The increased complexity and prosperity of Wilhelmine society opened new jobs to women and bettered the conditions of those in many of the old situations. More German women could now become teachers, albeit on the lower ranks of the ladder, and it was individuals from this profession who were to dominate the feminist movement. Female factory workers were enjoying shorter hours and slightly better pay along with their male counterparts. Women who worked in the fields did not, however, tend to profit as greatly from the rising standard of living.

In the 1890s, with their more optimistic atmosphere, select women began to take part in civic life. A bourgeois feminist society began to meet.[37] Women began to attend universities, though required to sit in the rear at lectures to avoid disruption. Among social democrats Klara Zetkin's *Gleichheit* (*Equality*) began to be published in 1891.[38] Rosa Luxemburg escaped from the East under a load of hay, took a Swiss degree, and settled in Germany, the center of world socialism.[39] She was but one of the children of the Ashkenazim who, beginning with Stephan Born, lead the socialist cause. Luxemburg and Zetkin, never really part of the official world of the party, were to become known as the only two "men" of social democracy. In these same years Lily Braun was gradually breaking with her Prussian-millionaire background.[40]

In a formal way social democracy went along with the feminist cause. The 1891 Erfurt convention decided for universal suffrage, reversing the 1875 position. Party clubs began to admit women, and by 1894 they had 7,000 members out of 240,000,[41] though still not legally permitted to attend meetings (they came dressed as men when necessary). The same year, when the Nuremberg *Bürgermeister* refused to allow female delegates, social democrats ostentatiously transferred their convention to more liberal Frankfurt.[42] Thus the party put itself on the side of truth and justice, without ever making the same commitment to women in terms of organizational help, newspapers, etc. that it made to men. In radical Berlin District One, Frau Grubela, otherwise unknown in party history, proposed in 1894 that social democracy's important central committee should add two women to its usual 5 men.[43] This suggestion was beaten down overwhelmingly in open convention as "reverse discrimination." There was unending trouble getting men to vote in even a few token female delegates to the annual conventions.

Next to prostitution, domestic labor, and fieldwork, that major women's occupation which worked the most hardship upon its practitioners was sewing. A seamstress' strike is thus something different from those previously treated. Miners, brewery workers, tobacco rollers all belonged to the fortunate in the proletariat, while those who ply the needle were among the forgotten. It is more difficult for the underclasses, who do not possess the respectability of the skilled laborer, nor his self confidence, his flat, or Sunday suit, or the spare cash he uses on party meeting nights, to take up the battle with authority. Nor were those who lacked respectability looked upon very favorably by social democratic authorities.[44]

However the 1890s were the first decade since the 1840s when propertied folk gave some attention to the underclasses. Such feelings account for the popularity of Hauptmann's *The Weavers*, which could be seen by bourgeois, but not by proletarian. The Kaiser had a very short "Left" period, and added a Saxon nobleman favorable to social legislation to the cabinet. Social democrats too fell under the influence of this climate of opinion, and championed, for a while, a cause not relating to male, skilled, Protestant working people.

Public action in this instance began when Johannes Timm, a man himself physically handicapped, put out a brochure on the condition of women who sewed for a living.[45] His effort was sponsored by the old union of tailors, and found a receptive public, part of it outside working class ranks. Germany had a large finishing industry; each year *Vorwärts* ran more advertisements for manufactured coats, suits, and dresses. Male tailors might still be able to make a living, but enterprising middlemen had begun recruiting women at far lower rates for the same labor. A third of German finished goods were exported to England, where they sold below the similar products of impoverished Russian Jews on London's East End.

A minority of these women were supplementing family income. During the stoppage, *Vorwärts* felt obliged to warn the comrades not to let their wives keep on sewing. However, most of the seamstresses toiled in single rooms and were part of Germany's "extra women." Most German females practiced the occupation of wife, but men were fewer than they, and men immigrated, joined the army or died young, and avoided a large family by marrying late.

Extra women were natural victims of the "putting out" system. The 1895 census counted 530,329 such.[46] They were not only numerous but helpless as well. An example which Timm gave was of a middleman paying his 20 seamstresses between 2-6 marks a week, while his own profits came to 100 marks.[47] Such wages only permitted individuals to subsist in a single room, often many stories up, likely without heat, on thin soup and potatoes. One widow told him the essentials of her situation: she could do two jackets a day by sewing from 4 in the morning until 11 at night. Each one was worth 70 pfennigs.[48] With this she had to feed her 4 children. Her greatest difficulty, however, was that after going three times to her agent's home, she had been told to stay away.[49] Not being paid was, in fact, rather common.

Vorwärts was only expressing common belief in saying that the only means of survival for many of these women was prostitution.[50] Lily Braun wrote of women earning less than 10 marks a week who had to do favors for the boss to live. The realities are hard to ascertain. Prostitution is conventionally defined too narrowly, and the late nineteenth century was a poor season for sexual candor. Princesses from the world's richest state used to be sent to live in Mongol yurts, to brave barbarian violence, and to accustom themselves to life on horseback, thus supplementing with their delicate bodies the protection which the Great Wall gave China. Was that prostitution? *Vorwärts* related a different type of case: a student liberated a prostitute from the police. In six years time, while studying medicine, he aborted her 6 times. When he refused to marry her after the last operation, she shot him and was jailed.[51] Middlemen in the finishing trade had the power to visit slow death through malnutrition on their workers; it would have been surprising had they not utilized some of that power. Thus a victory for the seamstresses would have been a gain for Victorian morality.

For a year the tailors' union worked to raise the sense of unity of these women, while bringing their case to public attention. It was a task which required patience, for the seamstresses lacked the comforting sense of solidarity which the factory generated.[52] However, legislation of 1891 which limited women's hours at the work bench had helped convey the idea that something might be done. Public meetings were arranged to coax the seamstresses along. Lily Braun attended one:

> So much poverty had probably never crept out of its dark corners before, and so many elegant women had never found themselves next to it...Old women with tired, red-bordered eyes stopped to make place for ladies with rustling silk...As Martha Bartels [imaginary name] spoke simply and almost dully, and told them the stories of their own lives...many wept. But these were not the fruitful tears of confession...these were the tears of despair, those which flow in church.[53]

At most Timm and his cohorts had brought together 3 percent of the Berlin sewers, though that was not an unusually low percentage of a trade to be organized in these non-union years. But having gone so far in stirring hope, they felt they had to take the next step. Late in January, 1896, meetings were held to decide what to ask of employers. The long-prepared cause was now met with a befitting response. Everywhere police had to handle overflow crowds.

"All that these women ask for," *Vorwärts* wrote, "is distinguished by self restraint."[54] Their first insistence was upon "an appropriate place to work."[55] The seamstresses, in other words, wanted to rise into the class of wage workers. Second, they wanted "a significant increase in pay." Their remuneration varied so widely that it did not seem possible to stipulate a particular percentage. They also wanted their money promptly, and according to a set schedule, and further, decent and humane treatment. The sense of the meetings was also that those who had extended "warm well wishes" should now transform their sentiments into hard cash. Leadership went to Timm, two other males, and two women.[56] The men being experienced, effective control of the stoppage gravitated into the cautious hands of social democracy.

By the end of the first week, 20,000 had quit. Packed meetings continued to be held. The best party orators went to entertain, and newspapers of the propertied classes spoke favorably of the women. Led by speakers from the aristocratic parties, the Reichstag concerned itself.[57] Deputies spoke with satisfaction of the fact that Germany led other lands in social legislation, and had even begun an inquiry into the finishing industry (1887). Richard Fischer put the case for the party. Behind the scenes, however, a less respectable reason for sympathizing with the strikers was floated. General von Kretschmer congratulated his daughter Lily Braun on helping the sewers, for he had heard that all the middlemen were Jewish.[58] Sociology was not always the strong suit of Prussian officers, but the same was said elsewhere. In 1871 at a particularly tense strike at Königshütte (Silesia), homes of Jewish people had been thrown down, but that is the only other sign of anti-Semitism to occur in this history of strikes. Of course, Jewish financiers were excluded from the coal industry.

The union began paying out allowances at 30 different stations. Six thousand strikers, presumably the wives of party-disciplined wage earners, renounced payments. Social democratic clubs contributed funds, and bourgeois newspapers set up collection points. Nonetheless, money did not flow in. In the second week of the walkout, Timm announced that 30,000 were needed to make up funds for the rather small allowances. In the third week, 45,000 marks were to be required.

At first the middlemen were unbending. They had a strong hand over the women, and did not want to lose it in their very competitive industry. Yet they had not the political influence of Ruhr magnates, they were losing money, and they could see the state of public opinion. Some even turned up at strikers' assemblies to argue the impossibility of setting up shops.

Already in the second week many bosses gave in, and sent representatives to deal with Timm. The sessions were long, as rank and file members appeared to explain their individual grievances. Both sides had much to gain from negotiations. The middlemen were worried over the unfavorable attention, while Timm's committee had insufficient cash. A compromise gave the seamstresses an increase of 12½ percent. The middlemen obligated themselves to follow normal business procedures by announcing their wage scales, and paying on time. Talk of shops was buried.

In the formal democratic way, ratification meetings were now convened.[59] This time political sophistication was not required on the part of party leaders, for the seamstresses knew nothing of meetings. They felt grateful to their

WOMEN'S SHARE of MAJOR OCCUPATIONAL GROUPS

(1895 CENSUS)

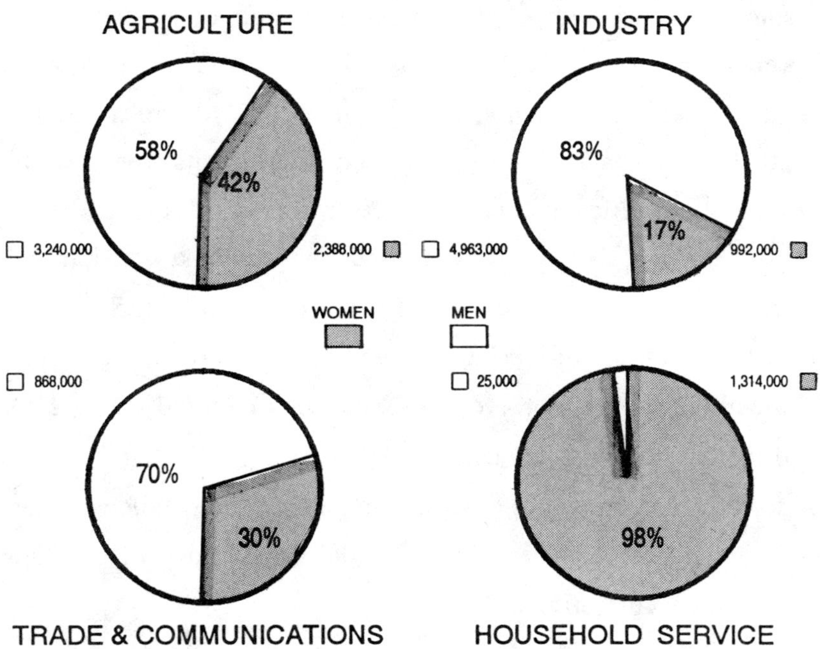

mentors, and perhaps more guilty than men at going on strike. The party line on this occasion was that a great victory had been won, and those on hand were said to have agreed.[60] Anarchists and other militants obtained the majority in one or two assemblies and they voted against this claim, but they could hardly prolong the conflict. After this petty gain the sewing women disappeared from sight. By fall *Vorwärts* admitted that almost nothing had been won for them.[61]

Presumably Timm had cut off the struggle short of victory because only 70,000 marks had been collected. That was just over 5 per individual on allotment. Neither bourgeois nor proletarian enthusiasts had contributed very much, and the small tailors' union could not sacrifice its treasury. It seems unlikely that the insufficient funds were the result of mass indifference, since German workingmen always gave; there must have been a decision high up in working class circles to preserve funds for more crucial struggles.

Those humble souls, the strikers, were not part of normal social democratic strata, indeed they were not even voters. They counted for less than did others. If the beer boycott had been launched as a genuine class struggle until tamped down by the big names of social democracy, the needlewomen's effort, given the weakness of the participants, could hardly have been aught but a petition with unusual features.

Such were several of the larger engagements in the doldrums between the prosperity of 1889-1891 and that more continuous surge of the economy which began around 1895. It was in Hamburg, a city with a long record of militancy, that the first great conflict of the new period was to occur.

Lying near the mouth of Germany's second river, Hamburg is almost an island, and its existence is sea-directed. The city was conscious of life in the

West, and freer of parochialism than Königsberg, Breslau, or Munich. Merchant princes had ruled this city republic for centuries. More than the rest of the nation, Hamburg existed to get rich, and in this decade German industry was seeking world markets through Hamburg. The city's foremost citizen was to wrestle for the trans-Atlantic carrier trade with J. P. Morgan himself. This was Albert Ballinn, self-made millionaire and court Jew to Wilhelm II.[62] Concentration upon money-making possibly blocked Hamburg from distinction in the arts. It was late in having a university, and native son Brahms lived elsewhere.

Being in touch with the world, enjoying a form of self-government, and free of absolutism, Hamburg workers were often more active in their cause than their colleagues elsewhere in Germany. They have also had two capable historians. Heinrich Laufenberg's three volume study soars above the usual local commemorative chronicle,[63] while Bürger's long account of the unions between 1865-1890 preserves much which has been lost elsewhere.[64]

In 1791 the city caught the fever of the French Revolution before the rest of the country. This Hanseatic Republic had then a population of about 100,000 and was governed as before by its leading merchants. Just below them in rank and wealth were the gildsmen; a master mason could well be a large contractor. The system was ossified, especially in that journeymen and apprentices could not easily attain their promised independence and tended to remain laborers. The law did not even permit a workingman to marry until he had an established income, and the rate of "illegitimate" children was correspondingly high. Aristotle has remarked how often great events proceed from seemingly trivial causes. A favorite apprentice had here prudently married into the boss' family. This youth always took more free time than allowed, which must often have been done under the ancient regime, with its more relaxed production standards. His fellow workers decided they had had enough of his special privileges and walked off the job to protest. Soon all the apprentices followed them. There was a street march involving up to a tenth of the population, including proletarians at some of the city's textile plants,[65] as Germany had its first general strike.

The first demand of the journeymen and apprentices was: no punishments for participation. They also wanted better pay, in the form of clothes supplied by their masters. Finally they desired their own customers, which is to say to reestablish the gild system as it had been earlier.

After the great demonstration the strikers retired to the hostelries of their trades. Their nerves were on edge, and they partied for a week. Meanwhile the propertied classes, observing how serious things had become in France, constituted a civic guard for this city which had never had a military. The new force marched to the gild quarter, and let off their muskets, killing two tailors. Bloodshed was more than the strikers had counted on, and they returned to their workbenches in defeat. But the outbreak of 1791 gave the Hamburg working class the tradition of having put on a general strike which only Breslau could match. The same year there was a general strike in neighboring Bremen,[66] but it does not appear to have left a similar historical impact.

Five days after the Berlin barricades went up in 1848, Hamburg had demonstrations. Political clubs for working people and union locals were soon set up, and the city became sometime home to Wilhelm Weitling,[67] Germany's Utopian Communist, as well as to Stephan Born. In the surrounding countryside farm hands went out on strike. Subsequently Prussian troops moved into the old non-military city and ended the year of revolution.

Following the repression of the 1850s, the Hamburg proletariat was heard from earlier than its fellows elsewhere. Artisans were the prime supporters of *Nordstern*, forerunner of the blue collar press of the future.[68] Strikes began in earnest in 1864, the chief of them at the Lauenstein wagon plant, where the working day was then reduced by an hour. So many stoppages took place that a council of strikers' representatives began functioning.[69] Hamburg's Lassalleans fought against these militant actions, arguing that they could not really raise the wages of workingmen.[70] Strike fever kept rising, however, until at one point there was a parade of 10,000 who had left their work benches. The men won some success, then the economy turned down in mid-decade.

Once again in 1868-69 Hamburg workingmen were going out in great numbers. Possibly these incidents of class struggle taught Bismarck that in the industrial age the old taboo on strikes had to be lifted. The men from Lauenstein struck again. Once again 10,000 took to the streets in support. After such a demonstration it was poor timing for management to announce a 25 percent cut in piece rates in July. The company claimed it was pressed to the wall, but the men would not yield. Thirteen thousand went out, 3,000 of them leaving town. Young men went from door to door with begging cups, and all the local gilds were approached for funds as before. Once again, in the historic Hamburg fashion, a parade was held. The men intended to hold out at all costs,[71] and they could feel that the city was behind them.[72] The Lauensteiners refused all terms except that they should be taken back, including the men in jail, at the old rates. They tried to publicize their case nationally, but were rebuffed by the telegraph office, which maintained that the strike was an "unseemly subject."[73]

More than in other cities, walkouts in Hamburg were plagued by replacement workers. Nothing was easier than to bring in men from neighboring rural Schleswig-Holstein or abroad, especially since the city had a reputation for high wages. After they had been out 7-8 weeks the Lauenstein workers grew angry at seeing hundreds of their livelihoods taken. Their courage was becoming depleted, and they were growing desperate. When had German proletarians been out so long? They assaulted the plant, beating everyone they found and destroying equipment as well. Strikebreakers had special lodgings, and they pulled these down. The home of Director Kirchmeyer was likewise attacked, for he was the boss.[74] Seeing the crowd coming, Kirchmeyer fired his gun and then fled. He hit a man who was the father of 6 children. Even this bloodshed, with its probable judicial consequences, did not shake the wagon workers. Lauenstein had to give in, and the men returned in triumph at the old rates.

Several thousand *thalers'* damage had been done. However the judges were either patriarchally minded, or believed that Hamburg had already suffered enough. Characteristic sentences were for 3-5 days. One man got 5 for having shouted Proudhon's dictum that "property is theft."[75] Since he had killed his man, Kirchmeyer had also to appear in court, but because he was a gentleman, he was permitted to do so in private. He was released, but found it prudent to leave town. After the strikes of the Wilhelmine period thousands of families had to leave their homes, but this is the solitary case where someone from management had to do so. Three thousand marched for the dead man's funeral, and social democrats granted the widow a pension.

If 13,000 went back, they did not thrive, for Lauenstein was indeed in trouble and the plant soon closed. Thus came to an end what was, with

Waldenburg, the hardest fought pre-1889 engagement. Seventy-five thousand workdays had been sacrificed, out of loyalty to the old Hamburg militant tradition. This was before social democracy and its unions had gained a grip on the minds of local proletarians.

In the 1870s much about Hamburg changed as it became the premier harbor of a rising industrial power. The ships serviced, the nature of cargoes, the pace of labor and the categories of workingmen were all different. One example was the appearance of "black" or coal loaders, for Hanseatic Hamburg had shipped no coal. The increasing number of port workers began taking part in the local class battles, fighting and losing two struggles in 1872.[76] In the bleaker 1880s there were signs that Hamburg workers, and especially those in the harbor, would let themselves be heard from again. Laboring folk emerged from the Exceptional Law period strengthened by the experience.[77]

At the end of the 1880s two blows fell on Hamburg working people, hurting their standard of living and provoking them in addition. After decades of profitable dodging, while taking advantage of the strong new Reich yet avoiding its tariff union, Hamburg was forced to become, in economic terms, part of the new empire. The price of food went up at once. Much of the working class budget went for food, so they were the ones who were hurt the most. In 4 years wheat, which meant bread, went up 12 percent, butter 58 percent, cheese 20 percent.[78]

The other blow affected housing. In the old days, with a sleepy harbor catering to sailing ships, most longshoremen lived by the water. But when Hamburg grew into one of the world's great ports, harborside land became immensely valuable. Those who controlled the city ordered urban renewal - clearing away the houses by the water. More than 24,000 people were uprooted.[79] It was quite ordinary for manual laborers to have to move, but these toilers regarded themselves as privileged and protected. Sociologists underline the strong preference of Germans for not leaving traditional domiciles.[80] Workers' memoirs abound with descriptions of their specially loved *Heimat*. Further, the transfer away from the river lengthened the *de facto* workday, prevented lunch at home, and created transportation costs.

Resentment over these twin blows, as well as exhilaration over social democracy's new freedom and election success, found expression in 1890. The issue which Hamburg workers adopted was the 8 hour day, freshly brought forward by the Second International. German social democracy insisted that the International call only for "manifestations" on the question, but in Hamburg many wanted to demonstrate in public. The city's proletariat was divided on the question and a large April meeting heard a speaker point out that Germans could not, after all, act with the freedom of Englishmen or Americans.[81] It was decided to ask party authorities for their opinion. Since the Exceptional Law still prevailed, that meant the Reichstag deputies. The police of Hamburg would have been more likely to approve a large demonstration than they! The deputies replied at once that a "general strike," as they called it, was not possible on May 1 and pleaded that the fruits of the recent electoral victory should not be endangered by an undue show of spirit.[82]

The deputies recommended only meetings. The following year their advice was of a similar nature.[83] Their preference was the usual: to conduct only so much of a class struggle as would not offend their opponents. However now that Hamburg was part of the Second Empire, its employers began to behave with a greater aggressiveness than before. Not yet reconciled to strikes, they began to hear what seemed like Utopian talk of a May 1 holiday for working people. They announced that not reporting for work on that day would mean layoff for an indefinite period. Police cooperated by forbidding further meetings, as agitation in Hamburg over this question gave birth to a national nervousness. In many cities troops were confined to their barracks on May 1, 1890, and others were posted that day at rail stations "just in case."[84]

The Hamburg police nonetheless tolerated one last gathering on April 25.[85] Neither the counsels of party chiefs nor the rather familiar actions of authorities sufficed to break the historic hold of militancy on the proletarians who assembled then. Even unionist Legien was caught up in the enthusiasm. Being more part of an international arena than was the rest of the country, the men of Hamburg voted as their ancestors of 1791 and 1869 would have.

On this first German May Day an impressive 40,000 men stayed away from their jobs in the old Hanseatic city.[86] This was a large proportion of the local proletariat, and also of all Germans who had taken the day off. Then on May 2, 20,000 of them found themselves jobless. For some only a short period was involved but in mid-May 8,500 were still not back at their jobs, in August 1,000 were still unemployed, as managements used the opportunity to solve some problems of their own. Support for the men locked out, which had to be raised locally, was to come to a rather large 470,000 marks. The men also took their losses from the judiciary. Eighty-one individuals were given 80 years, equivalent to one year terms for all the party members imprisoned under the Exceptional Law. Some working people were excited that a start had been made toward a real day of vacation,[87] while others were let down that so little had been achieved.[88] More typical was probably the tale of a memoirist who was regarded by his woman as a loafer when, around 1900, he took May Day off.[89] As for Bebel, he was relieved that the party's legality had not been endangered.[90]

The opposition of party leadership, the losses taken, and working class acceptance of the folk belief that it was wrong to miss a day's work combined to bring it about that nothing ever came of May Day in the Wilhelmine period.

One more event shook the Hamburg proletariat, as the scourge of Asia made a last visit to Western Europe. The port city drew in thousands who failed to get suitable employment, and hence could not afford housing. Those with poor or no income slept in cellars with a crowd of their fellows. The city had 50,000 roomers, most of whom inhabited quarters already overcrowded.[91] It was among these packed souls, eating inadequate food and sleeping below street level, that cholera, the disease of malnutrition, made its biggest harvest. It attacked the digestive system and killed within a few days. Eighty-five hundred men, women, and children died of this preventable illness in 1892.[92]

The rate of capital investment turned more favorable in 1894, and that in turn made work stoppages more likely. By this time the official union membership figure had risen to 409,000. The best years of the entire Wilhelmine period for working people were now beginning. Bit by bit more meat, cheese, and butter appeared on tables, and inflation was not to be feared. Most manual laborers would presently own a decent black suit for Sundays. Nor was there to be a serious threat, in the oncoming decade, that war would strip down the improving standard of living and take men's lives as well. As good times came, some of the first to know it were Hamburg proletarians. They had only to count ships in the harbor to have as exact an economic indicator as a statistician could devise.

As crucial to the Hamburg walkout as the economy was the national political climate. After Bismarck's fall, Caprivi had begun a slight liberal shift, but he was succeeded by the ancient Bavarian nobleman von Hohenlohe, who took the office under protest.[93] In his time the Right was able to assert itself under Saar industrialist von Stumm. The emperor had fallen under the influence of his authoritarian personality; both of them lacked Bismarck's ability to estimate the consequences of a political action. In the Saar, where von Stumm was looked upon as a monarch, a workingman could be blacklisted for life for having once glanced at a social democratic paper, and he hoped to extend such prohibitions to the whole empire. In the years of his dominance conservatives grumbled about universal suffrage, but lacked courage or ability to destroy it. This atmosphere of the later 1890s encouraged employers, even more than in the past, to resist strikes.

The Hamburg harbor workers were divided into many categories.[94] There were state and private piers, each with its own rates of pay and conditions. Boat crews moved commodities and baggage to and from the ships; for them there were regular loaders and warehousemen who stored goods. "Black" loaders handled only coal; among them "jumpers" used their bodies as balance to the coal being lifted from holds. Other workers kept the equipment in repair. In addition there were sailors, but they stayed aloof from Hamburg affairs.

The labor done in the Elbe River harbor had several pronounced characteristics.[95] It was exceedingly physical, as suggested by the travails of the "jumpers." It was irregular, in that almost no man could predict this week how many hours he would toil the next. The work was also seasonal. When a ship arrived, dock managers aimed to turn it around as fast as possible, no matter the cost. Over and over the material on the great strike refers to shifts which lasted from 3 a.m. to 11 p.m. Staying on the job for 48 hours, while laboring partly as a truck and partly as a crane, was not unknown. Nor was the 100-hour week. Hamburg was not short of willing hands, but, as elsewhere, German employers preferred keeping the same individuals to bringing on fresh ones. The men accepted, for economic reasons, the quick turnaround, but wanted some protections. They would often be alerted when a ship was expected, but after reporting they had to wait for hours. Only when they had loads on their backs would pay begin. They had commenced discussing overtime pay, a radical idea for the 1890s. Finally, their work was characterized by a high injury rate. Loads fell on them, and men tumbled into the holds and the river. The longer the hours, the more likely the accident. If every stone in the Great Wall cost a human life, every day in Hamburg's port brought serious injury.

There was more than a little resemblance between earning one's bread here and in the Ruhr. Both occupations wore men down and threatened their lives. Both were slightly romantic compared to those of men who worked at the same bench every day. Both miners and longshoremen were conscious of creating the new wealth of Germany. Longshoremen, for instance, loaded the luxury liners of Ballinn's Hamburg-America Line, its so-called, "New Yorkers." Both miners and the harbor workers developed solidarity beyond average.

By the mid-1890s, the blows which fell upon Hamburg had been absorbed, and the new prosperity was beginning to be felt. All the elements leading to the great struggle were in place. Once again, at the national union convention of 1896, it had been said that the "era of strikes" was over,[96] but this wish was not to be fulfilled. The men may have thought that they were still encountering the somewhat yielding bosses of the past, but in this they erred. In the later 1890s Bismarck came out of retirement nearby to inspect the city which he pronounced to be "a new world." Indeed the old Hanseatic Republic was no longer dominated by the "pepper sacks," as the old ruling class was called. Capital invested on the Elbe River docks had risen to ten times the total for 1870. It was the possessors of this new wealth who now called the tune, and who could count upon help from Berlin.

In the summer of 1896 Hamburg shippers indicated to their customers that higher fees for loading and unloading would shortly be posted. (Actually there were so many employers, and so many categories of work, and such complicated terms of payment, that changes were always taking place.) The announcement provoked two small strikes. In one case a thousand "black" loaders wanted to restore an 1892 pay cut and to get 5 pfennigs more an hour.[97] They were granted this boon. Pay cuts had been the rule for several years, but now conditions were improving. Everyone in the harbor knew at once of this small victory.

In the second instance an employer cut pay. The threat of a walkout by more than 1,000 men informed him that this was no longer 1892, and he backed down. These effortless triumphs had a most rousing effect, and after several hard years there was special resentment against the bosses. Sociologist Ferdinand Tönnies maintained, for instance, that the situation of the men had been declining, in absolute terms, for a quarter of a century.[98] A political incident stirred the men yet further. London dock strike leader Tom Mann came to speak for international cooperation among longshoremen, only to be deported by the local police.

As a consequence of these small events, loaders drew up pay and work demands, and submitted them in October. This was not prime season to tackle employers, for ice would presently close the port and, with the harvest in, substitutes would soon be at hand. But in the May Day demonstrations of 1890, Hamburg proletarians were to be led by their emotions.

Longtime Hamburg resident Carl Legien was to call the outbreak of the strike "completely unexpected,"[99] and he was followed in this by an academic writer.[100] Legien's declaimer, like Bebel's in 1889, was customary. But social democracy did not capture the heart of the Protestant working class by being blind and deaf. Legien had lived through the May Day crisis and knew the temper of the men. Already in October union leaders had been at pains to keep the longshoremen on the job.[101] On November 13, well along towards the time of freezing, leaders learned that their demands had been refused. A week later they held a mass rally. Legien and local union head Adolph Elm came armed with the stock argument that more would be gained by organization and discipline. They cited the low rate of union membership on the docks, and that the local's treasury had but 9,100 marks. Three thousand then voted to go out, and 40 to stay on the job.[102] The next day, a Saturday, several thousand did not report for duty. Union leaders condemned them.[103] Once the first contingent was out, the others followed rapidly, and by the end of the first week 8,000 were on strike. They were said to have 5,034 wives and 11,000 children.

The loaders wanted 5 marks for the day shift, 6 for the night.[104] That would have been an excellent wage, save that their labor was irregular and seasonal. They also asked that their hours be counted portal to portal, with a limit to hours, and more pay for overtime. Their money, they demanded, should be given to them at their place of employment, as was customary in Germany, rather than at seductive taverns. Their families were to be notified in case of overtime. Obviously the longshoremen were trying to rid themselves of survivals from early industrialism.

By the beginning of December, 16,000 had quit work. Although *Vorwärts* warned from afar that arbitration should be accepted lest the dispute turn into genuine struggle (*Kampf*),[105] union leaders had to go along with the men. The longshoremen prepared for difficult days. Assessments were levied on the few locals still on the job. Police forbade the usual door to door collections, but this restriction could be easily evaded. Strike allotments were set high, as single men received 10 marks, married 11, with more for each child.[106] Thus in off-season, the men were getting two-thirds of normal pay, more than many a Hamburg workingman. There were dock pickets and rowboat pickets. One day a small victory was cried about; 45 Italians had been persuaded not to scab,[107] surely a blow to their dream of high German wages, followed by a long trip back on plank seats.

Employers released figures suggesting that longshoremen brought home 1,000 marks a year,[108] giving them a pretty bourgeois standard. A strikers' meeting responded with show of hands:

Who had earned more than 1,000 marks a year;	3
Who had worked more than 300 days the past year?	0
Who had more than 5 people to feed?	60
Who lived in more than 5 rooms?	5 [109]

The degree of determination on each side has much to do with the outcome of strikes. From the beginning in Hamburg the employers were tough and resistant, while the middle class public, which looked benignly on the great miners' strike of 1889, was indifferent, if not cold, to the harbormen. It may be that the bourgeoisie was caught up in the conservative mood of the later 1890s. In that decade German employers began forming trade associations in earnest, and those from Hamburg were in the lead.[110] The Association of

German Iron and Steel Industry, a group second only to the Dortmund coal owners in political influence, was on their side. So was the Hamburg Senate, and behind it the Berlin government.

The owners of the docks proceeded energetically in the solicitation of strikebreakers. This being winter, their task was no difficult one. Already in December they had several thousand, coming largely from Scandinavia and Italy. These men received 6 marks a day for their unskilled labor. For their own safety, they were housed on ships.

Late in December 70,000 were out. Of these 7,200 were single. The high percentage of bachelors was doubtless related to the hazardous nature of the work. Half the single men were said to be hunting employment elsewhere. The married were said to have 18,000 children, no high figure for German proletarians, and suggesting that men could only take a certain number of years of the heavy work, and then had to leave. Through December there were ample allotments.

Legien's afore-quoted thought, with which other leaders were in agreement, was that two to three weeks was a suitable length for a walkout. This was the temporal aspect of the petition. That interval was cathartic for the men, and provided publicity as to the cause, while showing sufficient determination, yet stopped short of either a class struggle or a drain on the union treasury. But this time in Hamburg leadership had a larger problem than usual. The men, tougher than proletarians elsewhere, were intense in their quest for better conditions, and no inducement could bring them back to their docks and boats. From time to time compromise proposals had been aired, though never by anyone with power to influence the owners. Nevertheless, despite the poor prospects of such an endeavor, union and party leaders made a pre-Christmas effort to restore normalcy on the waterfront. They assembled the strikers on December 18.[111] The officials on the platform had nothing to offer save a proposal by the Hamburg Senate to investigate conditions. The longshoremen were told that after Christmas the walkout would collapse of itself, and were given the by now old bromides that their city was being hurt and that their organization might have to borrow to meet allotments. They pointed to the Bremen longshoremen who had gone out in October and had already settled on a compromise.

In late December the men were already much perturbed by the growing number of strikebreakers. But the loaders had pledged themselves not to be satisfied with anything short of victory.[112] Debate was long and furious. Every powerful social democrat of the area, save Bebel, was on hand to urge that calm and peace prevail. In an article filled with condemnation of the unorganized and the undisciplined, *Vorwärts* recorded that the resolution for return to work had been rejected 2-1, exactly 7,265-3,671. A complete tally, including the young men on the road, would undoubtedly have been more decisive. Social democratic calls for prudence and caution still broke upon the Hamburg tradition of the strike as it was understood in other lands. The day after this meeting the harbormen lined up shoulder to shoulder on the docks, and only 5 strikebreakers allegedly braved such a show of solidarity.[113] The great stoppage remained solid through Christmas, though picking up no allies. Some individuals renounced their payments. The longshoremen won a small and rare legal victory when an old law forbidding the quartering of human beings in the harbor was enforced against those taking their places. But rowboat picketing was now outlawed.

The new year produced no sign from the owners that they would ever negotiate. The dockers could count on no outside help. The two sides had taken their positions and neither was prepared to change. At the beginning of January *Vorwärts* denied plaintively and almost fearfully that the issue was power,[114] but the paper did not appear to be correct. Hamburg University's Tönnies prevailed on 6 other academicians throughout the university system to declare sympathy with the strikers, but this minute break in the ranks of Prussian officialdom was not sufficient to influence the outcome.

As the weeks wore on, the situation of the strikers did not improve. Money kept flowing in from the city and from the rest of the country. But the question of retaining their jobs was most worrisome. The Elbe had frozen, and there were but few ships. Inexperienced as the strikebreakers were, they could manage to turn them around. No striker knew whether it was his post, or that of another, which had been taken by a foreigner, and this uncertainty increased the anxiety.

For union and party leaders, the coming of January meant it was time to try again. Though they had enough money, they cut payments by a third, and they summoned the men to decide once again. The strikers disregarded the menace to their jobs, and the cut in support, voting to stay out by an announced margin of 72 to 28.

Leadership had now attempted three times to bring the men back, and they had tried lesser maneuvers as well. They did little to publicize the Hamburg conflict nationally, and undertook no widespread collection of funds. It would have been useful to have that one of Hamburg's Reichstag deputies who was then the greatest orator in the land rise to explain the fate of men who toiled 36 to 48 hours at a stretch. But Bebel remained in his seat and also did not visit the strike. Sophisticated maneuvers combined with neglect had not been enough, however, and social democracy failed to break the strike.

At the beginning of February union leaders simply ordered the men to go back under the old conditions.[115] The finest speakers were then dispatched to the many meetings - scattering the strikers had proved useful in Berlin. The many spokesmen for leadership could not point to a single concession, nor to the certainty of being rehired. They argued the prevalent shortage of money for allotments, which was not really true, and the menace to the future of the city should the walkout persist, i.e., the same national interest plea which was made in the great coal strike. There were not radicals on hand to contest their words. The men acquiesced, for they were weary and they worried about those who might have their jobs.

Though in the end rank and file allowed the defeat to happen, they did not like the taste of it. Saturday night after it was over the man gathered in great numbers, sought out the strikebreakers and roughed them up. As many as 150 of these unwelcome visitors were hurt.[116] That may have been a low figure, since injured workingmen drag themselves from a riot to avoid further trouble. The Hamburg judiciary treated the rioters with understanding.

When the defeated 16,000 returned to work that cold February, their troubles were not over. Six thousand were refused employment. The rest had to wait before they could start. Some had to sign that they would not join a union. Others found that their hours had been lengthened, or that their conditions had been worsened in some fashion. Everywhere the men were put down, sometimes by being required to address their bosses with the respectful "*Sie*" instead of the usual "*du*."[117]

Over 1,750,000 marks had been collected for the strikers, most of it from within the city. Had it been desired, the organs of social democracy could have brought the total to 3,000,000, for German proletarians were generous in such matters, and there had been no recent calls for funds. *Vorwärts* itself confirmed that the financial reasons given for ending the strike had been spurious.[118] The party believed that almost any method which might bring a return to normalcy was worthwhile, but in Hamburg the process of achieving that end, because of the militant traditions of the city, took longer.

Conscious of his party's role in ending the affair, Bebel was worried the first time he returned to his constituents.[119] He need not have been. Working people were wont to hang pictures of him and Liebknecht over the hearth. Nothing that party leaders did before 1914 shook that kind of faith, in fact much of it endured until 1933. Germany had no tradition of popular victory. Proletarians were accustomed to taking orders, to losing, then to adjusting.

Hamburg proletarians now joined unions in greater numbers than before, as happened after other non-victories in strikes. But there was a shift in attitudes. Both the May Day struggle and the dock strikes had been serious defeats, with thousands of lost jobs, for local employers had shown themselves to be formidable opponents. At this point in city history there comes a subsidence of activism, albeit temporary.

Wilhelm II loved to play emperor, and he was copied all down the line, from factory management down to union chiefs. These men, the most capable of their strata, had no taste for the difficulties which ensued when the men in their charge mounted and then continued a strike of major dimension. Legien first expressed his objections to such unruliness in *Vorwärts*, and then expanded his remarks in his book on the strike. He blamed hasty decisions of the masses for the unfortunate walkout; in the future, he asserted, leaders must find the courage to repudiate such actions. It was the line of Auer after the Berlin beer boycott, and others agreed with it as well.[120] According to Legien, those who had provoked the strike had not been union men, and there had hardly been one mark for each member in the bank when it all began. Ignoring the easily collected 1,750,000 marks as it they had been tainted, he reiterated the familiar gospel: without advance funds, no strike. The men of Hamburg were scorned for their enthusiasm, for Legien believed instead in comprehension and calculation, the characteristics of leaders. Legien and Bebel were not von Stumm or Wilhelm Hohenzollern, yet when an important conflict broke out, they did all they could to stop the perpetrators. Thus, in struggling for the petition and blocking the strike, they were part, though unrewarded, of the Wilhelmine power structure.

NOTES

1. *Corrblatt*, September 2, 1894.

2. *Corrblatt*, September 8, 1895.

3. *Corrblatt*, October 7, 1894.

4. One of the finer worker-autobiographers, Ludwig Turek, observing that men died on the Western Front, determined to become a deserter. See his *Ein Proletarier erzählt*. He disguised himself as a Pole, which he was in part, and thus was not taken by the general population to be a possible German soldier.

5. See especially Emil Struve, *Der Berliner Bierboycott von 1894*, Berlin, 1897.

6. Veit Valentin, *Geschichte der Revolution von 1848-49*, 2 vols., (Berlin: 1930-31), 1, 113-114.

7. Kuczynski, *GdL*, 3, 289.

8. Ignaz Auer, "Rückblick auf den Berliner Bierboykott," *Sozialpolitisches Centralblatt*, December 31, 1894. [Henceforth *SpC*].

9. The material here is taken from Eduard Backert, *Geschichte der Brauereiarbeiterbewegung*, Berlin, 1916.

10. Desai, *Real Wages*, 122.

11. R. Oldenburg, "Der Berliner Bierboykott im Jahre 1894," *Schmollers Jahrbuch* 20 (1894), 273-74.

12. *Vorwärts*, May 17, 1894.

13. *Vorwärts*, June 3, 1894.

14. See Richard Rösicke, "Das Ende des Bierboykotts und der Arbeitsnachweis der Berliner Brauereien," *Preussische Jahrbücher*, 79 (1895), 312-33.

15. *Vorwärts*, June 11, 1895.

16. Oldenburg, *Schmollers Jahrbuch*, 20 (1894), 289.

17. On the anarchists of this period see the remarks in *Vorwärts*, January 3 & 12, 1895.

18. *Vorwärts*, January 1, 1895.

19. Idem.

20. Backert, *Brauereiarbeiterbewegung*, 439ff.

21. Auer, *SpC*, December 31, 1894.

22. Struve, *Bierboycott*, 302ff.

23. Auer, *SpC*, December 31, 1894.

24. Conscious of this problem, Lily Braun began her classic study of women by discussing the want of adequate historical treatment of women. *Die Frauenfrage: ihre geschichtliche Entwicklung und wirtschaftliche Seite* (Leipzig: 1901), 1.

25. Des Gouges is thoroughly covered by Lily Braun in ibid., 79ff.

26. As part of the revival of feminist works, Hippel has been translated and reprinted. *Theodor Gottlieb von Hippel: On Improving the Status of Women*, Detroit, 1979.

27. Elizabeth Todt and Hans Radandt, *Zur Frühgeschichte der deutschen Gewerkschaftsbewegung, 1800-1849* (Berlin: 1950), 82.

28. Attitudes in the party toward women are given an almost premier discussion in Jean H. Quataert, *Reluctant Feminists in German Social Democracy, 1885-1917*, Princeton, 1979.

29. Werner Tönessen, *Frauenemanzipation: Politik und Literatur der deutschen Sozialdemokratie zur Frauenbewegung, 1863-1933* (Frankfurt: 1969), 30. Margrit Twellmann, *Die Deutsche Frauenbewegung im Spiegel repräsentativer Frauenschriften: Ihre Anfänge und Entwicklung*, Meisenheim am Glan, 1972, also has much useful information. The history of women, can probably only be recovered in the course of decades.

30. August Bebel, *Woman under Socialism*, tr. fr. 33rd ed. by Daniel DeLeon with introduction by Lewis Cosar, New York 1971.

31. This phrase, probably not unfamiliar at the time, has been taken from Hilda Lion, *Zur Soziologie der Frauenbewegung: die katholische Frauenbewegung* (Berlin: 1926), 38.

32. See Braun, *Frauenfrage*, 431ff,; also Juhacz, Marie, *Sie lebten für eine bessere Welt*, (Berlin: 1923), 29ff.

33. Ibid., 21ff.

34. Census figures are analyzed in Braun, *Frauenfrage*, ch. 5.

35. For an interesting if probably uncharacteristic account of these lowly folk see *Aus der Gedankenwelt einer Arbeiterfrau: Von ihr selbst erzählt*, ed., C. Moszeik, Berlin, 1909.

36. Braun, *Frauenfrage*, 387ff.

37. Richard J. Evans has made a fine commencement of the organizational history of the bourgeois feminist movement with *The Feminist Movement in Germany: 1894-1933*, London and Beverly Hills, 1976.

38. Clara Zetkin was not to be, like Rosa Luxemburg and Karl Liebknecht, a target of Pabst's executioners. She lived on to be buried in the Kremlin, but has yet to find a proper biographer.

39. There is the classic biography by J. P. Nettl, *Rosa Luxemburg*, 2 vols., London, 1966.

40. This story is the substance of the second volume of her autobiography, entitled *Kampfjahre*.

41. *Vorwärts*, May 1, 1894.

42. The protest resolution has been reprinted in *Dokumente und Materialen*, 3, 416-18.

43. *Vorwärts*, September 30, 1894.

44. See the articles in *Neuer Social Demokrat*, July 3 & August 2, 1872.

45. Johannes Timm, *Das Sweating System in der Deutschen Konfektions-Industrie*, Flensburg, 1893.

46. Kuczynski, *GdL*, 3, 328.

47. Timm, *Das Sweating System*, 15.

48. *Vorwärts*, February 6, 1896.

49. For a description of the situation of these women from a non-party source, see Alfred Weber, "Das Sweating System in der Konfektion und die Vorschläge der Kommission für Arbeiterstatistik," *Schmollers Jahrbuch* 10 (1897), 493-512.

50. *Vorwärts*, January 28, 1896.

51. Ibid., August 22, 1895.

52. Timm had argued for substituting factories for home work in his brochure. *Das Sweating System*, 22ff.

53. Braun, *Kampfjahre*, 102.

54. *Vorwärts*, February 5, 1896.

55. *Vorwärts*, February 11, 1896.

56. The Commission of Five is discussed in *Vorwärts*, February 9, 1896.

57. *RV*, IX Leg. Per., IV Sess., 899-925.

58. Braun, *Kampfjahre*, 103.

59. *Vorwärts*, February 22, 1896.

60. Braun, *Kampfjahre*, 2, 117.

61. *Vorwärts*, September 5, 1896. In this lead article the writer spoke much of the lack of all "sense of duty" on the part of the middlemen. The term was a last refuge after the fight was abandoned.

62. See Lamar Cecil, *Albert Ballinn: Business and Politics in Imperial Germany*, Princeton, 1967.

63. Heinrich Laufenberg, *Geschichte der Arbeiterbewegung in Hamburg, Altona und Umgegend*, 2 vols., Hamburg, 1911. A third volume was at the printer's when the Nazis came to power and was destroyed by them (information of Werner Blumenberg, longtime head of the German section, International Institute for Social History).

64. Heinrich Bürger, *Die Hamburger Gewerkschaften und deren Kämpfe von 1865 bis 1890*, Hamburg, 1899.

65. Heinrich Laufenberg, *Hamburg und sein Proletariat im achtzehnten Jahrhundert* (Hamburg: 1910), 108-114.

66. See Herbert Schwarzwälder, *Geschichte der freien Hansestadt Bremen*, 2 vols., (Bremen: 1975), 1, 513-515.

67. See Carl Wittke, *Wilhelm Weitling*, Baton Rouge, 1950.

68. Laufenberg, *Hamburg*, I, 237.

69. Bürger, *Hamburger Gewerkschaften*, 13-15.

70. Ibid., 34-35.

71. Laufenberg, *Hamburg*, I, 368.

72. Ibid., 368-378.

73. Ibid., 369.

74. *Social-Demokrat*, September 8, 1869.

75. Laufenberg, *Hamburg* 1, 376.

76. Ibid., 488-489.

77. Ernst Baasch, *Geschichte Hamburgs, 1814-1918*, 2 vols., (Stuttgart: Gotha, 1925), 1, 243.

78. Lothar Mosler, *Der Streik der Hafenarbeiter und Seeleute im Hamburg-Altona im Jahr 1896/97* (Leipzig: 1958), 36.

79. Ibid., 63ff.

80. Dahrendorf, *Society and Democracy*, 113.

81. Bürger, *Hamburger Gewerkschaften*, 475.

82. Ibid., 478.

83. Their February 4, 1891 statement has been reprinted in *Dokumente und Materialen*, 3, 356-57.

84. For this point, there is the selection from Ottilie Baader's autobiography, *Ein steiniger Weg*, in Emmerich, ed., *Proletarische Lebensläufe*, 351-52.

85. Bürger, *Hamburger Gewerkschaften*, 478.

86. Ibid., 491.

87. From Ottilie Baader's autobiographical fragment in ibid., 351-52.

88. Göhre, *Drei Monate*, 65.

89. Osterroth, *Vom Beter*, 138.

90. Quoted in *Vorwärts*, December 14, 1893.

91. Mosler, *Hafenarbeiterstreik*, 43.

92. Ibid., 47.

93. Quoted in J.C. G. Roehl, *Germany without Bismarck: The Crisis of Government in the Second Reich, 1890-1900* (Berkeley and Los Angeles, 1967), 121. But there was no "crisis"; the word is overused in German history-writing.

94. The first one of Tönnies two part series on the strike analyzes the jobs of the dock workers.

95. [Karl Vorländer], "Die Wahrheit im Streik der Hafenarbeiter und Seeleute in Hamburg im Jahre 1896/97," *Schmollers Jahrbuch* 21 (1897), 334-35.

96. Mosler, *Hafenarbeiterstreik*, 94-95.

97. Tönnies, *ASGS* 10 (1896-97), 675-79.

98. Tönnies, ibid., 190.

99. Carl Legien, *Der Streik der Hafenarbeiter und Seeleute* (Hamburg, 1897), 47.

100. Vorländer, *Schmollers Jahrbuch* 212 (1897), 337.

101. Tönnies, *ASGS* 10 (1896-97), 691ff.

102. Mosler, *Hafenarbeiterstreik*, 109.

103. Legien, *Der Streik*, 49ff.

104. Tönnies, *ASGS*, 10 (1896-97), 687.

105. *Vorwärts*, December 3, 1896.

106. Legien, *Der Streik*, 56.

107. *Vorwärts*, December 3, 1896.

108. Mosler, *Hafenarbeiterstreik*, 137.

109. Ibid., 147.

110. Saul makes the point that Hamburg employers were the toughest in the Second Reich. *Staat, Industrie*, 84-86.

111. *Vorwärts*, December 20, 1897.

112. Ibid., December 23, 1896.

113. Ibid., December 21, 1896.

114. Ibid., January 4, 1897.

115. Ibid., February 7, 1897.

116. Legien, *Der Streik*, 81.

117. *Vorwärts*, February 9, 1897.

118. *Vorwärts*, February 23, 1897.

119. Wachenhain, *Die deutsche Arbeiterbewegung*, 307.

120. Br. Poersch, "Zur Praxis des Strikebeschlusses," *DNZ* 16 (1897-98), 373-75.

5

CRIMMITSCHAU AND ITS TEXTILE WORKERS

Both objective and subjective evidence has it that the best years of the second Empire came just before and after 1900.[1] Capital investment was heavy, while unemployment was low. Real wages were climbing smartly, and the depressing rise in the price of staples was not to begin until 1903. Germany appeared to be expanding its international trade and influence in a world in which Europe enjoyed a natural superiority. Few thought that war might result from the competition of European states. Thus while the children were being born who were to die on the Western Front, peace and prosperity reigned in the Teutonic world, and not one hysterical party could gain footing.

Despite the good times, 20,000,000 proletarians were still concerned over wages and hours. Most men and women were now down to 10-11 hours a day, though they still had to toil for 6 days in the week. With the shorter day, there was more time for relaxation, which for proletarians often meant time with the children, in gardens or public parks, this being before the age of mass amusements (save for politics and lectures). Except for those in jobs which killed, men and women were living longer. For these additional years there was more money, as a sixth of the world's industrial production came from

Germany, and some of this wealth made its way down to laboring people. They were now eating more heavily, and drinking more healthfully than at mid-century.

Life had also picked up for working class women. Although they were still bearing more children than they wished,[2] they no longer had to spend most of the period between 18 and 35 in pregnancy. More children were surviving the crucial first year and sons were no longer so essential for their parents' old age, factors which drove down the birth rate. With fewer offspring, and more meat, cheese and butter, women were now stronger.

Around 1900 German laboring people had a degree of psychological security which was unusual for them. There were jobs for nearly all. Though Germany had surely its share of the unannounced unemployment, it meant something that 1899 was the fourth year in a row when official statistics showed joblessness under 2 percent.[3] By contrast, were that figure to rise to a mere 3 or 4 percent, which was high by late nineteenth century standards, then many more than the 1 to 2 percent affected would begin to fear. Other than that, parents could believe that their children would live better than they, and the army seemed to exist largely to give band concerts and march-by's. Historians are now maintaining that severe psychological tensions did not begin to infect European society until around 1910, and this date would seem to hold for the German urban working class.

Social democracy, a child of prosperity, continued its regular advance, gaining almost a third of the votes in 1898, and receiving a fifth of the mandates. When Liebkneckt died in 1900, there were capable men to replace him, though the newer generation was less ideological.

Unions profited even more from the same blooming economy, and men joined in numbers which dwarfed previous totals.[4] There had been 300,000 union members in 1890, but they were probably not well counted. Ten years later there were 723,000. Building trades people were losing some of their statistical predominance, and men from the middle-sized machinery shops were joining. Miners were still weakly represented, and heavy industry succeeded in keeping its men out. Men were not only joining, but were more willing to risk their livelihoods by striking. At the turn of the century both the Berlin government and the national union office began tabulating walkouts - it was for both a way of conceding that this unpleasant phenomenon could not be prevented. As the men grew more aggressive in wage and hour disputes, their leaders became more inventive in reining them in.[5] Locals now had to obtain national permission before striking, and the useful local collection of funds was ordinarily forbidden, for it made the strikers too independent.

Though Germans were now putting on more work stoppages than before, the inclination to strike remained much less intense than in other lands. About 50,000 British machinists went out in 1898, seeking a 48 hour week. Though they had the support of all the unionists in the British Isles, they were defeated after 6 months.[6] About 9,000,000 workdays were lost in this one engagement, roughly 9 times as many as in either the Ruhr conflict of 1889, or that in Hamburg in 1896-97.

A new factor was to affect strikes in Germany. The Right wing was always alive, and always alert for a work stoppage which could be used to threaten that revolution was coming. In the late 1890s the Right was on the march.[7] The emperor, the army officers, much of the bureaucracy, the large landowners combined with industrialists had effective control of two and a half political parties, which meant absolute power in the upper house of parliament, and veto power in the Reichstag. The East was largely loyal to the Right, and the East was the home of benighted beliefs. Down into the twentieth century in Silesia, one worker-autobiographer reports, children were taught to avoid Jews, lest they be caught and sacrificed.[8] In such terrain it was easy to believe that "socis" wanted to divide up property, abolish marriage, and destroy religion.

In the East a landowner could drive a man or woman 15 hours a day. Lily Braun's uncle, not the most backward of *Junkers*, horsewhipped a groom who had not tended his favorite mount properly.[9] Such an individual could well be perturbed on reading Bebel to the effect that workingmen would rule society in the future. Similarly Hugo Stinnes and von Stumm strove to keep "reds" out of their plants and mines. In England and France socialists Burns and Millerand were becoming ministers, but a Prussian heart which would feel no fear at the sound of French artillery might well quail at the notion of such cabinet officers.

Under aged Chancellor Hohenlohe the Right felt no curb, nor did the emperor. Bismarck's constitution had adroitly left the imperial role vague, and so it was easy for Wilhelm II to make his irregular and unpredictable interferences,[10] as he had in 1889. Early in the 1890s he told recruits that they might have to shoot members of their own families,[11] at a time when he may have been frightened by marches of the unemployed.[12] He spoke of himself as the greatest landowner in Germany, and behaved in many ways like a *Junker*. But he had also a clearly marked personality, with perpetual posing, flashing eyes, hourly change of resplendent uniform, speeches laced with threats, constant travelling. Those close to him recognized also an inability to work.[13] With his excesses of hunting and his clinging to the army, he appeared to suffer from *machismo*, possibly consequent on his withered arm.

Already in the nineties there were those who hinted at madness, but this was probably more a remembrance of Ludwig II of Bavaria than good analysis.[14] The Hamburg dockers had wanted nothing more than an easy, comfortable 18 hour day, and Bebel was such a traitor as to wink at plans for invading Belgium. But creatures of the Eastern latifundia like Wilhelm II and the *Junkers* were poorly conditioned to understand even modestly assertive workingmen, like those pictured in this volume, and rushed in terror to alarmist solutions. The sophisticates said then, as now, that Germany was well administered but poorly ruled.[15]

The strength and the aggressiveness of the Right manifested itself in the late 1890s in two pieces of legislation, both directed primarily at social democrats and unions. The first was thought control legislation, providing that critics of traditional views of marriage, the family, private property, religion and the monarchy were to be jailed up to two years. Such a law would have precluded discussion of any major social issue, and the more conservative Reichstag of the 1870s had refused Bismarck's plea to pass such censorship. Aged Chancellor Hohenlohe had not the force to block his imperial master on the question. The emperor's own contribution was adding the proposal that offenders would have to do "hard labor," possibly his notion of the worst fate that could befall a human being.[16]

Peace and prosperity were bringing on a favorable atmosphere for freedom of speech everywhere in Europe. Social democracy held mass protest meetings, and middle class parties agreed with the points being made, even if they did not campaign with the 'socis'. Thought control was easily defeated in the Reichstag, after which the emperor had the measure shunted to the Prussian legislature. Because of the three tier franchise, social democracy did not have one deputy here, but the legislation went down, 209-205, as the Right lost support even in its own ranks.

After this double defeat the emperor subsided temporarily, though at court there was talk of ridding the empire of universal suffrage and/or of a *coup d'etat*. However this was still the benign nineteenth century and nothing came of this chatter. Then the Hamburg dock strike persuaded the emperor and von Stumm to try for "right to work" legislation, i.e., the protection of strikebreakers. At this time standing outside a plant to keep men from going to work was in a grey area legally. So much as saying *Pfui* to a man entering a plant, or spitting wordlessly as he went by, could bring a short jail sentence.[17] Yet that tiny bit of leverage which the unions' sentinels of class struggle did possess was most crucial. Those without position, education or money found it most difficult to stand up to the boss. After they had taken their decision to do so, it was of the greatest importance that they be held to it. The errant, the timorous and the half-hearted had to be kept informed that their colleagues were in dead earnest. There were also those specifically employed to break a strike, but they might be turned away with words, blows, or the menace of a nearby crowd. Violence did occur, quite as the Right contended. A group of strikers did represent a threat to the unbroken arms and, more difficult for the police to detect, the house windows of an individual wishing to enter a factory. This was part of a good deal of violence in working class life, but *Vorwärts*, in discussing the matter, liked to make sarcastic reference to the well-known student riots, where not a single proletarian was involved. However the actions of the Hamburg longshoremen in preventing others from working, and the brawl which came at the end, had been given publicity everywhere in the land. Von Stumm and the emperor[18] proposed making it illegal to incite a person to leave his job, and once again hard labor was proposed for the guilty. The Minister of the Interior solicited major industrial firms for supportive funds.[19]

Social democracy distinguished between whether men had the right to strike and whether they should make use of it. Without an effective picket, in these days of small unions and inexperienced unionists, the strike would be effectively abolished. The party staged giant meetings to show how workingmen felt, and the Reichstag forum was used to the utmost. German newspapers regularly reprinted parliamentary discussions, so it was not as though Bebel and his cohorts spoke to empty galleries.

In his book on the unions Legien supplied samples from this 1898-99 debate. He believed that the legalization of unions in 1869 had not aided working people very much.[20] When there were disputes with management at factory or shop, laboring men were very likely to express their hatred for their betters, yet the law punished *grober Unfug*, which is to say, coarse expression. Judges were not accustomed to the language of the workplace and punished accordingly.[21] Nine-hundred and ninety-nine men had been apprehended for threatening to or using violence in the quiet years 1891-1896, the most common charge being that of cursing a strikebreaker. Of these 621 had been sentenced. About a quarter of whom were given less than 4 days while another quarter received 4-8 days.[22] Most of the rest received only slightly harder slaps on the wrist. Altogether those who were taken away by the men in *Pickelhaube* lost a week's pay, and may have had to hunt new jobs. Being presumably the younger chaps, that was not too great a hardship. The light punishments were true to the norms of the patriarchal state. In France, Austria-Hungary and Russia, men could die for going out on strike.

Yet such modest sentences hurt in another way. Earlier generations of working class captains, their thinking formed by the revolution of 1848, had done time in jail. While they felt this was unjust, they did not meditate upon this ordinary consequence of politics. Nothing in his autobiography[23] suggests that Bebel brooded over the years Bismarck gave him for self-education and during which he became a writer of note. In his seventies Liebknecht flirted with incarceration rather than bowing to Wilhelm II. By the end of the century, however, memory of 1848 had perished, as had the ragged conditions of mid-century life. Those of the second generation who headed the social democratic and union movements had good, regular salaries; to them imprisonment hardly seemed charming. Ludwig Schröder, mine union organizer often pursued by the law and finally framed, was of the modern type; a long term broke him. (See the addendum to this chapter where a case of shame and imprisonment is recounted.) With each annual raise respectability had a greater appeal. Among the low strata of the proletariat jail may still have seemed one of the regular hazards of life, but by the 1890s skilled workers who played the greatest role in working class politics thought themselves above having iron doors clang behind them.

When Legien argued here for the right to strike, he was doing so in a purely theoretical sense. More characteristic of his thinking was the point made in his same work that industry was better off with unions, which could do better than the state in restraining men from striking.[24]

When defending the working class against anti-picketing legislation, the party and the unions were more isolated than they had been in fighting off thought control legislation. Yet the legislation was defeated by the Reichstag in November, 1899, for by now the country wanted no repressive measures. The five year long threat to hobble the working class movement was now ended. The emperor would not try again, and von Stumm's influence waned. Social democracy had done more than the liberal parties in making this turn toward freer institutions. When von Bülow came on as Chancellor shortly after, he made a point of insisting that talk of a *coup d'etat* and all that went with it had to stop.

The attempt of the Right to crush unions had a strong effect, though not at all the one intended. Up to this time no more than 3 percent of manual laborers had joined unions. The low figure bespoke not only the fact that such associations were historically weak, but that unions had not been forcefully presented to the minds of proletarians. Then too they had only been quasi-legal. Wilhelm II and his cohorts compelled all thinking laborers to consider whether to join such associations with their colleagues. They did the work of hundreds of organizers. Then the Reichstag granted the unions a freedom which they had not been given in 1869. Proletarians could now feel that they were within the law when they signed up, and the more aggressive among them could also understand that there was a right to strike. Liberal and Catholic parties may not have wished to legalize unions, but the harsh campaign of the conservatives compelled them to do so. As Bismarck had rendered assistance over the long term to social democracy with the Exceptional Law, von Stumm and Wilhelm II had aided the unions with their campaign for new repression.

The Right now slowed its attacks on the workingmen's movement. The attempt to impede was not, of course, abandoned, for the head of the hard-line Central Association of German Industries, for instance, complained of "capitulation" by the state.[25] Von Stumm tried to control his employees' lives, spoke with almost unbelievable frequency in the Reichstag,[26] and acted as *de facto* Chancellor, although suggesting that he suffered from Messianism.[27]

When it turned out that the nation did not wish his leadership, he died (1901).

During the Hamburg dockers strike, Chief of Staff Waldersee had urged the emperor to lash out at social democracy 'before it is too late'. He went on to suggest that the world was on the eve of cataclysmic change. The second portion of his statement had all the realism which the first lacked. In the nineteenth century one may readily count the years which showed revolutionary impulses: in Europe they included 1820, 1830, 1848, with a flutter in 1869-71. In the twentieth century it is easier to tally the years of calm than those of disturbance.

Around 1900 the most vigorous revolutionary pressures came from China and from the effects of the Japanese victory over Russia. When Nigeria held the first African strike against the master race,[28] this was no harbinger of revolt, but a sign of the time. The Russian proletariat began to become active with large walkouts in 1896 in St. Petersburg,[29] and they drew support from German workingmen anxious for a change in Tsarist rule. There were major oil stoppages in 1903 in Baku region. In Europe there were unprecedented signs of increased radical activity, with agitation for universal suffrage in Austria-Hungary, direct anti-war campaigns in Italy, agitation for women's suffrage in England, and general strikes for suffrage extension in Belgium and Holland.

The subsidence of the temporarily defeated Right, and the rise of radicalism throughout the world changed the situation for the German working class. However in the 1780s, 1830 and 1848, when impulses had been given Germany from abroad, the response within the country had been insufficient to bring about major change.

In 1903 social democracy had almost spectacular election prospects, and thus began the partial radicalization of the Left. Rising food prices were being noticed by working people; party efforts to slow down tariff legislation, with its guarantee of rising prices, had failed in the Reichstag. But there was resentment in the country and on election night, Kurt Eisner, observing the results from the industrial centers, wrote excitedly in *Vorwärts*: "If the night continues as it has begun, a new day may be in the making in human history."[30] *Morgen die Welt*, it might be put! Embarrassed by this outburst, the party got out a new edition at once, and later released Eisner. The new day was, indeed, not to come in 1903 nor later. The counterpart to Eisner's notorious cry was that on election night a solitary wearer of the spiked helmet had sidled up to a well-known party official to whisper, "How are we doing?"[31] It seemed as if the majority of German males would soon be with the party, and thus the election gain contributed to the rise of radicalism. No one thought of a ceiling on growth.

In the textile industry the extensive use of women who were paid lower wages, the placement of many factories in rural settings, the ease with which a given type of cloth could be imitated and then sold at yet lower cost, and the availability of the raw material, had all combined to turn textiles into a low wage industry.

Among about 900,000 members of "free" (soc. dem.) unions (1903), textile hands, with 40-50,000 men and women, were one of the larger groups. They were, however, less than a tenth of the potential membership. About a fifth of them were women, which was very high, for normally only 4 percent of the organized were female. Along with mines and construction sites, textile plants were some of the few workplaces where the Catholic association had a good hold. But that membership was largely concentrated in a few towns in the

Rhineland. They had been responsible for major strikes at Kottbus in 1896 and Krefeld in 1898.[32] In the latter case Catholic and social democratic unionists, quite against their custom, had fought together and thereby managed to stave off a wage cut.[33]

The small Saxon community of Meerane had been the locus of class struggle beginning with a weavers' riot in 1842.[34] Bebel and Liebknecht had drawn early voting strength from this area, their supporters being weavers who had lost home employment. Forced into factories, Meerane men and women kept up the fight. In the 1890s their pay was cut, and union sources say that they took home barely 9 marks a week.[35] Then came 1902, a good year, and they were prepared for battle. They asked for a 25 percent pay increase, which would have restored their buying power of the 1890s and added a little more.[36] At first management, arguing publicly that their industry was too competitive to provide raises, refused to talk. The fight dragged on. Gradually the little town achieved prominence throughout Germany, and someone donated an unprecedented 3,000 marks, several times an individual weaver's annual pay.[37] Then after 3 to 4 months the employers surrendered and granted pay boosts of an astonishing 20 to 25 percent dimension. This was one of the great strike victories of the era, achieved by endurance.

Crimmitschau lies about seven kilometers from Meerane and there can be little doubt that the great gains of the smaller town had their influence upon the larger neighbor. The politics of Saxony also had its effect upon Crimmitschau. In 1903 social democracy had taken all but one of the Saxon Reichstag seats, as voters reacted against the loss of equal franchise in 1896 as well as the rise in food prices. More than ever this was the "red" kingdom. When social democrats had such an obvious majority, they may not have perceived how much men of wealth and position wanted to sweep back the social democratic tide in Saxony. But the kingdom's textile owners had been among early supporters of the Central Association of German Industries,[38] and were inclined to be hostile to universal suffrage and to unions.[39]

Like other area communities, Crimmitschau had a history of class struggle.[40] It was the center of the manufacturing hands union, which was not a gild successor, but a refuge for the unskilled. Created by Julius Motteler in the 1870s, this union drew both sexes into its ranks, and it was said that here a woman could learn to speak up.[41] In the same decade Crimmitschau was probably the smallest town to have its own party paper. The Exceptional Law did not crush working class organizations in remoter areas as it did elsewhere and already in 1882 textile operatives in Crimmitschau began consulting about the substance of their dreams, a shortened workday. They were then spending 14 hours at the factory, though two and a half were for breaks.[42] In the temporary boom of 1883 they asked for an 11 hour day and a 20 percent increase in pay. Their bosses refused to negotiate: they walked out briefly and then were granted the 11 hour day.

Agitation for a shorter day, alive everywhere in industry, did not die with this success. After 1896 bad times seemed to be banished, and pressure for 10 hours intensified. By the turn of the century most German factories were moving unhurriedly towards that workers' goal, and in Crimmitschau management knew that it lagged behind other textile centers in this respect. Nine hour shifts were by no means unknown and the Second International had made all aware of 8 hour days. Thus in 1900 if Crimmitschau was an old union town, it was also something of a social backwater. The local applied to the national union for permission to strike, in accordance with the union constitution. Since

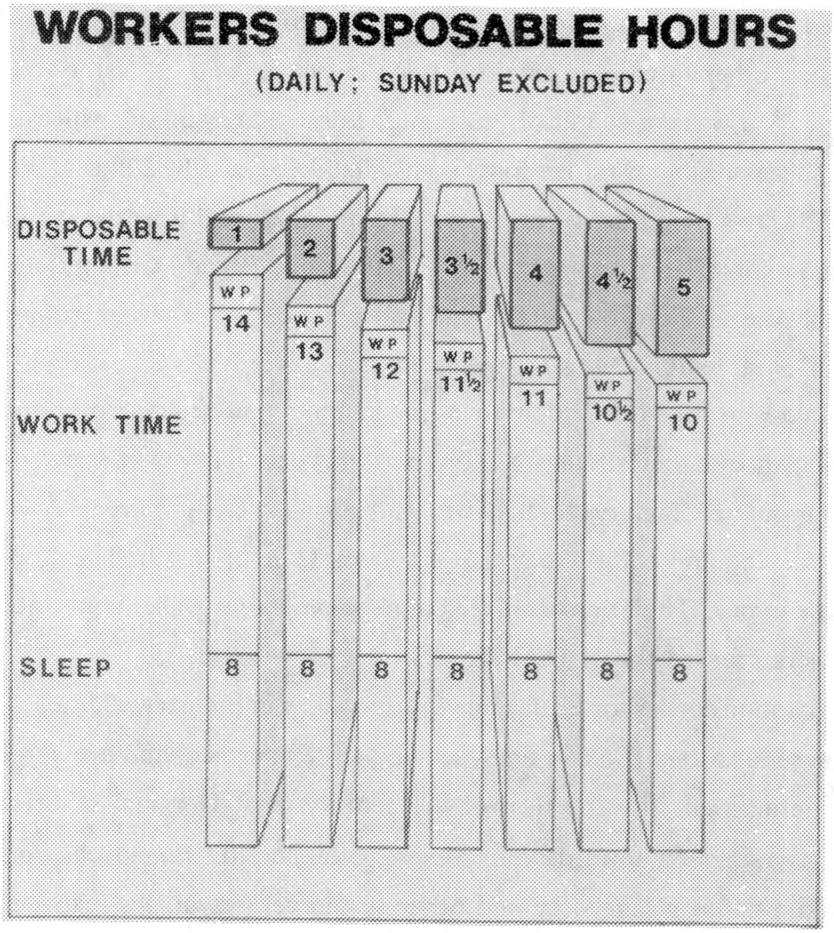
WORKERS DISPOSABLE HOURS
(DAILY; SUNDAY EXCLUDED)
DISPOSABLE TIME
WORK TIME
SLEEP
1
2
3
3½
4
4½
5
W P
14
13
12
11½
11
10½
10
8

the women and men of Crimmitschau had been extraordinarily patient in their campaign, since they had been so loyal in their actions, and since the 10 hour day was clearly on the horizon, the request was granted.

Each major work stoppage had its own tone. Hamburg dockers went out in a passion when ice was not far off, and whenever men left the pits in the Ruhr there was a loud tone and a hint of violence. Nothing of the sort in humble and isolated Crimmitschau. From the first their campaign had a pathetic ring as enshrined in their slogans:

> An hour for ourselves!
> An hour for our families!
> An hour for our lives![43]

Crimmitschau was making a sentimental, non-revolutionary appeal which gave union leaders no anxiety, while turning an almost lachrymose cheek to the bourgeoisie. The idea of the 10 hour day's importance for family life had already a certain currency in Germany.[44]

When a Crimmitschau *Hausfrau* left her one or two story house near dawn, allowing for walking time and breaks, it would be more than 12 hours before she would return. Eight more hours, at least, were taken by sleep. The shift was always arduous, so sleep was popular and insomnia likely unknown. Much of Sunday went for extra slumber. Thus during six days of the week, 4 hours were all that remained for personal activity, some of which had to be used for dressing, fetching water and washing. Poor laboring people hardly made a ceremony of eating, they were satisfied if something was there. A reasonable total for all these miscellaneous activities would be two hours. Thus males would have two hours a day free time. However the majority of hands in this Saxon town were women. Either by feminist conviction, or because it was good politics, their male leader conceded that these souls were subject to "double drudgery."[45] For upon their return from the mill, Crimmitschau females were expected to take up domestic tasks, especially that half of them who were married.[46] They had the normal responsibilities of cleaning, food preparation and child care. They did not have, during the week, "an hour for themselves," and it is very doubtful that a victory in the walkout to come would grant it to them. Single women, though expected to handle domestic tasks, did have some free hours. A 10 hour day would have given males 50 percent more disposable time for reading, visiting friends at the corner tavern, or simply sitting by the fire. Married women would only have suffered less exhaustion. All would have more energy on Sunday.

Union officials maintained that the 11 hour day was bad for the health. Crimmitschau women ordinarily began factory labor in their teens,[47] and were said to be spent and worn by 30. Their heavy toil led to a high rate of infant mortality, for in Crimmitschau 27 percent of infants perished in their birth year.[48] This Crimmitschau rate was far above the rapidly improving European figures of the day. In a neighboring location which had no mills, the comparable rate was only 11 percent. Mothers did not dare nurse their infants because of the long day, but suitable milk substitutes were not at hand. Heavy labor also affected the death rate, but on a textile based standard of living individuals were more concerned with today than tomorrow.

Social democracy had many reasons to back these mill hands. They hailed from the Saxon birthground of the party, had been promoting theircause for a generation with impeccable propaganda, were financially beyond reproach, and lacked any sign of worrisome aggressiveness. Accordingly the party supported them with both funds and an adequate publicity.[49] Throughout the long conflict *Vorwärts* never engaged in the usual heavy-handed moralizing that

CONFIDENT PARTICIPATION IN AUTHORITY
vs.
LIFELONG TRAINING IN SUBSERVIENCE

	WAGE EARNER	FACTORY OWNER
HOUSING	A crowded flat with numerous children adjoining others just like it. Clean, safe, but without privacy.	Spacious quarters inside and with grounds. Quiet and privacy possible. A secure haven for rest and recuperation.
CHILDHOOD	First consciousness that life is limited in space, food, enjoyment, attention of elders, money, free time, clothing, amusements.	First consciousness of priviledges with nurses, maids, playthings, adult attention, free time. Not without training in discipline.
EDUCATION	Strict and usually effective training in advanced verbal and mathematical skills in order to be useful to industry. No individualization to learning. On working class track.	Demanding gymnasium or technical training requiring many hours, but putting student on elite track. Possibility of wide educational horizon.
APPRENTICESHIP	Begun at 14, at low pay under double authority of master and factory. An early understanding that days of freedom are over.	No comparable experience. Brought up to enter economy in position of command and respect despite lack of experience.
EXPERIENCE of the WORLD	Except for the last of the journeymen, confined to working class quarter of one or two German cities. Knows only working people.	Travel, education, business experience, personal acquaintance possible on other parts of Europe, as well as with Germans in other elites.

CONFIDENT PARTICIPATION IN AUTHORITY

vs.

LIFELONG TRAINING IN SUBSERVIENCE

	WAGE EARNER	FACTORY OWNER
MARRIAGE	A work alliance established in twenties, with affection, without romance. Children soon limit the standard of living and of home comfort.	May be love or property arrangement. Marriage a great occasion, part of establishing one's place in the great world.
ARMY	Despite training which was often vicious, happy male years, away from humdrum, repetitive job and drab existence. No chance to become an officer.	Entry into prized officer or reserve ranks available for asking. Purchase out of army also possible.
EMPLOYMENT	Wage earner from age 14 to death. Advancement to pay possible in some positions, not in others. Little chance for independence.	Managing (though not necessary) and owning. A position of command, with money and social prestige, power in the world.
UNIVERSITY	Out of the question. As much chance as for a Jew to enter SS. Only self education possible.	University or technical training school assumed. Years of educational growth and fun.
ECONOMIC STATUS	Servitor status, but usually safe from unemployment. No opportunity to gain independence except for minority.	Prospect of ever increasing income. Secure and prosperous, with respect from society for economic position.

CONFIDENT PARTICIPATION IN AUTHORITY
vs.
LIFELONG TRAINING IN SUBSERVIENCE

	WAGE EARNER	FACTORY OWNER
VACATION	Not known to working people outside of Blue Monday and worrisome time of job change.	Watering places popular, also the Alps and Italy. A customary practise in the monied classes.
POLITICAL LIFE	Males could participate, and a small minority could have careers. Only within working class ranks, however. No contacts outside.	Assumed to be leader of mankind, so career in politics easily possible (Von Stumm, Stressmann).
ATTITUDE of POLICE, COURTS	Regarded by authority as lowly person and if active in public life, to be a suspicious person. Police regularly used to keep workers in check.	Authority used in support of factory owner stratum, to from real and imaginary threats. Never jailed during strikes.
RECOGNITION by SOCIETY	Expected to labor, to still, and to keep out of way of important people. Not mentioned in upper class newspapers. Recognition only within own class.	Organs of public opinion always glad to receive views of. Regarded as benefactors by society. State grants titles, honorific positions, etc.
SOCIAL CONTACTS	Limited by money and tight class lines to acquaintance only with other manual laborers. No contacts outside proletariat.	Acquaintance easily possible with any of the national elites, whether professional, military, scientific, political.

there were better ways to win than by striking. Above all, it was patience which had conferred legitimacy upon these Saxons. They had a favored phrase, "*Es muss doch gelingen*," which may be freely rendered as "We shall overcome." It is the slogan of the downtrodden who do not expect to conquer their opponents, but may somehow wear them down into some concessions. It was probably the extraordinary power of the Saxons to endure which made social democrats call off that internal time clock which usually led them to stop a strike after 2-3 weeks.

On July 24, 1903 women and men of Crimmitschau gathered under the sky to take up the 10 hour day. Police dispersed them for holding an open meeting. Next day operatives from 5 of the 90 local plants did not report, and their union asked for the 10 hour day and 10 percent increase in pay. Five days later their employers replied that, in view of prevailing competition, they could not grant such a request. They added ominously that they were discussing the matter with other Saxon industrialists,[50] i.e., the businessmen who had backed the law providing jail for picketing.

Crimmitschau employers now went on the offensive, requiring that their people signify willingness to continue under the old conditions. A further sign of how hard the fight was to be came on August 17, when city officials asked the union for membership lists;[51] there could be little doubt as to their destination. Early in August union officials had met with some state representatives and some non-Crimmitschau industrialists,[52] and there they gave ground, but were given nothing in return. The plant owners wanted pledges that the workers would return, and when they did not receive them, everyone was locked out. Crimmitschau thus qualified, in working class statistics, as a "defensive" action, and August 22 became listed, though erroneously, as its opening day.

Early in September a vote was taken. 5,596 favored continuing, while 115 wanted to return. Including those who spun or wove in their homes, the real number of strikers came to about 9,000.[53] There had been a dip in the economy in 1902-1903, but by now prosperity had returned. The moment for conflict was not badly chosen.

Save for the instance of the Berlin needlewomen, this was the only Wilhelmine labor dispute of any dimension where women were in the majority. At Crimmitschau they earned about 9 marks a week while men, who did some of the identical tasks, earned about 14.[54] If these were specially low wages for women, no specific complaint was made in 1903 on this ground. Three females served on the strike committee,[55] but the record suggests that men took the decisions.

Pickets were established and at first no one went to work in Crimmitschau.[56] The head of the action was Hermann Jäckel, long time chair of the local, who wrote up the strike and was to become a major party politician.[57] He would have settled the affair without the work stoppage, but he was far too outnumbered by partisans of the 10 hour day to proceed. Support for the union faithful was pegged at 8 marks, with 75 pfennigs for each dependent. Non-members received only 5 and 50 respectively, but were allowed to make up for their former neglect, and many now did. Crimmitschau was thus, despite its basic poverty, in the pattern of high support, with some few being allotted more than their former pay. As the weeks went by and national attention came to the town, money flowed in. Allotments were then raised 2 marks.[58]

Initially support required 60,000 marks a week. After the payout was increased, and more strikers came on the rolls, 100,000 was needed. In 1903 it was easy for the German working class to produce this sum. Another choice, taken at Waldenburg and often also in the Ruhr, was to go into debt by pressing merchants for credit. However, a stricter attitude towards money was normal among social democrats; in Hamburg the dock strike was in part ended so that the men might meet rent payments. Here too at Crimmitschau going into debt was thought to be reprehensible, and workers did not borrow, as capitalists surely did.

After speaking first of the Meerane strike, trade unionist Ottilie Baader recalled this moment in Crimmitschau:

> The strike brought to many, for the first time in their lives, a type of vacation. Mothers could have some hours of fresh air with their children. The benches in Bismarck Lane were filled with typical weaver figures, used-up, coughing women and young girls, with sewing or knitting in their hands.[59]

Coming in for their allotments, many commented how good it was finally to get one's sleep out.[60] Someone remarked that the town had become a health spa now that factory smoke was stilled.[61] But if there was mild humor, they all knew that it was patience and stubbornness which would win for them.

The Central Association of German Industries, having in mind the party's electoral win of 1903, boasted, "We are preparing such a defeat for social democracy in Crimmitschau as will cause them to meditate for a long time."[62] The men who owned the plants here were not powerful millionaires, but they seem to have been swept along by their greater brethren. Some of their losses were being covered by outside firms. The von Bülow government looked away from the strike.

The textile men might well have afforded the 10 hour day, which their competitors utilized and which brought them greater productivity. But they worried over loss of authority. In Heinrich Mann's *The Patrioteer* the chief character, small industrialist Fischer, idolized Wilhelm II, studied his habits, and spent his honeymoon trying to catch a glimpse of him. Within his plant Fischer tolerated no contradiction. There it was *voluntas regis suprema lex* (the will of the king is the supreme law) as the emperor liked to write in guest books. The desire of those with just a bit of authority was to preserve it, quite as Wilhelm II struggled to preserve his.

The autobiography of social democrat chief Carl Severing contained the detailed account of a walkout, which is rare for this genre. In 1896 at his Bielefeld sewing machine plant, the men heard of a competitor with a 10 hour day, and they knew their boss had made a million the previous year. They had no union and no funds, but they were not worried: "For the first months we have potatoes in the basement and smoked sides of bacon."[63] Half a century later Severing was derisive of such sacrifice, but he was not so at the time. The sewing machine builders decided on a 9 hour day with 15 percent more pay. Severing and two old hands were detailed to take these demands to owner Dürkopp, who was furious. "I let myself be forced by no man, least of all my workers," he shouted over and over again, hammering the table at each exclamation. After two weeks the men returned empty-handed, except for the tenth of them identified as trouble-makers and not rehired. At a final interview Dürkopp told Severing: "You remember what I said about not being forced. I shall do as you wish, but only gradually, gradually."[64] Thus the manufacturer deprived his men of a sense of victory, while preserving his notion of being absolute ruler. The little drama played out in Bielefeld in 1896 likely occurred hundreds of times.

With their regular staff locked out, Crimmitschau bosses searched for substitutes.[65] It was not easy to introduce strangers into this little community.

Potential strikebreakers were recognized at the trains, and were often turned back.[66] Unions were growing all over Europe, as was the argument against betraying the fellow oppressed. As usual, when replacement operatives were found, they were paid more than the regulars, and when strikers' allotments rose, so did their pay.[67]

From the first Crimmitschau authorities were active on the side of the owners,[68] especially as the *Bürgermeister* had married into a textile owner's family. Heavy police pressure began to be put on the strikers. In November, when bosses refused to talk with the workers' committee,[69] additional gendarmes were imported into Crimmitschau. The whole reinforced constabulary now commenced receiving a six mark a day "war pay" supplement, though there was not a shadow of violence and hardly a *Pfui* in all of Crimmitschau.

By way of increasing the intimidation, the police gradually became more strict. Pickets were forbidden to frequent the rail station, their most important watch post. It was not a real handicap, for strange proletarians were easily recognized. The police then forced anyone who seemed to be looking for outsiders to stand in a doorway, and, in a subsequent order, to remain inside. There was a saying that if a man put his toe beyond his threshold, he was off to jail. Peering out one's window was next outlawed.[70] Women were said to be distributing strike information from their baby carriages (not for the first time in proletarian history), so these prosperous females were forbidden to wheel their charges about. After all these restrictions had been placed on simple activities, conversation on matters of civic importance was banned in public places. There was a considerable employment of spies for enforcement of this provision. One striker was picked up for having identified a scab by mute language to those present in a tavern. Despite the good evidence against him, this individual was freed, for the law specified vocal language.[71]

By December there were strikebreakers in considerable numbers. Key skilled operators were being wined and dined by foremen to persuade them to return. One morning employers prepared a coup, blowing the whistles at the accustomed times, and putting on all the lights. No one from the town responded.

There was no violence, yet martial law was instituted on December 4. *Vorwärts* complimented the Crimmitschauers on their discipline, said correctly to be the fruit of long social democratic schooling.[72] Meetings of more than six were next forbidden. Thousands then trudged through the snow to a nearby Thuringian enclave,[73] and a cartoon honored their tramp. Dancing was further disallowed, since it was too hard for gendarmes to overhear what couples said. It was customary among each town's social democrats to brag that their locality had the worst police; in Crimmitschau they surely had the most ingenious. Working people took it all with humor, and the police were pedantic but shed no blood.

The pettiness of the Crimmitschau gendarmes caught the attention of all Germany. The comrades were in particular preparing a generous outpouring of support. Twenty-eight thousand *Stollen* (hard cookies) were shipped to the town's children at Christmas.[74] Police blocked distribution, an action well described in the current cliche as "counterproductive." Even papers on the Right thought this was sheer meanness to children, and the goodies were soon consumed by the intended recipients at a mass party where they received more presents than ever before in their lives.[75]

During holiday season Pastor Schink, local church leader, denounced the strikers from the pulpit. He was a gaunt, ascetic-looking individual who believed, with millions of his fellows, that the lowly should always remain such. A thousand were said to have left the state church in demonstrative protest against Schink, who was, however, backed by the rest of the Crimmitschau clergy.[76] This was a late but characteristic incident in the century long turning away of German working people from the state church.

Vorwärts sent an ace reporter, Friedrich Stampfer, to see how the poor folk in Crimmitschau were faring.[77] He spoke of those who had been ill the first days, for their bodies had not adjusted as yet to the absence of clattering machinery. He talked about those who had only half a pound of meat a week for a family of nine, whose staple was still potatoes. He described men who rented space under the roof to sleep, never fewer than two to a bed, exposed to wind and rain, hitting the rafters when they rolled over. Stampfer doubted that his native Austrians would tolerate the petty ways of the local gendarmes.

Through December the plant owners would not compromise. Payments were coming in from other industrialists, and were even raised.[78] *Vorwärts* wrote, as in the case of Hamburg, that small operators wanted to settle, but offered no proof. It seemed that German industrialists in general, even those who practiced the 10 hour day, were determined to crush the women and men of Crimmitschau. Some of the city's competitors were not even undertaking to seize the unfilled markets. Klara Zetkin's *Gleichheit*, with its large circulation, and its particular interest in Crimmitschau for reason of the women involved, remarked that beyond the 10 hour day lay the 8 hour day,[79] and this notion may explain some of the capitalist hostility to the movement in this unimportant locality.

Towards the end of 1903 it became difficult to turn strangers away. Local ranks were also softening, as women and men feared for their jobs. By mid-

January the distressing report was that up to a quarter of the workbenches were now occupied.[80] Worry about jobs mounted.

Party and union leaders had overcome their distaste for long conflicts this time - after the Meerane victory which was gained by persistence it would have been embarrassing to do anything else, and the 1903 elections put pressure on social democracy to achieve something. The growing militant mood of the working class may have affected a few at the top as well. Thus it was the national textile union officials who stayed loyal to the Crimmitschauers, while the local leaders objected.[81] In December Legien, the chief union figure in Germany, had gone to the stricken Saxon town and declared that there was no reason to halt the struggle. His approach, however, was that of the politician who asserts, "I shall never..."[82] immediately before reversing himself. Strike costs, often used as a pretext to call it off, were no issue here. The whole of the skilled working class stood ready to help, and those bourgeois contributions which had been lacking in the 1890s now flowed in. Great academic figures like Hans Delbrück and Lujo Brentano spoke favorably of the poor spinners and weavers.

At some point, nonetheless, the normal habits of the union chiefs could be expected to prevail over the unusual understanding they had shown toward the millhands. By mid-January the situation of the strikers had much deteriorated. Many jobs had been lost to strikebreakers, and the determination of German capital was unrelenting. When Legien came a second time to the beleaguered town, he had in his baggage a leaflet already cleared with other working class leaders. It was a document exemplifying much of the ideology of those who had clambered to the pinnacle of union bureaucracy.

In heroic terms the leaflet recounted the five months' fight of the "eight thousand," a compromise figure between those who began it, and those who finished it. They were said to have fought a great battle, despite every provocation, and to have much of the world on their just side. They had, in truth, won a moral victory. That is to say, as a petition it was magnificent, and of course a petition was not expected to be productive of gain until perhaps later. There had been, however, a serious difficulty with this struggle, in that the capitalists had made it into a power struggle, i.e., a genuine strike. By their willfulness they had gone so far as to threaten the whole economy of Crimmitschau. One fashion season had been lost, and if the now rapidly approaching spring season had to be sacrificed as well, customers would never return here to purchase the town's characteristic cheviots and velours. Especially those too old to move would be hurt. The time had therefore come to return "without conditions." The union could not afford to have the strike "crumble away."

Jäckel's history of this conflict echoes the idea of shying away from a real struggle.[83] Similarly *Vorwärts* wrote that the strike had become a "trial of strength" and a "question of sailing out into the unknown."[84] The *Leipziger Volkszeitung*, the major party paper on the left, asserted in its summary of events of the year that once the bosses had made Crimmitschau a test of strength, it was better to desist.[85] As before, the heads of social democracy flinched before a collision with the rulers of Germany, though it was very doubtful that in this case the Berlin government was concerned. No troops had been sent, no major political figure had called the situation dangerous. Textile strikes do not bring down cabinets - this argument was largely pretext. The humble folk of Crimmitschau had no dreams of power, and had they won their 10 hour day, they would have returned to work still a servile crew.

Neither the review of the contest, nor the compliments to the combatants were the substance of Legien's message. What he chiefly meant to say was that the class struggle had to be avoided. Such being his message the police made no problems about its distribution.[86] Although the tight organization of the strikers would have made a vote possible, Legien took no chances on losing. The announcement, accepted with stoicism by the spinners and weavers, ended the conflict. They had been born and bred to lose, which is not to say that they did not wish to win. Jäckel himself conceded that his people did not approve of the surrender.[87]

Legien's handouts hardly needed to say, but did, that revenge would now be taken on the strikers. "You know that all the difficulties of the fight are as nothing compared to going back humiliated," as one of the returnees said. Some had to hand over their union books.[88] Many others were told, "For you there is no work."[89] Legien observed a 40 year veteran of the mills who took it silently when informed: "your workbench has been taken." For him there would be no more pay days, and his old age would be meatless. About four hundred, that is, 4 to 5 percent were dismissed permanently, of whom 250 were said to be "fathers of families,"[90] fewer than at some other great conflicts. Someone calculated that time lost equalled three years' cutback to 10 hours.[91]

At its next convention the textile union discussed Crimmitschau without sense of tragedy.[92] The national office, which had sent 453,000 marks, appeared most complacent. Floor speakers agreed that it would have been imprudent to borrow. Back in Crimmitschau post-strike union rolls went up sharply.[93]

Though the great Saxon walkout ought to qualify as an incident of class struggle, both sides having striven to their utmost, the oft-spoken irony of history was to bring it about that Crimmitschau's greatest effect was a petition. For in 1908 the Reichstag, then more conservative than in 1903, voted the 10 hour day for most trades, excluding agriculture, and this measure was approved by the upper house. No event in national history had given more publicity to the shortened workday than the long stoppage in Crimmitschau. The excessive toil of young mothers, the petty restrictions of the gendarmes, the Christmas party where kids had almost lost their *Stollen*, all these had had their share in promoting the legislative action. A post-strike leaflet had said: "We shall triumph, in spite of everything," and the patriarchal state, acting in the manner of Severing's boss, had made the claim come true.

After August, 1914 a series of horrors descended upon the German people. About 1,500,000 lives were lost in the First World War, while malnutrition raged at home. After defeat came the uncertainties of inflation, followed by unemployment rising to a third of the work force. A destructive government next killed its people on and off the battlefield, and laid the country open to invasion and bombing attack. If aught is clear about those 32 years of horror, it is the Teutonic ability to endure. This trait was most highly developed among proletarians, who lacked the resources to evade calamity. A strike is a small war, and brings out high moral commitment, while calling on the capacity to sacrifice and the ability to endure fear. Working class folk had training in deprivation, for half the memoirists speak of going through malnutrition. Had they been asked, as part of the advancement of their class, to return to the more depressed level of earlier times, there can be little doubt what their answer would be. But their leaders trembled before the notion of asking rank and file for genuine sacrifice. They preferred to control and then subdue the average strike through payment of high support, which could then be withdrawn. Only at Waldenburg, which came too early to expect a victory, was the talent of German proletarians to suffer patiently called upon. Subsequently this weapon was shunned, as part of a genuine class struggle and as practiced in the other lands of the Western world, not to speak of the colonial world.

A WORD ON SHAME, STRIKES, AND CLASS CLIMBING

No social democrat left behind more autobiographical material than the gifted mason August Winnig. Here is his picture on leaving jail in 1899:

> I felt guilt weighing me down, and it was because of the strike. It had nothing to do with the fact that I had hit a strikebreaker and thus gone to jail. The feeling was of another sort: I had unleashed the fiery strike, it was I who had disquieted the men and upset their [normal] relationships. I had changed the world and I was responsible for what came of it. Since it was I who had led the men into dangerous paths, it was for me to suffer for my sins.[94]

The masons' walkout had lasted three months and was supported by the national office. Rank and file remained loyal to young Winnig, and greeted him upon his release. Likely he was incarcerated for running the strike, since little Blankenburg (Brunswick) probably did not yet tolerate walkouts as did Hamburg.

Winnig was the offspring of an elderly gravedigger, a man one notch above the ordinary workingman, for his position was official. Alas, August's brother had joined a tiny democratic party, and thus the family lost its place in Blankenburg officialdom. His mother, Henriette, a cowherd's daughter, had borne August as her eighth child. Her influence, rather than the paternal, appears to have been determinative for him. Winnig says of his childhood: "I was always hungry." His recent biographer, putting a psychohistorical emphasis upon his career, suggests that in youth he also suffered from Messianism.[95]

Wilhelmine society had no outlet for talented rebels. Since he was a proletarian, Winnig could not even aspire to teaching. Theodore Bömelburg, head of the masons, recognized his ability, encouraged him in union work and became his surrogate father. When the two individuals with the greatest influence over his life encountered each other, the cowherd's daughter told the great union official: "I know who you are. He went on strike once. Is he always supposed to do that?" Many times Bömelburg must have answered women who thought their men should toil every day without exception: "Mother, do you know how often we...came to the end of the week and had no bread? For that [reason] I will strike, that poor people should have some bread. That is my aim."[96]

Winnig's mother need not have been anxious. Erikson speaks of the ephemeral nature of German youthful rebellion;[97] like scores of others, Winnig soon learned to be an organization man. Once his home town chances for a job were gone, he lost his taste for heroics. He served a term in the army and then headed for Bömelburg's headquarters in Hamburg. At the flat of the rising leader he found such wonders as china, dinner silver, carpets, double curtains, and a clock faced with black marble. Soon Winnig too was emerging from poverty and the proletariat; like Bebel he began making up for lack of university training. His biographer explains his whole life, in fact, as pursuit of *embourgeoisement*. Possessed of a quick and colorful pen, he throve in an era with huge reading audiences, becoming editor of the masons' journal *Grundstein*, and moving from there to being a top official. By 1914 he was earning 3,000 marks, several times what a mere mortar board would have gained him.

When 1914 came Winnig had a yet larger bandwagon of respectability onto which to climb. He wrote poetry about nationalism. By 1918 he had moved so far as to join the Baltic *Freikorps*. Later, as a high Prussian official, he backed the Kapp Putsch. He advanced to being a columnist for a major Berlin financial journal and later welcomed the nationalism of the Nazis without joining them.

Winnig's career, if extreme, is illustrative of the impulses which respectable unionists, both leaders and rank and file, had toward meeting the norms of the prevailing bourgeois culture of the time. If they had those drives, and more of them did each decade, they then strove to avoid strikes, and wished instead to do everything which would lead them into the marvelous world of clocks with marble facings.

NOTES

1. On the rise of real wages, 1894-1903, see Kuczynski, *GdL*, 3, 361; Bry, *Wages in Germany*, 71, 74; Desai, *Wages*, 124-25.

2. The autobiography of Moritz Th. W. Bromme, *Lebensgeschichte eines modernen Fabrikarbeiters*, reprint of 1905 ed. (Frankfurt: 1972), makes very clear what a tragedy it was for a proletarian woman when she discovered that she was once again "of good hope."

3. Kuczynski, *GdL*, 3, 266.

4. In a recent article Gerhard A. Ritter and Klaus Tenfelde speak of the rise of unions in the nineties, "Der Durchbruch der Freien Gewerkschaften Deutschlands zur Massenbewegung im lezten Viertel des 19. Jahrhunderts," in Heinz Oskar Vetter, ed., *Vom Sozialistengesetz zum Mitbestimmung: Zum 100 Geburtstag von Hans Böckler* (Cologne: 1975), 61-110. They put things rather early: the second half of the nineties laid the basis for the rise of unions, and the break through to large numbers began around 1903. The large numbers were, of course, confined to certain areas of the economy.

5. For the list of constitutional restrictions which the various unions put upon their members' ability to strike, see Legien's *Koalitionsrecht der deutschen Arbeiter in Theorie und Praxis: Denkschrift der General Kommission der Gewerkschaften Deutschlands* (Hamburg: 1899), 143-158.

6. Cole, *Short History*, 258ff.

7. When the men could no longer be marched to the polls, Krupp management began making close analyses of their voting habits. See the reconstruction of how Essen voted in 1913 in Willi Bölcke, ed. *Krupp und die Hohenzollern* (Berlin: 1956), 117ff.

8. Marchwitza, *Meine Jugend*, 7. Marchwitza's mother rejected this widespread belief.

9. Braun, *Lehrjahre*, 1, 236-37. The *Junker's* attack was not very well advised, for a groom can always revenge himself on an animal.

10. For decades the standard biography of Wilhelm II has been Erick Eyck's *Das persönliche Regiment des Wilhelms II*, Zurich and Erlenbach, 1948. Eyck wrote under Weimar influence, attempting to be democratic, yet far from egalitarian in his approach. He did not regard the emperor as a man such as he was himself, but as a higher individual, yet faulted. Eyck stuck to politics in his biography, but since the emperor achieved almost nothing in a direct political way, this is a doubtful approach. The man needs, above all, psychological treatment, a first start at which is made by Virginia Cowles, *Wilhelm the Kaiser* (New York: 1963). More than one complicated effort is underway.

11. *Chronik*, 161.

12. *Vorwärts*, February 27 & March 6, 1892. *Vorwärts* showed alarm, for marches and minor clashes with the police were not in the style of social democracy.

13. The notable historian Ludwig Quidde published his essay *Caligula*, which is always taken to be a comparison with Wilhelm II, in 1894. The small work ended Quidde's academic career.

14. Maehl, *Bebel*, 515.

15. Roehl, *Germany without Bismarck*, 262.

16. Ibid., 221-22.

17. Saul, *Staat, Industrie*, 213-26, discusses how German judges handled picketing.

18. *Denkwürdigkeiten des Generalfeldmarschalls Alfred Graf von Waldersee*, ed. H. O. Meisner, 3 vols. (Stuttgart: 1923-25), 2, 388. Waldersee wrote the Kaiser twice about the strike; he was military commandant of the area. His comments bordered on the frantic though the strike itself was relatively quiet.

19. Bernhard Menne, *Krupp, Deutschlands Kanonenkönige* (Zurich: 1937), 207.

20. Legien, *Koalitionsrecht*, 17-22.

21. These are the comments in Saul, *Staat, Industrie*, 194ff.

22. Ibid. 24-28. Someone calculated in *Corrblatt*, January 22,1899, that the rate of strikers being arrested was 3.3 per thousand, which was felt in the working class to be bearable.

23. In his autobiography, Bebel uses a light touch to describe prison days. Of course, he was writing three decades later. *Aus meinem Leben*, 3, 227-28.

24. Legien, *Koalitionsrecht*, 17-22.

25. Quoted in Saul, *Staat, Industrie*, 27.

26. Hans Jaeger, *Unternehmer in der deutschen Politik 1890-1918* (Bonn: 1967), 62, fn. 163, has found that von Stumm's rostrum appearances exceeded all other industrialists. Hammacher was similarly addicted.

27. In the safety of private conversation and in their diaries, social democrats doubted that von Stumm was sane. See Paul Mayer, ed., *Bruno Schönlank, 1859-1901: Reformer der sozialdemokratischen Tagespresse* (Hannover: 1971), 118. Wilhelmine society, of course, afforded exceptional circumstances for the expression of conservative extremism.

28. This first African walkout has been described by A. G. Hopkins, "The Lagos Strike of 1897: an Exploration in African Labor History", *Past and Present*, 35 (1966), 133-155.

29. The *Leipziger Volkszeitung's* call for support of the St. Petersburg strikers has been republished in *Dokumente und Materialen*, 3, 454.

30. The same June 17 *Vorwärts* contained a different but no less startling outburst of enthusiasm. "The victory of the German proletariat is the victory of German culture, *(Unser das Reich - unser die Welt)*." This is to say, "Ours is the [German] empire - ours will be the world."

31. Stampfer, *Erfahrungen*, 82.

32. *Vorwärts*, January 8, 1899, described the issues in Krefeld; it was largely a question of wage cuts. See also *Corrblatt*, February 23, 1902.

33. The Krefeld victory is described in *Corrblatt*, April 13 & 20, 1902.

34. "Der Weberaufstand 1842 in Meerane," *Die Spindel* [Glachuau], 1959, Heft 8, 2-6.

35. *Corrblatt*, November 3, 1902.

36. *Vorwärts*, December 13, 1903; *Corrblatt*, January 26, 1903.

37. *Vorwärts*, October 21, 1902.

38. Hartmut Kälble, *Industrielle Interessenpolitik in der Wilhelminischen Gesellschaft* (Berlin: 1967), 12-13, fn. 41.

39. Saul demonstrates that it was only a certain part of German industry which was reluctant to concede human and political rights to their workers. Many of these hard-liners outside heavy industry were in textiles. *Staat, Industrie*, 56.

40. See the academically oriented, non-social democratic study by Erich Schaarschmidt, *Geschichte der Crimmitschauer Arbeiterbewegung*, Dresden, 1934.

41. Hermann Jäckel, *Der Crimmitschauer Kampf um den Zehnstudentag* (Berlin: 1905), 60-65.

42. These early events are recorded in *Der Weber-Streik zu Crimmitschau*, 3d ed. Munich, 1883.

43. The lore of the long battle at Crimmitschau, (and it had more than other strikes) was lovingly collected in *1903-28: Blätter der Erinnerungen an Sachsens Bedeutsamsten Arbeitskampf*, Berlin, 1928.

44. E.g., *Corrblatt*, February 1, 1891.

45. Jäckel, *Crimmitschauer Kampf*, 60.

46. *Gleichheit*, August 4, 1903.

47. *Gleichheit*, September 2, 1903.

48. *Gleichheit*, September 9, 1903.

49. The appeal of the national unions is reprinted in *Dokumente und Materialen*, 3, 101.

50. Jäckel, *Crimmitschauer Kampf*, 24.

51. Ibid., 28.

52. Idem.

53. Woldemar Wagner, "Zu einigen Fragen des Crimmitschauer Textilarbeiterstreiks von 1903/04" *ZfG*, 1 (1953), 574.

54. *Gleichheit*, October 7, 1903.

55. Wagner, *ZfG*, 1, 576.

56. For an analysis of strike conduct in general see Siegfried Nestriepke, *Die Gewerkschaftsbewegung*, 3 vols. (Stuttgart: 1920-21), 1, 378-402.

57. Jäckel, *Crimmitschauer Kampf*, 19ff.

58. *Gleichheit*, December 9, 1903.

59. Baader, *Ein steiniger Weg*, 83.

60. *Gleichheit*, December 9, 1903.

61. Idem.

62. *Vorwärts*, January 6, 1904.

63. Severing, *Mein Lebensweg*, 1, 45.

64. Ibid., 46.

65. *Corrblatt*, January 25, 1903.

66. Jäckel, *Crimmitschauer Kampf*, 46.

67. *Gleichheit*, December 23, 1903.

68. Wachenhain, *Die deutsche Arbeiterbewegung*, 390.

69. *Vorwärts*, November 6, 1903.

70. *Gleichheit*, December 23, 1903.

71. *Vorwärts*, December 16, 1903.

72. Ibid., December 9, 1903.

73. Ibid., December 13, 1903.

74. Schaarschmidt, *Crimmitschauer Geschichte*, 125.

75. *Gleichheit*, January 20, 1904.

76. *Vorwärts*, January 7, 1904.

77. Stampfer's articles may be found in *Vorwärts*, December 24, 25 & 29, 1903.

78. *Gleichheit*, December 23, 1903.

79. *Gleichheit*, November 18, 1903.

80. *Vorwärts*, January 10, 1904.

81. Schaarschmidt, *Crimmitschauer Geschichte*, 124.

82. *Vorwärts*, December 20, 1903.

83. Jäckel, *Crimmitschauer Kampf*, 67.

84. *Vorwärts*, January 19, 1904.

85. *Leipziger Volkszeitung*, January 10, 1905.

86. *Vorwärts*, January 21, 1904.

87. Jäckel, *Crimmitschauer Kampf*, 73.

88. *Corrblatt*, February 4, 1904.

89. *Gleichheit*, January 27, 1904.

90. *Corrblatt*, April 3, 1904.

91. *Gleichheit*, January 27, 1904.

92. *Corrblatt*, April 3, 1904.

93. *Crimmitschau, 1903-1928*, 103.

94. August Winnig, *Der weite Weg* (Hamburg: 1932), 41.

95. Wilhelm Ribhegge, *August Winnig: eine historische Persönlichkeitanalyse* (Bonn: 1973), 30.

96. Winnig, *Der weite Weg*, 133.

97. Erik H. Erikson, *Childhood and Society*, 2nd ed. (New York: 1963), 335.

6

THE RUHR STRIKE OF 1905

In the 1890s fortune smiled upon the Ruhr coal owners, particularly the largest among them. Production bounded ahead, so that by 1900 the valley was turning out 60 million tons annually, more than half of all German coal. The product was in demand, profits were excellent, and capital was on hand for expansion. What made the coal barons additionally powerful was that they had had the wit to form a cartel to set production quotas and market prices.[1]

Already in 1857 Ruhr coal firms had discussed common marketing.[2] Agreement took decades, however, for the temptation to cut the competitor's price was too great. Finally in 1893 Emil Kirdorf, manager of the huge Gelsenkirchen pit, succeeded in bringing together most of the firms in the Rhine-Westphalia Coal Syndicate with the declared purpose of setting production quotas for each company and vending the output of all. This was a much more ambitious goal than that of previous trade associations. Over 80 percent of the valley's output was covered in the initial agreement. *De facto*, the new cartel was able to set prices for all Germany. There was in this way also a better chance to take markets from the British, whose annual tonnage still far outdistanced that of the Second Empire.

The prosperity of the later 1890s enabled the fledgling association to consolidate itself. Its strength was shown when no one cut prices during the mild depression of 1900. A further trial came in the decennial renewal year (1903) when the troublesome production quotas were reassigned. The syndicate emerged from this trial stronger than ever, with more pits within its fold. In these years of bloom it became the world's most forceful economic association and included many of the wealthiest and most powerful men of the Second Empire. A 1911 listing, for instance, put Krupp's capital, some of which was in coal, at 215 million, the greatest fortune in the land.[3] Thyssen was credited with 45 million and Stinnes with 30. Most of this money was of very recent accumulation.

Ownership of Germany's most valuable resource, just as the Empire was becoming the world's second industrial power, gave a handful of Ruhr magnates very great power. They knew how to cultivate political influence as well. In 1889 both Bismarck and Wilhelm II had floated the idea of nationalizing the mines, but after Kirdorf's syndicate was on guard, nothing more was heard of this. Krupp manager Jencke wrote his superior in 1893 that the sole duty of the state was to preserve order, and to protect those willing to work against "terrorism."[4] He went on to extol the firing of suspected social democrats. Krupp forwarded this epistle, with its hardly novel ideas, to the emperor. Thus four years after the great rebellion, the case was reversed, and Ruhr barons were instructing the emperor how to behave. These were men of very great determination.

Being quite sure of its economic and political bases, the coal syndicate moved on to vertical expansion.[5] The great new growth industry of the day was steel. Between 1889 and 1914 German steel production was to triple, while outstripping that of England. This new industry was the best single customer for the black diamond, and the profit in combining the two would accordingly be very large. Already in 1903 the fight over syndicate renewal had pitted the large, aggressive, technically advanced firms which wanted to go beyond coal against the smaller and more limited traditionalists who were satisfied with late nineteenth century ways. Once the magnates won in the cartel, they were ready to buy into iron ore, of which Germany had an insufficient supply to guarantee steel production over the decades, or in case of war. The handiest source of iron was France, and the first approach of the big Ruhr coal owners was by way of purchase.[6] The French rejected them.

The *Hibernia* affair demonstrated the considerable strength the Ruhr barons had in internal affairs.[7] Finally coming to realize the force of the syndicate, the Berlin government decided in 1903 to buy into it. But once the state's bankers began purchasing *Hibernia* stock, the magnates got wind of the plan. They wanted no bureaucrats interfering with their quotas and prices. They mobilized the rest of *Hibernia* shares and prevented their sale to the Berlin government. In this simple fashion they turned back the formidable Second Reich.

When Bebel had spoken of irresistible Ruhr barons he was thinking of but 20. By now there was a yet smaller circle of decision makers. One of these half dozen was Hugo Stinnes. The house of Stinnes was founded by Matthias, whose boats plied the Rhine before 1848.[8] After the Tariff Union of 1834 was born, he prospered and the family gradually moved into other lines of business without becoming spectacularly wealthy.[9] Hugo Stinnes succeeded to the headship of the family in the late 1880s. Of all the active magnates of the Ruhr, Hugo Stinnes, who went into every detail of his firm's progress, and had even done a shift or two *unter Tage*, was the most exaggerated case. One of the first businessmen to use the telephone, he was said to have had a mind as much like a machine's as Morgan's. He made inventions, was not afraid of unconventional markets, and bought up sick companies to restore them. Albert Ballinn, who knew much of such matters, said that as some children cannot keep their hands off candy, Hugo Stinnes could not keep his off the property of others. Accumulating was his life, and he did not ordinarily stop to enjoy.

In 1904 Stinnes recognized a very ordinary problem at his *Bruchstrasse* pit, which had a quota from the syndicate and therefore had to function just as efficiently as possible. The not uncommon difficulty was that *Bruchstrasse's* best veins were getting to be further and further from the entrance. The solution of choice was to lengthen the miners' unpaid working time. Accordingly notice was posted at the mine in December, 1904 that normal shift time would be increased by 30 minutes. There was no consultation with miners, though by this time mechanisms for such negotiations were available.

In this first decade of this century, the German industrial workday was continuing its long decline. Stinnes was bucking the national trend, and he scorned the usual apologies for increased hours (depression or price declines). Ruhr diggers all believed that the historic shift, coming down from the Middle Ages, was 8 hours, and they resented already the payless minutes spent going to and from the mine face. When Stinnes made his announcement, the men at *Bruchstrasse* went out on strike. He may have anticipated this result, for memory of the family's 1868 strike was unlikely to have disappeared from table conversation.

Whatever his reasoning, Stinnes now backed off, contemptuously alleging one of his wife's many pregnancies. Of course he had to check on cartel support, for a friendly biographer concedes that "his enemies [were] as numerous as a swarm of mosquitoes."[10] Had he continued to reverse himself, he would have lost some of his sense of being a ruler, and perhaps also some standing among his colleagues.[11] Love of authority was, at the time, by no means confined to Teutonic lands. Stearns quotes an entrepreneur from a nation with stronger democratic feelings:

> I do not intend for my workers to discuss my conditions of work; if these do not suit them, let them go elsewhere, I have hundreds to replace them. Besides, I am the Master...I intend to be the Master and I will be in spite of everything.[12]

To retain such control as this French employer required, Stinnes reissued his proclamation two days before Christmas, postponing the effective date until February 1, that those who wished to change pits might do so. If Stinnes reckoned that his miners would now strike, it may have been because he was aware of the recent rise in activism in Germany. He would hardly have noticed the beginnings of a worldwide revolutionary wave.

Ruhr miners of 1905 were no longer the desperate coalies of 1889. They had been granted much of what they then sought and the improvements altered their lives. What had done the most for them was the reduction in hours. They were now *unter Tage* 9 hours, including that dangerous, hurried, crouching journey on hands and knees which gave them "buttons" on their backs.[13] They still remembered that Hammacher had promised pay for those terrible minutes. Pay had also advanced. The owners, given their exceptional financial situation, found it easier to hand out money than to cut hours.

Kuczynski has written of a "labor aristocracy" (as have others), and the miners were now in that category. In 1900, he said, their wages were about 26 percent higher than in the 1883-1892 cycle.[14] More recently Desai gives Ruhr diggers an average 1890 wage of 865 (1895) marks and then of 1,065 marks of similar value in 1905. Since miners' standard of living in 1890 was among the best for proletarians, they were doing fairly well by 1905. However, most of the improvement had come by 1900. Following Desai, in the earlier years wages advanced 15 marks a year, so men could observe about 70 pfennigs more each pay period.[15] In the new century the increase had declined to about 30 pfennigs per two week pay period, with hackers pulling about 4 marks a day. Diet was now richer than before, there was more time for relaxation, and the pride of the Ruhr - that wives did not work for money - lingered on.[16] The unmarried could have an alcoholic weekend, followed by "blue" Monday, giving them a 5 day week.

Increments to pay came to that quarter of miners who had company houses. Providing them had been an idea of Alfred Krupp's for better control of the work force. A mine with a reputation for bad air or poor safety could have a complete turnover in a year, and company housing might reduce that figure. Families everywhere could take in a lodger (for which companies often paid a subsidy), keep a pig and have a garden. Those who saved their cash might have a chance to buy their house,[17] while those who gave the company trouble could be evicted.

Conditions within the mines had improved somewhat. The men no longer tolerated abuse such as they had suffered in the 1880s, or as prevailed still in the Saar and Silesia. However sanitary facilities were slow to improve, and safety was no better than in the 1880s.

A sign of bettered conditions was the existence of unions. For it is not the most miserable of men who creates them, but those who have had an awakening of self confidence. The several miners' associations which had mushroomed between 1889 and 1891 had then collapsed,[18] but after 1895 they were slowly rebuilt. Three of the four of them turned out to be significant.

Forty-three delegates gathered at Halle in 1890 to form the German Mine Workers Association which, by virtue of a few months' seniority, became known as the "Old Association."[19] For political reasons, but not out of preference, this group insisted that it was neutral both as to parties and as to religion. Such was the social democratic union, widely believed to be hostile to religion. It called itself "free" since no one had to espouse any doctrine to become a member. Prior to 1914 the "Old Association" was the largest of the four, and holding its opening convention near the lignite fields, with a few Saar miners present, suggested that it wanted to expand.[20] Its constitution spoke, in the preamble, of "limitless exploitation" by capitalists and the Prussian state.[21] This outburst out of the way, the real demands were stated: an 8 hour day, portal to portal, with shorter hours in hotter places. They sought a 4 marks minimum, to be paid weekly. Among further demands was an end to *Nullen*, a national mining code, and the outlawing of the blacklist. At this first meeting, but not later, there was a call to end the "capitalist ring", which meant the proto-cartel of the day.

When the "Old Association" met again in 1891, the bloom was off,[22] as delegates met in Bochum, a city evenly split between Catholic and non-Catholic.[23] Few delegates came from outside the Ruhr, and there was no pretense at national membership. Schröder was in the chair and the ambiance was social democratic. The previous year's (estimated) membership of 200,000 had now shrunk to 56,000. Perhaps two-thirds were up to date in their dues, for it was notoriously difficult to get money from miners.[24] The "Old Association" now belonged to the General Commission of German Trade

Unions (soc. dem.) though actually the miners went their own way. By 1895 declared membership was down to a suspiciously round 5,000.

Aside from the independence of their dues-payers, the mine union was plagued by German authority. Schröder, Bunte and Siegel had all been fired despite their august role as petitioners. Siegel migrated to England, where pay was better and there was no blacklist. Schröder was to fare worse.

In the years of decline, bitterness between social democratic and Catholic unions grew more aggravated. The fewer the interested men, the harsher the fight for their allegiance. So Schröder came to pay his way into a Catholic meeting in February, 1895, bent on cannibalism.[25] He had friends with him. In the chair was August Brust, a man who never shied from controversy. As soon as the meeting began the "reds" began their heckling. A generation before, their fathers would have thrown chairs and steins. Brust had anticipated this, and had seen to extra police. He ordered Schröder and company out. By way of defiance the social democrat stopped at the door for a refund, which was refused. During the ensuing argument, Officer Münter approached Schröder from the rear, and threw him to the floor. When he arose, he was kicked down again. Schröder knew something of German justice to workingmen. Though Münter had a reputation as an alcoholic and as a sadist, he was uniformed. Schröder's only choice was to run out. Thus the incident as remembered 25 years later in *Vorwärts*.[26] The Catholic historian Imbusch was reluctant to describe the incident.[27]

When the Old Association's journal printed this version in 1895, Münter charged libel, alleging that he had not touched Schröder. He won his case, testimony about his character not being permitted. The same happened in a second trial.[28] Then the zealous prosecuting attorney charged that Schröder *et al.,* in contradicting an official of the state, had committed perjury. Once again social democrats tried to establish the facts, but their case was damaged by the unwillingness of Catholics to testify. "What," *Vorwärts* remarked indignantly, "Fifty witnesses who did not manage to see, all set apart by itself, the most interesting thing that happened all night?"[29] Schröder and his friends were all solid, hard-working family men while Münter was an SS type brute, but the jury voted with the uniform. Schröder was given three years at hard labor, with head shorn, and one of his comrades received five and one-half. The mine owners' *Rheinisch-Westfälische Zeitung* complained that social democrats put loyalty to party above common honesty.[30] None of those sentenced petitioned for royal grace, and all served their terms.

The party was accustomed to about 80 years annual political sentencing, but this was specially raw. *Vorwärts* wrote: "No case in recent times has made a deeper impression upon the comrades than [the one] by the bourgeois jury in Essen."[31] A 1911 retrial heard both Catholic miners who repented their earlier silence and police who had grown ashamed of their lies, as *Klassenjustiz* eased just a bit in the prewar years. Schröder, then too old to appreciate his official vindication, even received modest compensation.

Mayer, second in command in the Old Association, was likewise jailed for perjury. When the Saar miners' union was crushed in these same years its chief, Warken, was imprisoned. The most successful miners' association of the mid-1890s was the Saxon, which had 9,200 members in 1894[32] despite the small size of the field. It was now abolished by government action, though it had survived the Exceptional Law period. Its principal leader, Sachse, was jailed for a year, though Saxony did not ordinarily incarcerate working class leaders.[33] Thus within a short period in all areas of miner strike activity union leaders were jailed, in a way which was quite out of character for the patriarchal state. Hue made the distinction between warning terms of a few days, and the longer sentences which might ruin a man's effectiveness,[34] if not the individual as well. There is no comparable instance in Wilhelmine history where all a trade's best organizers were imprisoned at once, and it raises the question of whether Kirdorf's new cartel might have arranged these concurrent sentences so beneficial to itself.

Since it was the progress of the economy more than the agitational abilities of the leaders which determined the fates of unions, the jailings in any case fell short of their probable aim. After about 1897 the Mine Workers Association (soc. dem.) began to thrive. The national office gave the men a sense of solidarity and provided them with supplementary funds in case of sickness, death, unemployment and also strikes. The coalies were, however, more independent than other proletarians, and signed up only very slowly. By the end of the century the Old Association had 40,000 members, by 1905, 90,000, or roughly 27 percent of the Ruhr force. There was only minor membership in other fields: the Saar, Silesia, Aachen and the lignite fields remained essentially closed to the union. Cash balance went up smartly each year, with total wealth passing 1,000,000 in 1905.[35]

In the second half of the 1890s the miners began to profit from their courage in 1889. The country's new prosperity built the organization. Shepherds of the effort were Sachse, Hue and others of the self-educated, not one of whom was ever sacked for dishonesty or incompetence. As they began to amass millions in the various social security funds, however, they began to have proprietary sense toward these monies, having been around in the bitter days when only "5,000" were on the rolls and prosecuting attorneys might seek out the leaders any day. They had no desire to revert to the days of penury and danger and it was a long time since they had made a shift. Small strikes they might tolerate, but large scale walkouts they thought of as a menace to the organization they believed that they had built. They were more prone to measure the well-being of the union by its bank account than by the longevity of its members. Otto Hue, who became the historian of the Old Association, said in 1899 that one could take comfort that there was no talk of a work stoppage, and he was a trifle more militant than the others.[36] The mine union had that constitutional clause common to German unions, according to which the central office had to approve all walkouts.[37] Yet the men who sat at clean desks and never had to worry about a fire or a coal fall, knew that they could not control miners, as, for instance, plumbers might be reined in. They presently found themselves approving what was to become a very significant struggle at Neurode.[38]

If there was money in the bank and the police were not at the door, there was yet the daily, nagging, apparently insoluble problem of religion. The conflict with the Catholic union went on every day. As formal advocates of the class struggle, the Mine Workers Association was appalled at the split. In the words of one of their pamphleteers:

> If one of the bosses suggested that [they] should organize by religion or by nationality, the others would be sure to let him know that one of his screws was loose.[39]

Sometimes the Old Association approached the Catholics with proposals for common action, but cooperation became difficult in meetings where rank and file liked to show off their newly acquired irreligion, and jeer at believers.[40]

Another quicksand was nationality. Germans who love Poles occur about as frequently as Greeks with an affection for Turks. Though the party might subsidize Polish workers papers, in line with the formal commitment to internationalism, other attitudes were just below the surface. Ignaz Auer was candid when others were not: "We couldn't do the Polish workers a greater favor than to Germanize them, but one may not say so."[41] Polish *Gastarbeiter* were commonly thought of as wage-cutters,[42] which may have been true, and was a bitter charge to live with. The Old Association found it hard going when trying to enroll Polish miners, who came to the Ruhr in increasing numbers.

Second in importance was the Catholic union, speaking for a sub-group of 30 percent of the population.[43] After Bismarck's assault on them in the 1870s, Catholics thought in terms of self-defense, for which purpose the Center served very well. Unlike other parties, this one had to straddle class lines, and Catholic bourgeois, peasants and workers were among its voters, which made for peculiar compromises at times.

The 'permanent' Reichstag districts which Bismarck drew up gave the advantage to rural areas, and thus, though it was not the Iron Chancellor's intention, to Catholics. A map of Germany would show 'Black' areas in a thick 'L', with stem along the French border, and with an even thicker base going east across Bavaria.[44] The 'L' included a quarter of all Reichstag seats, but the Center could only keep them for itself by acting as a coalition. Should one segment defect, others might follow. In the 1890s, for instance, falling agricultural prices had made Catholic peasants threaten to form their own organization.[45] A similar peril was that 'Black' proletarians would not hear the siren song of class struggle, as did Catholic workingmen in France and Italy in these decades. The Ruhr had six Reichstag seats, and retaining them was a *sine qua non* for the Center.

In his great encyclical *Rerum Novarum* (1891) Pope Leo XIII had urged the formation of associations of religiously minded workingmen who could thus protect their interests while not colliding with their employers. The "new things" which the Pope proclaimed were not quite such, for a strong minority of German Catholics had promoted similar ideas since the 1840s, but the Papacy, with its primary strength in Mediterranean agricultural lands, had been tardy in responding to industrial issues.

The Catholic miners of the Ruhr founded the neutrally titled *Gewerkverein* in 1894, based it on the principles of *Rerum Novarum*. This association offered the same social services as the "free" unions, with provision for the sick, for burial and for unemployment. Men might join regardless of class or religion, though the association did call itself "Christian." Thus businessmen and also priests could become members but not social democrats, who were specifically excluded. Top officials always belonged to the Church, the first head being August Brust, a miner.

The *Gewerkverein* was even less sympathetic to strikes than the Old Association. When there was talk of a walkout in 1899, Johann Effert, second in command, resisted the idea at that year's convention.[46] Their *Bergknappe* had a milder tone than the "free" union's *Bergarbeiterzeitung*. For instance, on the eve of the 1905 outbreak, the latter inquired how it could be that Bertha Krupp could have an income of 30,000,000,[47] equivalent to that of 30,000 miners. Such a cut at the capitalist system would not have been found in *Gewerkverein* journals, where they liked to speak about personal and family affairs. Doctrine played no great part in their journalism and at moments they were downright naive and prejudiced. Thus when the massive Austrian miners' strike of 1900 occurred, *Bergknappe* hoped for their victory, one reason being

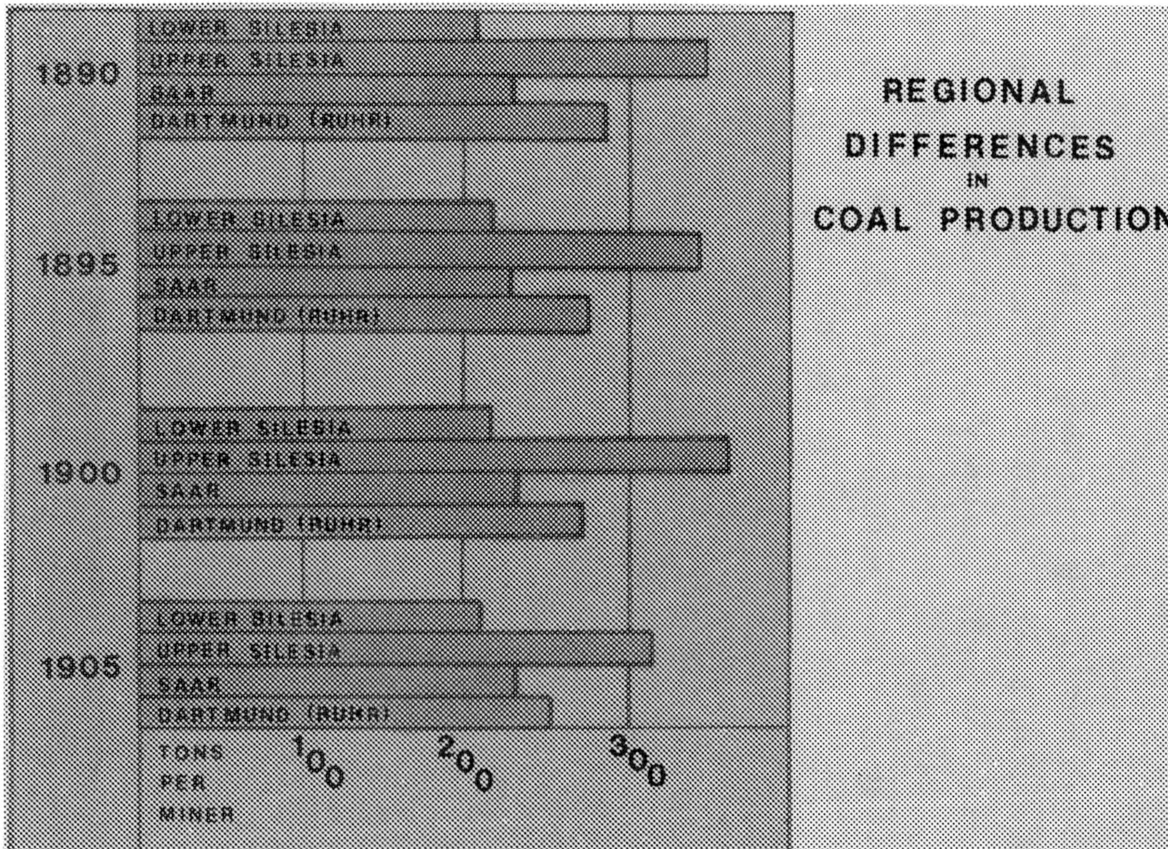
REGIONAL
DIFFERENCES
IN
COAL PRODUCTION
1890
1895
1900
1905
LOWER SILESIA
UPPER SILESIA
SAAR
DARTMUND (RUHR)
LOWER SILESIA
UPPER SILESIA
SAAR
DARTMUND (RUHR)
LOWER SILESIA
UPPER SILESIA
SAAR
DARTMUND (RUHR)
LOWER SILESIA
UPPER SILESIA
SAAR
DARTMUND (RUHR)
TONS
PER
MINER
100
200
300

that victory would mean the Austrian miners (presumably Slavs) would remain at home, and not bring diseases among the Germans.[48]

The *Gewerkverein* had low dues, the treasury being occasionally augmented by the donations of rich friends.[49] The benefits program was modest. Like the Old Association, it grew apace with the economy. In the mid-nineties there were but a few thousand on the rolls, then prosperity, and the attention given unions by the emperor and von Stumm did their part. By 1905 44,000 were in the ranks, about 14 percent of the Ruhr force - though not quite all members came from the valley. Catholic proletarians joined not only to be part of a union, but because they did not want to be swamped by social democrats, Prussians and modern industry.

The Polish Association of Miners drew its recruits from the Slavic tenth of the Second Empire.[50] Population was rising rapidly in Poland and Russia, but there were not opportunities for employment for many more in agriculture. The more energetic males came first from Polish parts of Germany, and then from Polish parts of the Tsarist Empire, heading first to neighboring Silesia, and then to the Ruhr. They travelled in cattle cars, and arrived in territories not only alien, but hostile. Their housing was very crowded, and they were often cheated on rent.

Before women began to follow the men in numbers, they had to subsist on food to which they were unfamiliar. In the mines they often got the worst assignments, and warning signs were printed only in German.[51] Outside the mines they were looked down upon, to which their response was heightened sense of fraternity. They tended to settle in certain cities, especially Recklinghausen, Herne and Gelsenkirchen, where they soon had their own churches, priests, and societies of all types,[52] (so many of the latter that the Berlin government began to worry). Fighting to maintain their own culture, they taught their children Polish, though only German could be used in school.[53] "We came here with two great pearls," said one of their leaders, "our language and the faith of our fathers."[54] Such individuals were not ready for Auer's Germanization.

Nineteenth century Poland had a tradition of revolution beginning with Koscziuszko in the 1790s and continuing through 1830 and 1863. Many tens of thousands had died in these wars, and it was quite to be expected that some of the passions felt then would carry through into the trade unions of later times. A bit of it showed at Herne in July of 1899.[55] The whole valley was then looking for a raise but instead take-home declined because of altered social security payments. Explanations of this change were only in German. The Poles rioted in the old-fashioned way. Two thousand troops arrived and, since the rioters were not German, shot and killed two, while injuring a known 29 more.[56] Previous to this the decade's only strike casualty had been a female onlooker at a Silesian pit.[57] *Vorwärts* was concerned that Herne might produce more riots and revived the slogan of Exceptional Law days: "Do not become provoked,"[58] but the Berlin paper could have had but scanty influence here. Heavier sentences than usual were dealt to about 50 Poles, and they received a total of 37 years. Those fired came to 191, of whom 29 were identified as Germans.[59]

The affair at Herne prompted the birth of the Polish Association of Miners,[60] which was at first secret, but then came into the open with institutions such as other unions had: a paper, dues, insurance benefits. The Polish association grew and had by 1914 property worth a million. Religion gave it a natural alignment with the Center Party and the *Gewerkverein*, and originally its constitution forbade membership to social democrats. However, these immigrant miners were more rebellious than their German colleagues, and also easier victims of the cartel. The anti-red clause was soon dropped, and the Poles were subsequently more the allies of the Old Association than of the Catholics.

The Hirsch-Duncker group, veteran of Waldenburg, had by 1905 2,000 adherents in the Ruhr and then 10,000 marks. They were treated with outward courtesy by the other unions, but lacked consequence.[61]

Together the four unions had enrolled just over half the Ruhr energy producers by 1905. The four had different goals and were unaccustomed to cooperation. In common, however, their leaders feared strikes. They hardly seemed to have the strength to stand up to the most powerful economic organization in the world. But if they lacked experience, unity, cash and aggressive leaders, these unions, with near to 300,000 members, had their positive sides, for the men were conscious of their importance to the German economy, more devoted to class struggle than other proletarians, and remembered their victory in 1889. Furthermore, the lines of division by religion (though not by nationality) may have been more apparent than real, a part of official positions taken by organizations, but not entirely shared by rank and file. When Levenstein sampled proletarian opinion, Ruhr miner respondents denied the existence of God by a 6-1 margin.[62] These were not simply the replies of godless social democrats to a poll ignored by Catholics, for in the same sampling of opinion Saar miners, in that almost entirely Catholic area, called themselves atheists by a margin of 4-1. In Silesia, loyal to the Church, where few workingmen would have listened to lectures on Darwin, 126 miners asserted a belief in God, while 227 denied it. However that may be, a long term trend was at work, for the influence of religion was in decline, while unionism was on the ascent, developments which had the potential for making the differences between the two major miners' unions decline in intensity.

In May, 1889, by way of covering their retreat, the Ruhr miners' chiefs had said that if the companies did not respect the agreement, they would recommend another walkout. Actually one such came in 1891 when 20,000 men went out.[63] At this time the miners had not yet made many of the concessions which were expected of them. However when the 20,000 saw that they were not being followed by majority, they returned to the pits, and the Ruhr remained quiet until 1905.

The Saar was away from major roads, without a large urban concentration, lacked a university or other cultural distinction, and was something of a cultural backwash. The region had no history of political activism, and patriarchal controls were accepted as readily as in the East. Peasants' sons adapted easily to mining here, the more so in that wages at the state pits were higher than elsewhere. Yet in 1889 Saar miners made a start at militant action by going out for a few days.[64] That was more difficult here than in other fields, because of the watch which was kept on working people. "Even the flowing water and the free air belong to him," wrote a Saar worker.[65] "Him" was von Stumm, friend of authoritarianism and advocate of concentration camps for social democrats. Von Stumm liked to control "his" workers: for instance their brides were given dowries, but only if they were certified virgins.[66] Such gifts would not have come to much expense in the Ruhr, where half the brides gave birth within five months of marriage.[67]

In 1892, a year of downturn, Saar miners had had their wages cut. Union-educated areas would have comprehended that a recession was at hand, and that they had better adjust, but the Saar was not such. Instead they became aroused, and late in the year Bebel was invited to speak. He who had spoken in every German city of 100,000 and many lesser now made his first appearance in one of the nation's chief industrial areas. (So slight was social democratic penetration here that when the strike broke out *Vorwärts* had to pirate reportage from bourgeois papers.) Bebel spoke outdoors to men who attended at peril to their livelihoods. The crowd was enthusiastic, but he took the standard approach of recommending a political solution for their economic woes.[68]

Excitement grew among these isolated and inexperienced miners without organization or funds, but not without a certain bravery. They came from a small field, which could not brake the German economy, it was becoming winter, and they were opposed by both von Stumm and the state. Their chief spokesmen were presently arrested. Disregarding all these obstacles, on the first workday after Christmas, thousands stayed home, and by the day after New Year's, 25,000 were out. This was an astonishing display of militancy, given the quiet history of the Saar.

What these miners wanted in 1892 was primarily more money. From the first they had difficulty raising cash to pay for the walkout. The Mine Workers Association (soc. dem.) issued an appeal,[69] but at this low point for mine unions, there was no association which could help 25,000 men. A further handicap for the work stoppage was that the miners did not really live in an ordinary part of the Second Empire. Men who lingered on the roads for any reason were under suspicion of being pickets.[70] All had to fear for their jobs, and many thought it best to go back before their neighbors did. Rumors of a major crackdown spread rapidly.

MINE UNION GROWTH

RUHR TO 1905

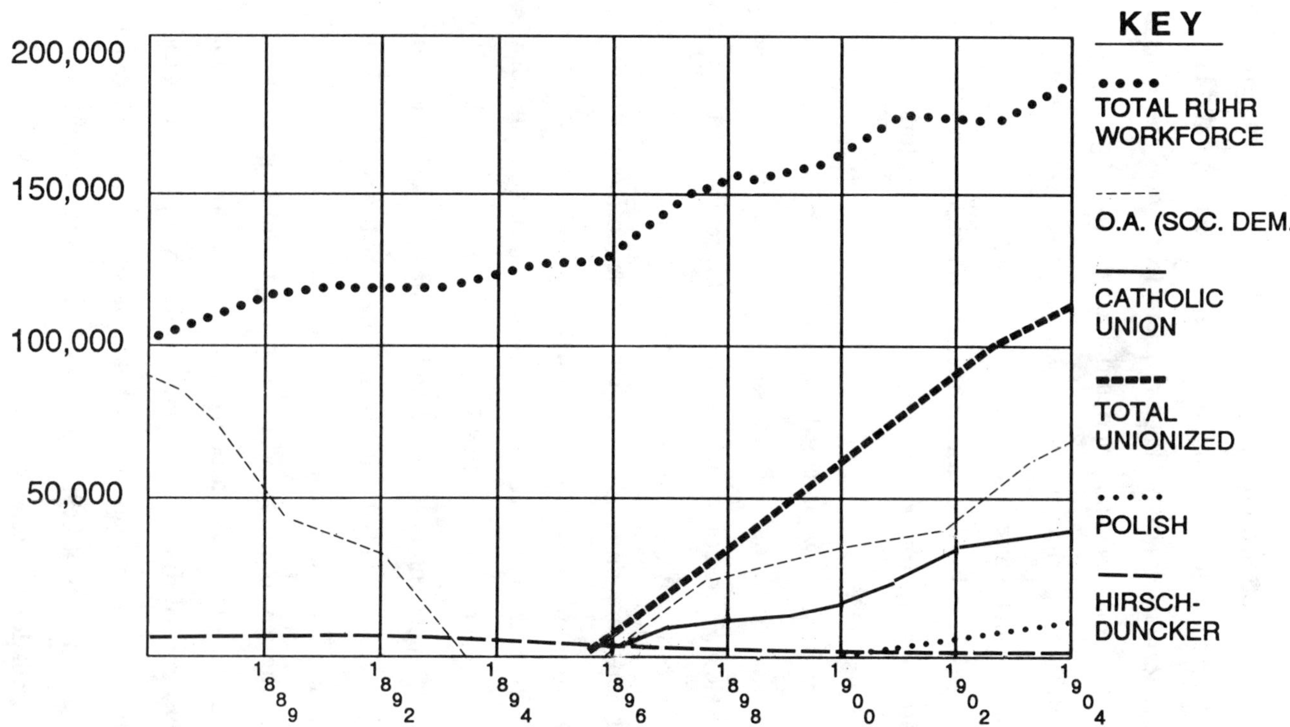

Legien's paper said the usual: the Saar strike had come unexpectedly.[71] This time it was probably true. Meanwhile the Prussian ministry acted as if wishing to end threats of strikes forever. Five hundred men who were identified as the ringleaders were told that they would never again work in the Saar. Another group, 2,457 men, were to be deprived of employment for some weeks.[72] The firings were so large that an exact count was not possible, but 15,000 men, women and children were said to be "breadless." [73] There had been no such mass dismissals since Waldenburg (1869), and in the Saar they were succeeded by judicial proceedings. The valley then lay quiet for a generation.

Those who retained employment began to fare more poorly than before. Saar mining wages had been high, and in 1892 the men received half the value of what they dug. By 1902-1903 their share was under 40 percent, when the comparable figure for the Ruhr was about 55 percent. The Saar miners also had to bear with such abuse and corruption as no longer existed at the other fields. Social democrats and Catholics quarreled with each other over responsibility for the strike,[74] and over lagging organizational attempts in the stricken area, but neither proceeded to remedies.

Towards 1900 the cartel pushed the price of coal upwards, and in 1901 the black diamond averaged nine marks. Since pay did not rise accordingly, the men talked strike, but there was no action. Union officials preached against a walkout, the Herne shootings had an intimidatory effect, and the Prussian government had recently made the conciliatory gesture of an improved sanitary code,[75] as the companies were now required to install showers and locker rooms. Toilets were to be built both above and below, and medical personnel to be hired. When the temperature was 29° Celsius, shifts could last but 6 hours. These reforms, long sought by the men, helped avert a turn of the century walkout.

Austrian miners, with long shifts and lower pay, labored under yet worse conditions. Diggers tended to be Slavs (especially Czechs), and owners German, so national hatred was intense. In 1900 70,000 of them, most in what is now Czechoslovakia, walked off their jobs. They had no union and they had no funds. Relying solely on their endurance, they held out for a quarter of a year until Vienna intervened and gave them a 9 hour day. If this was not the 8 hours they sought, it was still a very great gain. What they had done had an influence in Germany, particularly over the border in Silesia.

At Neurode, in a part of Silesia with a tradition of activism, the miners had gone out in 1904. Neither Germans nor Poles were willing to tolerate any longer the excessive hours and extra shifts, as if 1889 had not happened. They knew their pay and conditions lagged behind most of Germany and even Austria. Their demand was for 2.8 a shift, hardly 60 percent of the going Ruhr rate, though their veins were more productive. Also they wanted shorter shifts and more decent treatment. Sachse of the Old Association came to talk them out of it,[76] but their secret ballot showed 931 for a strike and 75 against.[77] They were opposed by a very determined manager, but one of a singular type, who did not imagine himself an emperor. He simply declared that he had seen a strike before, and that he would wait them out.[78] The families at Neurode had to tighten their belts, for it was 3½ months until the Count who owned the mine was ready to settle. The 1,800 won both higher pay and some concessions on hours. There were some firings, but this was the most successful mining Silesian strike.

It was not the Saar, nor Austria, an alien land, nor the small struggle in

Neurode which moved the men of the Ruhr. It was their own situation which did that. After 1900 the Rhine-Westphalian Coal Syndicate had slowed its rate of pay increases, confident perhaps that the men would not respond. But there began in 1903 that long and damaging climb in basic prices which was to culminate in 1923. Between 1903 and 1914 the cost of staples which working people consumed were to rise by about 30 percent. In the first years of that increase, Hue reckoned, the cost of a kilo of potatoes went up from 51 to 62 marks. Both he and the Catholic historian Imbusch calculated that miners' real pay fell about 70 marks between the high of 1900 and the strike.[79] Other statisticians suggest that there had still been some little improvement in pay in the first years of the century, but this was not the perception of the miners.

If the miners were exercised about pay in 1905, they were less so about hours. The years of desperation had passed, though the issue of what justice required as to hours *unter Tage* had not disappeared. One Max Glotz related that on his first day below the temperature was 31° Celsius.[80] The men would occasionally strip, wring out their trousers, then put them on again. Tenfelde reports that just below the surface the Ruhr is 9° Celsius;[81] for each 25 meters further down, the temperature rises by a degree. Thus 600 meters, which was quite ordinary, 30° was normal. Over the years excessive heat, constant perspiration, as well as the arduousness of the toil wore men down. It was still the case that only young men went below in the Ruhr. The streets were full of those who could no longer bear the toil. The companies remained slow in installing health equipment, and relied on the miners' strength and the trains from the East. In part the miners went along with Herculeanism, picturing themselves as strong, masculine types, and accepting their work fatalistically. To get some of the best wages granted proletarians in Germany, they would overlook early invalidism and death. Though medicine might give the men some improvement in their condition, the larger gain, there being no thought of mechanizing the mines, had to be achieved through shorter hours.

The men had also become aroused over the "worm." This agent of a kind of low-grade cholera, thriving on heat and on filth, had recently been at epidemic levels in the valley. Most miners took tea or another beverage to work, but what they brought could not suffice for a hot shift. When fatigued and overheated, they would grab whatever liquid lay about, and thus catch the "worm." In 1903, the worst year, 10 percent had been afflicted. They had to go through a painful purging and lost several days' pay. They resented the fact that had the companies spent a few more marks on clean water, the disease would have disappeared.

More accepted than the abominable "worm" were accidents, many of which were preventable.[82] Of all the lands around the North Sea, Germany had the highest casualty rate for mining. Between 1893 and 1902, 2.14 of every 1,000 men who went below died there each year. The comparable English rate was 1.32, and even Austria could match it.[83] Judging by the British Isles, each year 300 Ruhr miners perished for want of better precautions. Figures on the permanently crippled in Germany and in other advanced industrial lands presumably say the same thing, but are not available.

More inspectors, surprise visits and heavy penalties would have reduced death and injury rates. Tests for explosion danger and precautions against coal falls, which together led to just over a third of the accidents, would also have had their beneficial effect. The men needed time to work on their own security, there had to be instruction on the question, with disciplinary action against those who did not heed. But Germany needed coal, and the cartel was run by determined men. Orwell remarks:

> There are still living a few very old women who in their youth have worked underground, with a harness around their waists and a chain passed between their legs, crawling on all fours and dragging tubs of coal. They used to go on like this even when they were pregnant. And even now, if coal could not be produced without pregnant women dragging it to and fro, I fancy we should let them do it rather than deprive ourselves of coal.[84]

In Wilhelmine times, the calls for safety from the miners always came near the end of the list. At strike time the demands of the day came before those of the decades, and the coal barons were allowed to be frugal at the cost of miners' lives.

The owners were similarly reluctant to give ground on the single most annoying issue, that of *Nullen*.[85] When the haulers brought the carts to the lift, the load would be chalked to the credit of the individual team. Occasionally one was refused for being insufficiently filled (there was always loss en route), because it contained too much rock, or because the foreman wanted to be tough. When a cart was thus annulled, four men lost several hours' effort. They often labored in a lying position, or on their sides, and were never comfortable. They had to handle great weights in darkness and heat. They were forever bumping into things and there was always danger. All the despair felt at earning their bread in this grim way could be crammed into hatred of *Nullen*, that deprivation of pay for labor cruelly performed. A likely estimate was that only 2 to 3 percent of loads were cancelled out, but there were mines which cut their costs by annulling as many as a tenth. The amount of cash involved in the *Nullen* being small, it could readily have been absorbed into general costs, but the owners preferred to take the punitive road. The men responded with hatred.

Early in the century yet another issue had come to the Ruhr. When Stinnes had ordered the *Bruchstrasse* shift lengthened, his action had one more meaning for the coalies. Near *Bruchstrasse* was a small mine about to be closed, and under cartel rules its quota would be absorbed by the survivor. Making *Bruchstrasse* more productive meant causing unemployment elsewhere. So far 7,000 men had been laid off through the valley as mines closed down. Unions had already had a conference on *Stillegen*, as it was known. Hue had addressed the Reichstag on the question, and his words had been much commented upon.[86] For a decade there had been but minor unemployment, and working people were terrified lest the figure rise. Since the mine owners were known to be wealthy, public sympathy was with the miners on the question of *Stillegen*.

Altogether the case for a strike was not nearly as clear in 1905 as in 1889. Pay was not advancing in an obvious way, yet it was quite high. The true 8 hour day was not on hand, yet it seemed to be coming. The "worm" and the *Nullen* affected but a small minority. Thus when the men started streaming out of the pits, the *Rheinisch-Westfälische Zeitung* exclaimed: "There can't be a strike - there's no issue!"[87] But this was the twentieth century and men became aroused more easily. Stinnes who, along with Kirdorf, were the two magnates who were most disliked, had also done their share.

Stinnes had ended his proclamation with the words: "My will must prevail." Ruhr miners, whether of peasant or proletarian origin, had been taught by life to submit docilely when one of the gods of this world said something of the sort. So it was when their fathers had that role and subsequently when they had to obey the teachers in school.[88] In first jobs or during apprenticeship they had also to conform if they wished to stay on. Next came the army where, if they did often enjoy themselves,[89] they were under the tyranny of non-coms who enforced a discipline as severe as any in the world. In all these 20 odd years a youth from working class was trained to fill a certain place in German society, but not to develop himself, which was beside the point. His army uniform laid aside, he returned to factory or shop, where foreman took the place of drill sergeant. Later in the twenties came marriage, after which recurrent financial woes added to the forces controlling the individual.

Ways to rebel were few. Levenstein's poll found that 6 percent of workers in other trades thought alcohol indispensable for life, but 20 percent of miners did, the highest total being in Silesia.[90] A contemporary analyst of miners' psychology thought that among those who dug coal, the men who lived by booze formed one of the largest sub-groups.[91] Job changing was another option. Half the personnel of a mine often turned over annually. Fleeing the coal region altogether was not often attempted, the leavers just went to another pit. By the end of the century immigration was on the decline, and running away from wife and children was frowned on socially, and infrequently attempted. Of outlandish solutions workingmen suicide was rare,[92] and anarchism never caught on in Germany. If, despite all this education in passivity there was somehow sign of rebellion, social democracy, unions, state and church were on hand to channel it into meetings, elections, and strikes of short duration.

Altogether the German forces to keep workingmen obedient were the most efficacious on the continent. Everywhere the uniform reminded men of the duty to submit. The system was wonderfully reinforced by the economic success of the Second Empire. There was enough to eat, and save for the under-classes, all proletarians had roofs over their heads. Thus life came to be filled with petty cares, such as bills to be paid, whether wives were pregnant again, etc.

A first break with the psychology of submission came in 1872, which was but a partial strike. A more thorough rebellion came in 1889. The final generational uprising was that of 1905. Over the years hope and courage built up, and men could remember how they shook the world the last time, so that even the emperor had to take an interest. Those who had lost their jobs would be forgotten, and a crowd of young militants would be on hand. However even this generational rebellion could only take place under favorable circumstances, and thus not in Silesia or the Saar.

The psychology of Hugo Stinnes in approaching the strike would be one quite opposite. Every situation he met at home, during his education, in society, in business or politics made it natural for him to say "My will must prevail." At bottom proletarians accepted that Hugo Stinnes or Wilhelm II should, as exceptional beings, command them. Neither in union or social democratic literature is the idea of equality given much play. Lacking such a belief, it took a long train of grievances lasting over a generation before workingmen could bring themselves to cast aside the mental habits of their whole lives and release the rebellion which was in them.

Kirdorf had been annoyed[93] when Stinnes postponed his *Bruchstrasse* decree. The new shift-lengthening notice was then actually issued later in December. It began, pedantically enough, "We envision a codicil to the works order," and towards the end of the 200 words came the provoking phrases:

> The time for the cable run is to be changed. As a rule, the trip down will take place one hour before the beginning of the shift and the trip back at the end of the shift.[94]

This was posted on Christmas Eve and the miners of *Bruchstrasse* were invited to state by December 28 whether they intended to look elsewhere for employment. A few days later, the men having ceased to report for work, it was announced that free coal would no longer be made available to employees. Stinnes seemed to indicate, with this additional small sign of ending a traditional institution which was decades, if not century-old, that he was prepared to fight.

Already in December, as word of the *Bruchstrasse* situation circulated, union officials had their trouble keeping men at work at other pits. The year-end issue of the *Bergarbeiterzeitung*, official union journal, urged the men to "Be united!", meaning that no minority should commence striking.[95] *Vorwärts* noted that unions were already being charged with cowardice by the men.[96] Feelings were further exacerbated when the *Rheinisch-Westfälische Zeitung* commented unwisely (Jan. 1) that "as long as the unions have the present leaders, there will be no strike."[97] In January the miners themselves began to take command of events. The next pit to go out was the *Hercules*, whose management had recently dismissed its union leaders.[98] The Mine Workers Association (soc. dem.) suggested that legal action be tried to recover the jobs, but in the atmosphere of 1905 this proposal seemed too weak and ineffectual. *Bergarbeiterzeitung* confirmed that everything possible was being done to reduce tension.[99] Wilhelm Düwell, social democratic reporter from Dortmund, explained how excited the men were. Alarmed party deputies were later to fix on this one not very important individual as being responsible for the walkout to come.[100]

Excitement increased in the first week of January. By its end 4,000 were said to be out.[101] *Bruchstrasse* had voted 360-10 for a strike,[102] the men having also long-standing sanitary grievances. *Germania*, daily voice of Catholic Germany, took a calmer view than the social democrats and believed that the companies wanted a strike to get rid of surplus coal and to hurt the union.[103] Hue, Sachse, their lieutenants, and the chiefs of the Catholic association were out every day, talking to the men to stay on the job. In turn they were accused of *bremsen*, or putting on the brakes. It was an old charge.

After the first weekend (the men tended to make up their minds then), 10,000 were out. The first moment of incredulity having passed, the *Rheinisch-Westfälische Zeitung* began printing bulletins from the strike zone,[104] as if it were a war. In the second week the pattern changed, and the Monday total doubled on Tuesday, as did Tuesday's on Wednesday. More than a sixth of those who toiled *unter Tage* were now out. Yet caution still ruled for many. Miners would watch what the next pit did, and whether the passion of the evening meeting would suffice to keep neighbors at home in the morning. Gradually the union's effort to keep the men at work lost out. As for the constitutional provisions giving veto power to the national office, these had become impotent.

The *Gewerkverein* (Cath.) was not founded to promote the class struggle, and had only slowly and occasionally been brought to approve walkouts. (Such a desire for class conciliation did not prevent Kirdorf from maintaining, perhaps with Austria in mind, that Catholics were often more militant than social democrats.[105]) In this month Catholics often shared platforms with social democrats, trying to stem the tide.[106]

When it was not quite certain that there would be a strike, Hermann Sachse, head of the "Old Association," addressed 25,000 Dortmunders,[107] condemning the walkout which he described as the action of the unorganized.

Carried away by his anxieties on a day when 40,000 were out, he even suggested that paid spies had brought on the conflict. The discussion following his address went on until three in the morning though only a handful supported his point of view. *Vorwärts* was to iterate endlessly that it was the non-union people who brought on all the trouble,[108] and there was probably some truth to this, for many of the active miners felt too independent to join unions.[109]

A recent historian of the Seattle general strike of 1919 notes that as soon as workingman arrived in a leading position, he turned against continuation of the struggle.[110] Although conflicts between those who held forth in the shop and those who lived in the union office were common in Wilhelmine times, they were somewhat more likely in the miners' union than elsewhere. Sachse sat behind a desk, his finger nails clean, and he was without a worry that a sudden fall of coal might orphan his children. He had more job security than Wilhelm Hohenzollern! He could travel to conventions, including some abroad, and he had not the humiliation and crisis of a job loss to be concerned about.

What Sachse and the other officials could recall was the days when they were closed down by the state. That happened in the seventies, the eighties, and for part of the nineties. This was not an unreal fear: German unions were disbanded once again in the 1930s. Union chiefs could likewise remember when total union membership was under 10,000, and many of those doubtful dues payers. But between 1904 and 1906 the Old Association increased its holdings from 735,000 to 1,235,000 marks, a gain of 73 percent, while the Catholic union improved its property position from 271,000 marks to 508,000 (58 percent). Should such fortunate and unprecedented gains in strength be sacrificed to the emotions of a few out in the field? Even the Poles were taking in more money, and apparently adopting more of a Teutonic way of handling their affairs.

As long as they could, the men of the desks made their almost frantic effort to block the walkout. *Vorwärts* denied that it had encouraged the work stoppage by as much as a single word. Legien's *Correspondenzblatt* spoke regularly of the strike as a "catastrophe." One issue quoted a different opinion: "[The strike] is a struggle against the bastion of industrial absolutism, and a victory would be of service to the entire working class."[111] The succeeding issue then reverted to normal: "With justice everyone asks: did this great struggle have to break out? could it not have been avoided?"[112] The *Bergarbeiterzeitung* speculated that the walkout came because the cartel wanted to reduce its surplus, and declared that not a single leader favored it. The Old Association wailed that it was already paying out 12,000 marks in the prolonged battle at Neurode. Only when the union fund appeal was sent out over Sachse's signature was the self-pity finally muted, and a tone of more dignity adopted: "We begged them not to strike, but the anger was too great."[113]

By January 21, 70,000 were out. The decision having been taken by the men, 74 delegates from the Old Association, 67 from the *Gewerkverein*, 7 Poles and 3 Hirsch-Dunckers met in Essen to consider the situation. Any minimal respect for historical accuracy should cause those 151 to be designated the followers, and the 70,000 the leaders. These few gathered in meeting had been overwhelmed by events, and were wary of each other, for their tradition was of mutual hostility. A few months back, in 1903, Hue had taken the Bochum seat from the Center, for that party had been compelled by its peasant supporters to back tariffs on food. Then in 1904 there had been rough election struggles among miners for the post of "elder." (The acute Winnig believed that leftover excitement from that campaign touched off the walkout.[114]) As for the Poles, they may have been slightly more pro-strike, but they had no reason to trust the Germans.

The 151 accepted their only choice and cast aside mutual hostility while joining in disgust at what the men had done. Their 250 word proclamation bespoke distaste for the strike in every phase.[115] They condemned the miners for insubordination in not properly seeking permission to leave the pits. They admonished them to observe "iron discipline" in the future. Regretfully conceding that events could not be reversed, they ordered the men still at work to remain there. They further announced that demands would be made on the owners and that if no suitable reply was received within 5 days, they would issue a strike call! There was mention as well of an appeal to Berlin. A commission of 7, representative of the 4 unions, was to run the strike. Not one syllable touched upon the cartel, *Nullen*, or sanitary conditions, and there was no reference to possible victory, though "an end to the action" was spoken of.

Chairman of the Commission of Seven was the Catholic Effert, perhaps to refute the idea that it was a "red" walkout. This was a choice of some consequence, for Effert was in secret touch with the Berlin government before and during the strike.[116] One more Catholic, two social democrats, two Poles and one Hirsch-Duncker made up the Commission. Once they were constituted, they began slowly to assert the normal domination of the organization over the members. As a first step, the Seven consolidated those demands which the miners had been making in their meetings,[117] above all the true 8 hour day. They suggested it could be eased in over two years. *Nullen* was to be entirely forbidden. A minimum pay scale was to be established, with 5 marks a day for the skilled, descending to 3 a day for horsedrivers. The Seven asked that the men be given a voice on safety questions. After miscellaneous items came the final and hopeless ones: no dismissal for strike activity, and union recognition. The list was not complained of in mass meetings, and there were protests when items were dropped. Apparently the Seven had divined what the men wanted.

The coal barons replied at once in a curt statement possibly copied from their 1889 refusal to bargain.[118] They said that the men had now broken contract, and that the condition of the mines did not require correction. Dissatisfied individuals were advised to talk it over with their bosses. Should the changes the miners desired take place, however, it would "ruin" the industry. *Vorwärts* meanwhile reprinted an optimistic Bourse report that disunity among the miners would cost them the day.[119]

Men continued to leave the pits. By the time the owners' answer was received, 70 percent of those who toiled *unter Tage* were out, and they had been joined by about 30 percent of those who worked above ground.[120] On Wednesday, January 18, the day the strike was officially proclaimed, 190,000 stayed home. On Thursday the total passed 200,000. For three weeks thereafter the number of strikers hung around the 213,000 mark. Of the black faces from below, 85 percent were out, as were about 40 percent of those who worked above ground on coke briquets, or who cleaned and sorted the coal. All the latter operations had been growing in importance, but those who labored at them never attained the *camaraderie* of the men *unter Tage*.

Fund collection proceeded moderately well. Over 1,864,000 marks were donated. About half came from non-mining unions and city-wide strike committees, and another quarter was assembled through the massive social democratic newspaper network. Thus in the year of revolution (1905), party and union officials overcame their historic fears of making mass appeals which might encourage indiscipline and more walkouts. Men from the more poorly paid trades poured out marks for those of greater income. Several construction unions, veterans of strikes, were particularly generous. As for the Old Association, its treasury had been protected, and actually its reserves were to grow this year. The Catholics had no tradition of supporting the strikes of others, and lacked the will to do so. The Poles were simply short of cash. About 158,000 marks arrived from abroad. The amount of 60,000 is said to have been donated from outside the working class, though it is hard to see how this could be exactly known. One or two of these contributors deserves a note. Archbishop (later Cardinal) Kopp[121] of Cologne, himself a scion of the working class, early and publicly contributed 1000.[122] The city councils of Frankfurt and Stuttgart sent cash, as did the scapegrace son of notoriously tightfisted magnate August Thyssen.

What was collected came to half a week's pay and, beginning on the 27th, was distributed to all claimants.[123] The men could also rely on their regular pay for the first half of the month, which was handed out later. It is probable that the money contributed helped more with morale than as cash. "The almost unanimous sympathy of the bourgeoisie for the strikers was an exceedingly important factor, which raised their moral power of resistance," wrote Hue.[124] There was, of course, no such unanimity, but when it was possible to cite an Archbishop, city councils and the son of a magnate, such donations were worth many times their money value. For the humble who seek a better life, the sympathy of the lords of the world is apparently of the greatest importance. For those who conduct a class struggle, a mark would be a mark.

The valley was quiet during the big walkout. Owners called for troops to protect that exiguous minority still going below, but Chancellor von Bülow was not fond of confrontations and did not supply them. The emperor's inclination and ability to influence events had by now waned. Had soldiers been sent, and behaved as those of 1889, 40 lives would have been sacrificed. On the other hand, if the men had gone below in normal fashion about 24 lives would have been lost. It was a bloodless January in the Ruhr, and the men had a rest. After a two month walkout elsewhere a striker wrote: "Our pale cheeks had become colored by the time it was over, and we had been enormously strengthened."[125]

One report had it that wives sympathized with the strike.[126] The matter is of the greatest consequence, for unhappy mates could force the men back earlier. However, there is a paucity of information. Clearly the women of the Ruhr knew that work *unter Tage* ground their men down and led to premature aging, and they were surely aware that the price of staples was climbing. Yet many of them were new to the Ruhr and imbued with the inherited belief that a good provider should toil every day for the family. Like as not the women of the Ruhr were split in 1905.

The march of Russian peasants on the Winter Palace and the resultant slaughter which opened the Revolution of 1905 took place in the strike's second week. Social democracy met to discuss this event in the major cities and, with overtones of anti-Slavism, *Vorwärts* wrote of the Russian state as the enemy of the "civilized world" (Kulturwelt).[127] Ruhr miners were not usually exercised over international questions, nor do they seem to have been so this time. Winnig remarked that they looked upon the party as nit-pickers from Berlin and Saxony.[128]

As in 1889 there was a question of what the Prussian government would do. This time, however, there was no Bismarck, and the emperor had withdrawn in part from political life. However, as early as January 14th the Reichstag had put the strike under discussion. Worker-historian Otto Hue was the natural spokesman for the miners, and he took the encyclopedic approach in making his interpellation. He praised the regime for not intervening for the coal barons and he blamed them,[129] in particular Stinnes, for acting illegally in not consulting with their men before changing the contract. While maintaining that the union had always done its utmost to keep the men at work, he spoke at all points in defense of the walkout, recalling once again the famous 8 hour promise Hammacher made in 1889. In regard to *Nullen* he cited the rawest cases, such as that of a man who had a load cancelled when he was at home. In general, he said, in industrial society the average age of miners had fallen by 6 years, and overwork was forcing them into early retirement, so that half the men going down into the pits were under 30. Only 5 percent managed to survive the pace and the danger until they were 50. A self-educated individual with the ordinary literary pretensions of the day, he challenged the nation to honor the Schiller anniversary by giving miners their freedom.

The Reichstag kept at the question for several days, but there were no outbursts against the miners, as in 1889, and much understanding of their situation. The debate was characterized by more maturity than in the past when a strike was the topic. There was a hint of the cartel's isolation in German society.

Von Bülow's reply to Hue was in consonance with this tone of the Reichstag. It was appropriate as well in view of the peace and prosperity

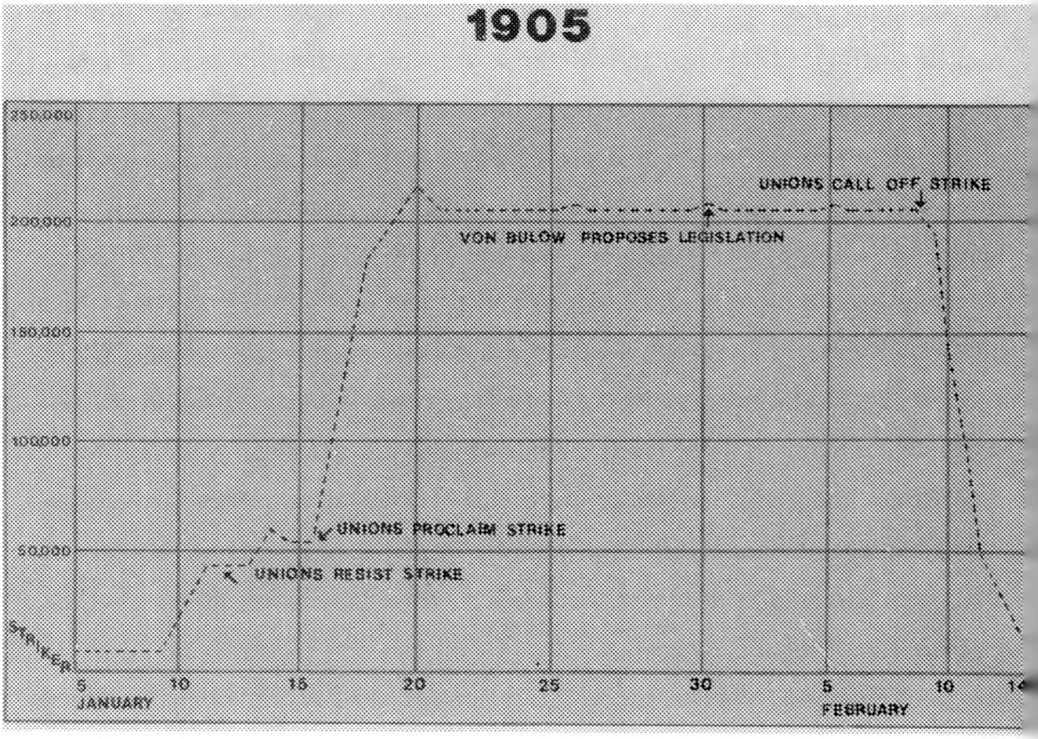

1905
250,000
200,000
150,000
100,000
50,000
STRIKER
UNIONS CALL OFF STRIKE
VON BULOW PROPOSES LEGISLATION
UNIONS PROCLAIM STRIKE
UNIONS RESIST STRIKE
5
10
15
20
25
30
5
10
JANUARY
FEBRUARY

which Wilhelmine Germany had been enjoying, as well as for the momentary subsidence of hotheads on the Right. The duty of the state, he maintained, was to see to law and order and to attempt conciliation.[130] Thus he had not sent troops, but an investigatory team, for which there was ample Prussian precedent. The state representatives were appreciated by the men, but regarded as an interference by the owners. The Chancellor further declared that some of the issues the miners raised required legislative action. These were: overtime, fines, worker advisory committees, *Nullen*, and hours of work in overheated conditions. These questions, he said, would be handled in the Prussian parliament. It was Prussia which, in the past, had established the mining rules for the country. Taking up the matter in its legislature had the advantage of excluding social democrats from the discussion, while strengthening the Right. In the Prussian lower house Catholics could, of course, speak for the miners. Von Bülow's artful ploy was a grim blow to the social democrats.

Miners had petitioned the state in 1868, 1869, 1889 and now 1905. They finally had something of an answer, and it was mildly favorable. Three days after von Bülow made his promises, the chairman of an Essen meeting suggested making an end to the strike conditional on recognition of the Seven.[131] He was howled down, for that would have left the 200,000 with nothing. The men did not trust their leaders and could not believe that Stinnes would sit down with Sachse and Brust. However, effective control over events had by now passed into the hands of the union officials.

The Seven now called together second line leaders, whose opinions were presumably more reliable than those of mass meetings. Many of them were union employees whose future lay with their chiefs. Others represented the miners directly. They debated long, and then announced they were reducing the original demands to five, while relying upon the Prussian parliament for the rest.[132] What they retained was the pay demand, no firings, humane handling and guaranteed coal for homes. They took this step backward although there was not yet a sizeable movement back to work, and although troops had not appeared.

Not much was achieved with this concession, for it was taken as a sign of weakness.[133] A recent historian remarks that unions lacked the power to trim the arrogance of the *Herr im Hause* (master of the house) industrial lords.[134] Actually no one in Germany knew how to do that. If the men had the potential power, their leaders lacked the will. Meanwhile behind the scenes von Bülow was exerting pressure to end the strike.

For their part the 200,000 stuck to their somewhat shrunken cause. They had their December pay, and the real money crunch lay ahead. They were more united than in 1889 and if there was a minority which preferred to go back, this time they went along with the majority. The companies did fear public reaction if they evicted in mid-winter, so that menace passed. Donations continued. In one Ruhr town police declined to help those who wanted to enter the pits.

When the second line leaders met on February 9, many of them were social democrats who believed that the miners' cause had already achieved a befitting public recognition and a governmental promise, which was as much as could be expected. In their minds there lived on the idea of the non-dangerous petition. Meanwhile their internal clocks kept ticking on towards 3 weeks, the time limit for a proper petition-strike. As for the Catholics, their historian declared: "the *Gewerkverein* had always had the honorable desire to live in peace with the *Arbeitgeber* (providers of work), as its whole activity shows."[135] Cartel members would by now have spoken to Catholic businessmen, their inferiors in the German economy, to press the need for the union to go back. Effert, Chairman of the Seven, would have heard the same from von Bülow, whose creature he was in part. Polish leaders would understand that if the police were to fall upon anyone, it would likely be they.[136]

Thus the February 9 gathering consisted of a heavy majority of experienced union hands who never wanted the strike, and a minority who would have to report back to militant locals. Sachse made it sound very grim:

> Leaders are convinced *that either we break it off* next week, or there will be troops. Had we not paid out sufficient money, *the result* would have been soldiers *and shooting,* and our movement would have been miserably destroyed.[137]

Thousands of strikes had taken place in the period described in this volume, and there was nothing in their history to justify Sachse's argument that a cut in payments would bring riots, and that troops would then crush a strike. Beyond this attempted intimidation by dishonest means, the Seven had other tactics to ensure a favorable decision: they gave themselves unlimited speaking time, while confining those of the floor to 5 minutes apiece. The debate was to be reported only in the union paper, where it could be censored. Some of the miner delegates remarked that the walkout was even stronger than before. Anent gains already received a Dortmunder growled that "we don't even have a sparrow in our hands."[138] Earlier Catholic *Germania* had written that in Bochum they were fond of saying of von Bülow's remarks that "a promise is not a bargain."[139] But these were stray comments, and the Seven had assembled their people carefully. The vote to return was a convincing 164-5, with Hue allegedly one of the minority.[140]

The Seven had prepared for this favorable count. Already they had printed 250,000 leaflets explaining why the great rebellion of 1905 had had to be called off. Their argument was quite of the cut of similar documents.[141] As at Hamburg, Crimmitschau and also at the Ruhr itself in 1889, reference was made to the evil effects of the stoppage on the national economy. It was said, and no doubt truly, that the coal barons would not soon give way. The Seven pointed to promised Prussian intervention, and noted that public opinion backed the strikers, and these were crucial points for those who were really petitioning their betters, not going on strike. It would be impossible, the leaflet said, to ask for further sacrifices though here, as before, no one had had to sacrifice very much.

The unions had no constitutional provisions for ending a strike, or determining what the majority felt. But it was soon clear that many miners, despite the fact that they were losing money, and feared the blacklist, had invested the courage of a generation and felt they had little to show for it. They wanted the true 8 hour day, raises and the honor of a victory. "The great mass," wrote Catholic historian and strike leader Imbusch, "which had had the spirit to hold out until now, could not grasp that suddenly while the struggle was at its high point, everything was brought to a conclusion without victory."[142] In Essen the 250,000 brochures printed in advance were seized by irate miners and thrown on the street, where they blocked traffic for several hours.[143] Sachse had to have police protection when he left the key meeting. Like Legien in Crimmitschau, when breaking off a strike he was on state business, and so this former jailbird was accompanied by men in *Pickelhaube*. Two assemblies held in predominantly "Black" Essen voted overwhelmingly to continue the walkout: *Vorwärts* called the city a "center of indiscipline."[144]

The word "traitor" was much in use after February 9, and not only in Essen. Sachse had later to explain that he had not halted the work stoppage to please the Catholic *Gewerkverein*.[145]

Vorwärts praised the "disciplined calling off of the strike...[as] a very promising tactic," though actually it had been done many times before. The distinguishing feature here was that strikebreakers could not be blamed. The bellweather paper, relieved that the crisis was past, repeated a few days later: "We agree with most of the bourgeois press that the leadership of the strike is a page of honor in the history of the...movement."[146] The paper was here in curious company, but reverted to more ordinary social democratic *patois* in saying that the walkout was a "moral victory."[147] Catholic papers were similarly elated that it was all over, but expressed their feelings more suavely.

The men gradually adapted themselves to the decision to abandon the conflict when there was no compelling reason to do so. Their surrender grew out of a certain mentality. Blue collar memoirist Adam Scharrer began his work:

> I have nothing special to say about myself. I went the way of the proletarian child who as the first of about a dozen and a half children of parents who had a tiny piece of land. I became superfluous, and 'went among the people,' as did many thousands....[148]

Scharrer caught here some of the individual proletarians' sense of being anonymous and of being subject to constant defeat. The Ruhr miners, half of them from the East, were surely among those most accustomed to losing. If they not only lost the battle, but their faith in Sachse, Hue, Brust, Effert, and the others, there was little to be done about that either. Stinnes could fire a man, but they could not fire their leaders, protected as the latter were by all too complicated election procedures. They had no alternative and so they disposed themselves. Furthermore, while they had hesitated to go out, they rushed back. No one wanted to be classified as a "ringleader." The morning after the Essen mob dumped the leaflets on the street, 10 percent of them were back. These gave the signal that it was all over, and the others began to recall the penalties they might face, such as fines, lowered crew rates, *Nullen*, etc. Saturday an astonishing 60 percent had returned, and Monday the total was 86 percent. Many were rudely received, and hundreds were told to come back later, and thus they were given the taste of defeat. As in 1889, they felt resentment. Hue and others talked of holding out, [149] but nothing was done.

Wilhelm Reich believed that social democracy was based on the conservative instincts of ordinary workers, who acted in contradictory ways:

> The average worker is a contradiction in himself. [He] is neither a clearcut revolutionary, nor a clearcut conservative, but stands divided. His psychic structure...derives from the entire atmosphere of authoritarian society.[150]

It is not necessary to rely upon interpretation from a quarter which historians may consider suspect - though Reich was himself for a time a minor leader of the working class movement. In 1868, while meeting in a city which exceeded all others in loyalty to unions and to strikes, Lassalleans actually voted against both. The Eisenachers wooed the Waldenburg strikers, then reverted to putting near impossible conditions on strike support. Such examples may be multiplied. Manifestly German proletarians were of two minds - better said, of two emotions - about walking off the job, though ordinarily their leaders were resolutely against such action. The anonymous rank and file might rouse itself finally to settle scores with the boss. However the rupture of normal habits, the psychological burden of disobedience and the fear of losing employment would be too much for them. Time and time again they could be manipulated into going back.

Hardly two weeks after the greatest work stoppage in national history ended, Hue spoke in Bochum, saying that the leaders had only done what needed to be done. Everyone agreed and the resolution passed unanimously. Not only was the resentment gone, but new members were signing up. Alone in 1905 22,000 joined the Mine Workers Association - which had after all distributed 23 marks per member during the strike[151] and proportionate numbers signed up with the Catholics.

That summer the Old Association held its convention in Berlin. There are no mines near the Prussian capital, but the city has charm and is distant from unruly rank and file. Here Hue described breaking off the strike as a "masterful" action; this time he gave the reason as lack of funds.[152] (Winnig, never at heart a party man, once asked what the union had actually done for the miners.)[153] The convention of delegates, hand-picked as usual, backed the decision to end the strike.

The miners went back undefeated, and took only minor losses, having kept their houses, and their jobs, and not been subject to arrest. Von Bülow delivered their lesser gains, as the *Nullen* was at last outlawed, the day cut for those laboring in excess temperatures and a voice on conditions given to the men. They could not yet close a dangerous shaft, but they had made a start. The larger boons came from the cartel. Pay went up smartly after a few months, and averaged 5 marks a shift for hackers by 1907. Annual wages rose by several hundred marks, and the Ruhr clearly led the German proletariat in pay. Such a large gain, made at the cost of 3 weeks' wages, was an investment of which any of the great magnates might have been proud. Meanwhile hours kept being shaved towards the true 8. In every respect the miners had done exceedingly well. An astute recent observer of the German working class notes that the miners' victory was *staatserhaltend*,[154] i.e., tending toward the preservation of the state. For if some miners had revolutionary impulses, the way their victory was doled out like charity, and the satisfactory size of that triumph, probably served to check such impulses.

However from 1905, as not from 1889, the men had learned something of their own power. City councils, archbishops, professors, Chancellors, magnates had jumped to support them. They began to perceive that no one could send them *unter Tage* against their will. They had not, however, tamed the most powerful economic association in the world, which could still make the pretense of granting wage increases out of benevolence rather than because of the miners' *force majeure* and still refuse to treat with their representatives. The Commission of Seven in particular had helped bring it about that the great magnates would not have to bow down to mere workingmen. Thus, for instance, when the men came back to *Bruchstrasse*, short of money and fearful of the blacklist, Stinnes had an announcement for them. They were to be fined their first 3 shifts' pay for breach of contract. His will was still prevailing.

NOTES

1. Tenfelde, *Sozialgeschichte*, 205.

2. Hue, *Bergarbeiter*, 2, 107ff.

3. *Vorwärts*, December 31, 1911.

4. This letter of January 17, 1893, is reprinted in Bölcke, ed., *Krupp und die Hohenzollern*, 72-77.

5. See Fritz Fischer, *Germany's Aims in the First World War*, tr. unknown (New York: 1967), 259.

6. Ibid., 257-59.

7. Charles Medalen, "State Monopoly Capitalism in Germany: the Hibernia Affair," *Past and Present*, 1978, No. 78, 83-112.

8. Gerd von Klass, *Hugo von Stinnes* (Tubingen: 1958), 24ff.

9. The Stinnes family collided with what now seems an archaic form of the class struggle in the revolution of 1848. Earlier they had dispensed with the peasants who pulled their boats with teams when the Rhine was difficult and replaced them with steam power. The peasants responded in 1848 with a cannon turned on the hated modern boats, only to have the Stinnes family respond in a characteristic way, by securing the support of Prussian soldiers.

10. Ibid., 10.

11. *Bergarbeiterzeitung*, January 7, 1905.

12. Such situations are mentioned in all the sources. In particular consult Lorenz Pieper, *Die Lage der Bergarbeiter im Ruhrrevier*, Berlin and Stuttgart, 1913.

13. Orwell, *Wigam Pier*, 25.

14. Kuczynski, *GdL*, 3, 326.

15. Desai, *Wages*, 111.

16. Oldenburg, *Schmollers Jahrbuch*, 14, 625.

17. Tenfelde, *Sozialgeschichte*, 323ff.

18. Otto Hue, *Neutrale oder parteiische Gewerkschaften* (Bochum: 1900), 99, speaks of the miners' independence, which made it difficult to build permanent unions.

19. Hue, *Bergarbeiter*, 2, 410ff.

20. Ibid., 2, 414-15.

21. The constitution of the Mine Workers Association has been reprinted as Supplement 6 in ibid., 754-56.

22. Ibid., 415, 16.

23. Tenfelde, *Sozialgeschichte*, 52.

24. Marchwitza relates how the organizers had to go running after him for dues at a later period when men were more disciplined. *Meine Jugend*, 242ff.

25. In his history Hue repeatedly complained that Brust was too contentious a man to come to agreement with. This was then confirmed by Heinrich Imbusch in his autobiographical statement in *25 Jahre Christliche Gewerkschaften*, 125-132.

26. *Vorwärts*, January 31, February 1 and 2, 1911.

27. Imbusch' *Arbeitsverhältnis* is a long and detailed work, but the author slid over this famous incident.

28. *Glückauf*, July 6, 1895.

29. *Vorwärts*, August 15, 1895.

30. *Rheinisch-Westfälische Zeitung*, August 19, 1895.

31. *Vorwärts*, August 20, 1895.

32. *Corrblatt*, March 31, 1895.

33. Hue, *Bergarbeiter*, 2, 345. *Glückauf*, the Mine Workers Association paper, said, August 24, 1895, that the Saxon union had not been so menaced under the Exceptional Law as it was in 1895, and this seems to have been true.

34. Hue, *Bergarbeiter*, 2, 448, fn. 73.

35. Ibid., 736.

36. Johann Fritsch, *Eindringen und Ausbreitung des Revionsimus im deutschen Bergarbeiter-verband (bis 1914)* (Leipzig: 1967), 68.

37. Ibid., 74-75.

38. That the Old Association was paying support to Neurode was mentioned in its *Hilferuf an die Zentralvorstände der Gewerkschaften Deutschlands*, issued in January, 1905.

39. Quoted in an undated "3 x 4" brochure attacking the Catholic union and entitled "Bergarbeiter Aufgewacht!"

40. Karl Schirmer, *50 Jahre Arbeiter* (Duisberg, 1926), 33-34, gives examples.

41. Quoted in Nettl, *Luxemburg*, 1, 133.

42. Patt, Johannes, *Ein Bergarbeiter Schicksal*, 120, complained that Polish workers submitted too easily to the foreman.

43. See David Blackburn's "The Problem of Democratization: German Catholics and the Role of the Center Party." in Evans, ed., *Society and Politics*, 160-183.

44. Paul Hirsch and Bruno Borchardt, *Die Sozialdemokratie und die Wahlen zum Deutschen Reichstage* (Berlin: 1907), map the election districts conveniently by color of winning party.

45. There is a description of this phenomenon in Ian Farr's "Populism in the Countryside: the Peasant Leagues in Bavaria in the 1890s" in Evans, ed., *Society and Politics*, 136-159.

46. *Bergknappe*, February 15, 1899.

47. *Bergarbeiterzeitung*, December 10, 1904.

48. *Bergknappe*, February 3, 1900.

49. Imbusch, *Arbeitsverhältnis*, chs., 2 and 3 cover this period.

50. Murzynowska, *Polskie Wychodzstwo*, 143ff.

51. Christoph Klessmann, *Polnische Bergarbeiter im Ruhrgebiet, 1870-1945*, (Göttingen: 1978), 272.

52. Also Hans-Ulrich Wehler, "Polen im Ruhrgebeit," in his *Krisenherde des Kaiserreichs, 1871-1918* (Göttingen: 1970), 219-238.

53. Stephen Hickey, "The Shaping of the German Labor Movement: Miners in the Ruhr," in Evans ed., *Society and Politics*, 217.

54. Klessmann, *Polnische Bergarbeiter*, 111.

55. *Vorwärts*, June 28, 1899.

56. Klaus Tenfelde, "Die 'Krawalle von Herne' im Jahre 1899," *Internationale Wissenschaftliches Korrespondenz*, 15 (1979), 82.

57. Hue, *Bergarbeiter*, 2, 258.

58. *Vorwärts*, July 14, 1899.

59. Tenfelde, *IWK*, 15, 88.

60. Klessmann, *Polnische Arbeiter*, 110.

61. Hue, *Bergarbeiter*, 2, 288ff.

62. Levenstein, *Die Arbeiterfrage*, 334.

63. Hue, *Bergarbeiter*, 2, 430ff.

64. Ibid., 376.

65. Parvus [Alexander Israel Helphand], *Die Gewerkschaften und die Sozialdemokratie* (Dresden: 1896), 46.

66. Karl Alfred Gabel, *Kämpfe und Werden der Hüttenarbeiter-Organizationen an der Saar* (Saarbrücken [1921]), 239.

67. Pieper, *Die Lage der Bergarbeiter*, 239.

68. *Vorwärts*, September 27, 1892.

69. *Glückauf*, January 7, 1893.

70. *Vorwärts*, January 3, 1893.

71. *Corrblatt*, January 1, 1893.

72. *Chronik*, 165; Hue, *Bergarbeiter*, 2, 439.

73. Imbusch, *Arbeitsverhältnis*. 104-05.

74. Trade union accusations that the party undercut the Ruhr strike were repeated by Von Elm in *Vorwärts*, December 8, 1893; Auer replied to such charges in the Hamburger *Echo*, and his remarks were then reprinted by *Vorwärts*, November 21, 1893.

75. Hue, *Bergarbeiter*, 2, 553-54.

76. *Bergarbeiterzeitung*, December 17, 1904.

77. Ibid., December 10, 1904.

78. Ibid., December 17, 1904.

79. Imbusch, *Arbeitsverhältnis*, 567; Hue, *Bergarbeiter*, 2, 582.

80. Levenstein, *Aus der Tiefe*, 57.

81. Tenfelde, *Sozialgeschichte*, 220.

82. Kuczynski, *GdL*, 3, 373.

83. Hue, *Bergarbeiter*, 2, 652.

84. Orwell, *Wigam Pier*, 30.

85. There is a discussion of *Nullen* in Pieper, *Die Lage*, 91ff.

86. *RV*, XI Leg. Per., I Sess., Speech of Otto Hue of April 21, 1904, III, 72.

87. *Rheinisch-Westfälische Zeitung*, January 11, 1905.

88. Lloyd DeMause cites from Preserved Smith the case of a school-teacher who reckoned that he had assisted his pupils' education by "911,527 strokes with a stick, 124,000 lashes with a whip, 136,715 slaps with the hands, and 1,115,800 boxes on the ear." DeMause, ed., *The History of Childhood* (New York: 1974), 41. The same sort of experience is readily documentable from workers' autobiographies, where the references to 'beating-teachers' are frequent.

89. Göhre, *Drei Monate*, 120-21.

90. Levenstein, *Die Arbeiterfrage*, 247.

91. Mücke, *SM*, 1910, 1381-82.

92. The family of Franz Louis Fischer, author of *Arbeiterschicksale*, a memoir, was suicide prone, but they were an exception.

93. Von Klass, *Stinnes*, 136.

94. Reprinted in Imbusch, *Arbeitsverhältnis*, 571.

95. *Bergarbeiterzeitung*, December 31, 1904.

96. *Vorwärts*, January 10, 1905.

97. Quoted in *Corrblatt*, January 1, 1905.

98. *Vorwärts*, January 3, 1905.

99. *Bergarbeiterzeitung*, January 14, 1905.

100. Matthias and Pickett, *Die Reichtagsfraktion*, 136. For the emotions of party leaders, as exhibited in private, there is the summary protocol of union executives conference, held February 19-23, and printed as *Allgemeine Deutsche Gewerkschaftsbund*, "Partei und Gewerkschaft," a supplement to *Vorwärts*, August 11, 1906. Henceforth Supplement, *Vorwärts*, August 11, 1906.

101. According to the table in Fricke, *Die Ruhrbergarbeiterstreik*, 163. He has used the figures in the employers' house organ, *Glückauf*, which are said by Imbusch in *Arbeiterhältnis* always to understate.

102. *Rheinisch-Westfälische Zeitung*, January 7, 1905.

103. *Germania*, January 4, 1905.

104. *Rheinisch-Westfälische Zeitung*, January 9, 1905.

105. Heinz Josef Varain, *Freie Gewerkschaften, Sozialdemokratie und Staat: die Politik der Generalkommission unter der Führung Carl Legion (1890-1920)* (Düsseldorf: 1956), 42.

106. Imbusch, *Arbeitsverhältnis*, 576; for an example see *Bergarbeiterzeitung*, January 14, 1905.

107. *Vorwärts*, January 11, 1905.

108. Hue's speech to the Mine Workers Association, summarized in *Corrblatt*, 1905, No. 23, contains this line of approach.

109. Göhre, *Drei Monate*, 102, noticed this phenomenon.

110. Jeremy Brecher, *Strike* (San Francisco: 1972), 112-13.

111. *Corrblatt*, January 22, 1905.

112. Ibid., January 29, 1905.

113. From the *Hilferuf an die Zentralvorstände der Gewerkschaften Deutschlands*, which was intended for mass distribution.

114. Winnig, *Der weite Weg*, 171.

115. Reprinted in Fricke, *Ruhrbergarbeiterstreik*, 164.

116. Ibid., 68.

117. The demands are reprinted in *Dokumente und Materialen*, 4, 131-33.

118. Reprinted in Schmidt, *Der Weg war lang*, 42.

119. *Vorwärts*, January 17, 1905.

120. Detailed figures, taken from the owners' *Glückauf*, and breaking the Ruhr into constituent areas, may be found in Koch, *Die Bergarbeiterbewegung*, 143-45.

121. See the full and sympathetic obituary in *Vorwärts*, March 9, 1914.

122. *Germania*, January 21, 1905.

123. *Bergarbeiterzeitung*, February 4, 1905.

124. Quoted in Ribhegge, *Winnig*, 51.

125. Hue, *Bergarbeiter*, 2, 621.

126. Fricke, *Der Bergarbeiterstreik*, 104-06.

127. It was normal for *Vorwärts* to exclude Russia from the pantheon of the civilized world. There is an example in the issue of January 22, 1905. Five days afterwards, seeking shock effect, *Vorwärts* printed the letter of a soldier who was defending massacres of the Namibian people, then fighting against German troops. No conclusion as to level of civilization was drawn.

128. Winnig, *Der weite Weg*, 154.

129. *RV*, XI Leg. Per., I Sess., vol. 5, 3903-17.

130. Ibid., 3919-21.

131. *Vorwärts*, January 31, 1905.

132. Ibid., February 7, 1905.

133. Ibid., February 8, 1905.

134. Kaelble, *Industrielle Interessenpolitik*, 79.

135. Imbusch, *Arbeitsverhältnis*, 593.

136. Murzynowska, K., *Polskie Wychodzstwo*, 160ff.

137. Imbusch, *Arbeitsverhältnis*, 593.

138. *Bergarbeiterzeitung*, February 13, 1905.

139. *Germania*, February 2, 1905.

140. Fricke, *Ruhrbergarbeiterstreik*, 139-141.

141. The declaration of the Seven may be found in *Dokumente und Materialen*, 4, 137-38.

142. Imbusch, *Arbeitsverhältnis*, 158.

143. Idem.

144. *Vorwärts*, February 12, 1905.

145. *Vorwärts*, February 16, 1905.

146. Ibid., February 10, 1905.

147. Ibid., February 11, 1905.

148. Adam Scharrer, "Auch eine Jugend," in *Das Vier Männer Buch* (Berlin: 1929), 191.

149. Imbusch, *Arbeitsverhältnis*, 591.

150. Wilhelm Reich, *The Mass Psychology of Fascism*, tr. Vincent R. Carfagno, 3rd ed., (New York: 1970), 217.

151. *Vorwärts*, March 1, 1905.

152. Otto Hue, *Unsere Taktik beim Generalstreik* (Berlin-Bochum, n.d. [1905]), 24-25.

153. Winnig, *Der weite Weg*, 171-72.

154. Ribhegge, *Winnig*, 52.

7

BEFORE THE CATASTROPHE

At Lassalle's death (1864) there had been 4,000 in the social democratic movement. This figure rose to 493,000 voters in 1877 and to 1,427,000 when the Exceptional Law went out of effect (1890). The party received just over 3,000,000 ballots in 1903, 4,250,000 in 1912. A change in the associations law made huge membership possible, and a million had presently joined the party. These figures were the glory of Bebel's organization. The opposite side of the coin was that in five decades of party history there had not been one idea first promoted by social democracy, then brought to public attention and finally converted into law. Social democrats were not genuine participants in German political life, they were merely suppliants standing outside the door.

The inability of social democracy to achieve political gains opened a place for the trade unions. They were aided by the continuing prosperity; the needs of German business for capital were no longer so great, and wages did not need to be held down. The turn of the century legitimization of the unions had helped their membership grow, and it was not lost on proletarians that von Bülow had not sent troops to the Ruhr in 1905. Given also the slight relaxation of police pressure, and that Bebel's doctrine of the future society was growing as antiquated as the man himself, all factors conspired to bring it about that "Gomperism," the doctrine of more wages and shorter hours, should finally have its day. It was a first introduction of American ideas to the continent which normally scorned them. Social democratic or "free" unions passed a million in 1904, and the surge had come to 1,800,000 by the time of the 1904 downturn. Some hundreds of thousands joined other groups, especially the Catholics, who were concentrated in a few trades and areas. When the economy picked up again, the rolls commenced growing, so that by 1912 the "free" unions had 2,500,000 in their ranks, while the others added 500,000 more.[1] Such a stampede to sign union rolls was only equalled in the Western world by the early days of the CIO. By 1914 a quarter of all organized proletarians of all lands were German.[2]

In 1912 social democracy, while nearing its permanent ceiling, gained almost 40 percent of the Reichstag votes. The party then sought the meaningless second presidency of that body, the sort of post which should long have been theirs. All other parties combined to deny the pariahs this small success. But in 1912 every German workingman knew that the black-faced diggers of the Ruhr were getting 5 marks a day, and that union strikes had aided them. Auer had said that Germans would not chase mere wages and hours, and Bebel had expected "revolution," but many activist workers would have found them in error by 1912.

The unions which were growing massively in the last prewar decade came from areas of historic party strength: Prussia west of Berlin, Saxony, and Hamburg.[3] Catholic and Polish unions tended likewise to be Prussian-based. Bavaria, the Empire's second largest state, which had never had a major strike, was under-represented with about 9 percent of the "free" unions. The East provided very few members. Seven unions comprised about 70 percent of the

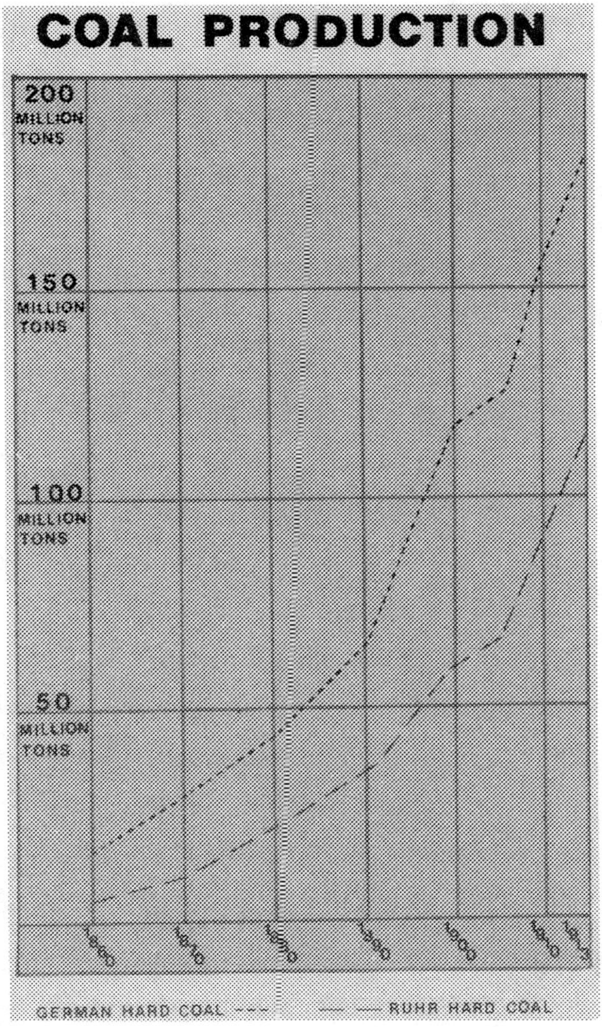
COAL PRODUCTION
200 MILLION TONS
150 MILLION TONS
100 MILLION TONS
50 MILLION TONS
1860
1870
1880
1890
1900
1910
1913
GERMAN HARD COAL ---
— — RUHR HARD COAL

"free" in the prewar years:

Miners	118,000
Textile Workers	140,000
Wood Workers	193,000
Factory Workers	205,000
Transport	216,000
Building Trades	336,000
Metal Workers	536,000 [4]

Although they retained the name of the founding organization, most of these were conglomerates. Metal workers had absorbed the machinists, plumbers and the ancient smithing trades, putting them together with both small and middling machine plants and making themselves large and rich. In 1912 they took in 57 marks a member, which came to 18,000,000.[5] The next largest group, the building trades, had sponged up most of the original social democratic faithfuls. Wood workers had similarly absorbed everything connected with their own trade and much besides.[6] Despite the impressive totals, the percentage of organized often remained low, as for instance among the miners, where Saar and Silesia remained outside the ranks.

In the better situations, when an individual joined a union, a man had someone who would negotiate for him. Especially in construction, authoritarian attitudes were less pronounced, and contracts common.[7] In 1896 the book printers, then still leaders among the skilled workers, signed a first written agreement with their principals. Doctrinaire social democrats were alarmed at this compromise with capitalism, but could not thwart it.[8] After the turn of the century contracts became ordinary, so that by 1914 two million men and women had gained this security of employment. National union offices maintained that their members had the advantage of achieving 1.75 marks a week when contracts were negotiated without a strike.[9] Union locals averaged

385 members, rather large for individual self-expression, if useful for economic struggles. Locals from various trades would form cartels in metropolitan areas. This type of organization was autonomous within the unions and had been specially generous at the time of the 1905 strike.

Catholic unions also gained after 1905, though not in the dimensions of "free" unions. Their members were drawn from small towns, and they did not emphasize class struggle, both of which factors may have inhibited growth. Their highest prewar membership total was about 400,000, and their strength was in the Ruhr, in Western textile towns, and among Catholic construction hands. As their minority situation grew more and more obvious, they insisted upon independent approaches, lest they be swallowed by the social democrats.

Hard line capitalists, particularly in heavy industry, set up company unions.[10] But despite funds from above, and privileges for members, these so-called "yellows" did not prosper.[11] Decades before workingmen had said: 'whose bread I eat, his song I sing,' but in the last years before the war bowing to patriarchalism was on the decline.

No matter how low the payments, Germany had been the first industrial nation to provide working people with social security. The better situated manual laborers, realizing that socialism would not arrive in their lifetimes, began looking for supplements. They found them through unions, successors to those gilds which had supported members in sickness, old age and other emergency.

The union pension funds presently began handling large sums. Between 1891 and 1920 the "free" unions paid out 120,000,000 marks in social benefits.[12] Of this 45,000,000 went for sickness, and 41,000,000 for unemployment, the latter being specially important because the Berlin government paid nothing at all. The old journeyman concept was preserved with the payment of 11,000,000 marks for travel. Apart from these social security funds there were strike benefits, of which 80,000,000 marks were distributed by 1910, which is to say two thirds as much. Many demands were made upon the strike funds, and the national offices watched them closely. Too large or too frequent walkouts might bring pressure to tap the social security monies. Bernhard Adelung who, as a printer, was a not untypical skilled laborer, wrote in his memoirs how these various payments softened life: "[social security benefits] cemented us together and made us strong."[13] The payments were made honestly and efficiently, and without the condescension to be expected from Wilhelmine officials.

A corps of desk workers handled the funds; in 1900 unions had 260 central office employees, which grew to 2,867 by 1914.[14] No scandals concerning these persons have been reported. What was more significant were the attitudes which those handling millions developed. Once poor boys, the union heads had become bankers. They became most cautious about their responsibilities and they were mistrustful of the possible demands of the members. Naturally honest, they now grew conservative in the defense of the funds they guarded. Above all they wanted to avoid political crises. The state had seized union treasuries in 1878 and had von Stumm had his way, he would have done the same around 1900.

All these onetime proletarians had become, through their own virtue and hard work actuaries, politicians and financial experts. It was only natural that they should wish to be compensated accordingly, though not on the scale of what a coal company executive might expect. Already by 1905 many union leaders were drawing more than 2,000 a year for their complex roles,[15] which was still only a third higher than the average Ruhr miners' pay. Subsequently their pay began to rise more splendidly, with gains regularly exceeding those of rank and file.

In respect of pay, the example had been set by August Bebel, the continent's most famous working class leader. While a politician, he had never relinquished his machinist business, and he was very well paid for his performance as orator.[16] His writing brought in a fine income; by his death *Woman and Socialism* had gone beyond a thirtieth edition. He had been the recipient of a gift from a will, and with it he purchased a villa on a Swiss lake, which was, for his day, a conventional opulence. Alexander Schlicke, head of the giant machinists' union, was a natural born bureaucrat, and it would have been surprising had he not had contempt for Bebel's ideas. But he doubtless believed that his services should be as well compensated as those of the party chief. In money as well as political rank the union chiefs were advancing towards 1914. In 1893 only Legien and 4 others from the unions belonged to the Reichstag *Fraktion* (delegation). By 1912 this number had increased to 36.[17]

These responsible union chiefs were part of a society headed by an emperor more conscious than most rulers of his role. The most popular institution in the country, the Prussian army, the coal cartel, even the Social Democratic Party, all exalted leadership. All German society taught that leaders should lead, and followers should follow. After a year heavy with strikes (1906), Schlicke explained this theory to his convention. His words hardly differed from Auer's after the Berlin beer boycott:

> Judgement about correct tactics requires the experience and observation of the trade union battlefield over many years. This sort of experience is possessed only by a small portion of colleagues, and principally by those who have the leadership of the whole movement in their hands. For this reason it is mistaken to leave the

> leadership to a group which has emerged out of an accidental election. Those offices which have to care for the means and support of a struggle are those which are called to its headship. Establishment of tactics in each individual case should in no circumstances take place in great assemblies, but only in the narrow council of war of the administration, and among those trusted men whose experience entitles them to this [role].[18]

Of 125 who listened, 72 were union employees.[19] Such conventions were, in fact, regularly referred to as "bureaucrats' parliaments."[20] These individuals could hardly be expected to endanger their jobs by objecting to his elitist emphasis. Adolph von Elm, veteran of the Hamburg strike, was another to say openly that because of their emotionalism the masses must not be trusted with the major issues.[21]

When the exclusion of ordinary members from decision-making was discussed, there was not usually mention of the type of question meant. But there were no quarrels over travel allotments, unemployment benefits and the like. Restrictive provisions were related to strikes. Since Legien had tabulated restrictions on the rights of locals to walk out, the list had grown.[22] Restraining techniques included waiting periods, required reports, secret balloting with high percentage required to start or continue a walkout, etc. In Schlicke's union this percentage was three quarters of all on the books.[23] As strikes multiplied, new methods were devised, the most favored of which was control of strike funds by the national office.[24] To keep locals dependent, union chiefs frowned on public collection of funds.[25] But when the number of men was large enough, and the intensity of feeling was very great, all these provisions could be swept away, as in the Ruhr in 1905.

The average machinist local had more than one thousand members, but the average number of these who engaged in offensive (*Angriffs-*) walkouts was rather small:

1900	75
1905	122
1906	114
1907	87
1908	41
1909	53[26]

Schlicke's association was evidently successful in keeping larger groups on the job.[27] The fewer who went out, of course, the more manageable the affair, the less the cost, the reduced danger of police intervention. There were also defensive strikes, usually aimed at overcoming pay cuts or worsening conditions. National offices were more likely to approve these.

In one decade Bebel had written books on Fourier, on the Moslems in Spain, and his history of women, for he was a literate man of the nineteenth century. The second generation of working class leaders, the desk-sitters, did not specially care for wisdom. As cited previously, the initial issue of the machinists' journal had said that the men wanted shorter hours and higher pay.[28] Union constitutions all had phrases about raising men up out of "spiritual misery,"[29] and the individual who enrolled might well have been the mental superior of those who did not, but such education was left to the individual, as it might not have been earlier. By 1913 Legien's *Correspondenzblatt*, which had begun with 16 pages, was now immensely expanded and had annual supplements to provide information: 220 pages of statistics, 224 on legal questions, 100 on proletarian literature, and 40 of addresses. One could not find in this principal journal of the unions, however, an analysis of their situation in the Second Empire, nor of the power of the Reichstag, or the place of the Hohenzollerns in German society, the nature of working class education, the situation of women, or any number of other serious issues. Long on organization, short on thinking, such were the German unions.

In being dull but diligent, German unions were not alone. G. D. H. Cole had described the "friendly societies" of Britain which proceeded the New Unionism of the nineties as follows:

> Societies of this type were compelled to have high rates of contribution and to be very careful of their funds. The latter obligation led them to discourage even justifiable strikes and forward movements, and to place all their reliance on conciliation and arbitration; [they] had an even more serious drawback in that [they] practically restricted their membership to those who could afford high contributions - that is, to a limited group of relatively well paid and highly skilled workers.[30]

Cole's was no mean description of Wilhelmine unions. The Second Empire census of 1907, the first in 12 years, counted just over 28,000,000 employed persons.[31] Of these 9.8 million were in manufacturing and the handicrafts, and 8.6 million were in agriculture. These figures indicate that after German unions became the world's most numerous, not 1 in 10 workers had joined. German unionism, like that of other nations, had more to do with not-belonging than with belonging.

The chief characteristics of that 90 percent who remained outside can be readily established. Unions did not thrive in heavy industry, as Krupp, von Stumm, Ballinn, Siemens and their colleagues took very great pains to keep their plants from being organized. Their methods were usually quite simple, but thoroughly applied. They paid well,[32] but were ruthless towards those who wanted to organize. It made the German unions appear weak that they could not crack Krupp or Siemens.

Most German working people lived far better than their ancestors; they were better nourished, their lives were more interesting, and they could look forward to 10-15 more years of existence than their forebears had. However 2,000,000 laborers on the fields of the East, most of them women, had been excluded from these gains.[33] This was especially true of homeless wanderers after the harvest, who never had suitable housing or medical care. They were fortunate if they saw 500 marks in a year. For those who labored bent over in the field, there could be no talk of self education or participation in civic life. Escape to the West, and particularly the Ruhr, was their only real hope of advancement.

Seeking new areas for increase in votes, social democrats began to take an interest in the farm laborers of the East. A union paper, *Landarbeiter*, began to appear, and publicize, for instance, that the injury rate on large estates, where much machinery was used, was nearly as bad as in the mines.[34] Each year 2,000 agricultural laborers died from work accidents, and 10,000 were injured. Likely the real rate was higher, for accidents could easily go unreported in the countryside. At best such field hands earned very little. One report from Mecklenburg said the men there received 240-350 marks a year.[35] No wonder the Ruhr could draw men from the East! In the East men could be fined for not bringing their wives to the fields, where they were paid much less than males.[36] At one of the emperor's *latifundia* women were required to toil 5 hours in the afternoon, receiving 40 pfennigs for their efforts, with each of their children receiving 20. *Vorwärts* found these conditions out of consonance with Wilhelm II's pronouncements that a woman's place was in the home.

Children were normally supplemental earners, and birth control was little practiced on the large estates. Sizeable families resulted, though with filthy hut for residence and heavy labor requirements there was a high rate of infant mortality. Little else was to be expected when a mother was required to be back in the fields a few hours after giving birth. In some areas up to 60 percent of the infants died.[37]

In prime season labor lasted from 4 in the morning until 9 at night. The hands were expected to recover off-season. Diet was often wretched, as in this recollection of childhood meals:

> Potato soup, buttermilk and potatoes, kohlrabi and potatoes, cabbage and potatoes, turnips and potatoes, potato puffs, potato balls, all in the finest potato harmony. Meat there was but once or twice a week, and then only a snippet.[38]

Toil in the land of the *Junkers* brought special humiliations and hazards. One estate owner's wife converted her morning milk bath into noonday soup for the hands. *Vorwärts* told of a man who was shot when he went to collect his back pay (1908). It was not a crime to kill a workingman in this area, and no charges were filed.[39]

These usually humble field hands did not develop the ability to express themselves which skilled workers did. Nonetheless, one of the finer memoirs came from Ludwig Turek, who spent many years bent over crops:

> Lack of [political understanding] weighed like an alp on the rural worker. He struggled bravely though all the petty troubles that a workingman has, yet I never heard of one who really had it out with a landowner. Among Polish migrants one finds a trace of class consciousness. If they ever had been particularly openly cheated, they would come together, put their demand to the masters of the estate, and not take up work again until their demands were realized. In general the Poles showed a certain recognition that only through sticking together could they deal with a *Junker* who had no conscience. Among German landed workers this kind of wisdom was a very rare article in prewar times.[40]

Over the decades the urbanized skilled workers who composed the party had occasionally made half-hearted efforts to evangelize among their rural brethren. But when the First International had, in a burst of ideological enthusiasm, approved collectivization of agriculture (1869), social democrats were burdened henceforth with the reputation of communism while not having gained one single vote thereby. For two decades thereafter they had been too absorbed in fending off Bismarck and the blows from the economy to venture outside the town base. Then in the 1890s there came a renewed push by Vollmar for peasant votes, and he needed something more appealing than the communist albatross of 1869. The dominant majority from Prussia, Saxony and Hamburg would tolerate no tinkering with principle and voted down Vollmar's bid to the peasants.[41]

From time to time devoted party comrades would use Sunday afternoons to hunt rural supporters. The narratives of such expeditions do not vary greatly. Sometimes the "reds" were run out of villages by rural police, but quite as often the alleged enemies of religion, marriage and private property were chased out with pitchforks and manure. These latter were not formidable weapons, but they did bespeak cultural differences. Urban and rural branches of the working class were raised, educated, married and, for that matter, exploited in quite different ways. They had antagonistic views on hundreds of matters. Down through the Second World War tavern owners kept peasants and proletarians in different drinking rooms, for the better protection of their property. *Junkers* and industrial lords found it easier to frame common policy than did those who created their wealth.

The Reichstag passed, with difficulty, a new public associations law in 1908, and it made unions possible for agricultural workers for the first time, though they were still forbidden to strike. Previous to this only 2100 rural and forest laborers had had the courage to join. The "free" unions now determined to make up for lost time (geographically, Catholic unions could not expect to do well). With enthusiasm Legien's *Correspondenzblatt* plagiarized Engels' 1895 comments:[42]

> From the day when millions of landed workers arise and demand full equality, a new epoch of cultural and human history will begin. From that day will come the collapse of the *Junkers*.[43]

Actually Engels was being over-excited. Those who have the Prussian army at their disposal do not collapse quite so rapidly. Union energies and subsidies were put to work, though there was a shortage of men with rural backgrounds who could campaign effectively. Strikes being out of the question, publicity and lawsuits were preferred. Newspaper exposes were sometimes useful, for the gross practices of the *Junkers* had rarely seen print in the past. A new monthly, *Landarbeiter*, began to make the case for rural proletarians.

The *Junkers*, who had often flattered themselves that they had loyal "hands," resisted. But they were not in the favorable situation of the coal cartel for they could not raise prices, being in competition with the freshly ploughed soil of Argentina, of the American Middle West and the plains of Canada. Paying their harvesters a decent wage would have put many an estate on the auction block. Fear for their own financial position was doubtless behind the often-expressed irrational claim that social democratic influence would make the Eastern peasants into poor soldiers.[44] Aristocrats worried as well that their laboring class would shake off its lowly view of itself: "All landed workers bear the mark of servitude throughout their lives," wrote Lily Braun,[45] who grew up among them. That old mentality, the product of centuries, and the power of the *Junkers* over the whole lives of their field hands proved far superior to the amount of force which the "free" union could exert. By the end of 1913, only 17,000 had joined the new union, and of them a mere 57 toiled on *Junker* estates![46] Before 1918 there was to be no major change for farm workers, male or female.

The 1907 census listed just over 10,000,000 employed women, a sharp increase from the 5,600,000 of 1882.[47] Of these 216,000 belonged to social democratic unions, with much smaller totals in the Catholic and Polish groupings. Thus not one employed woman in 25 had a union book. Of those who did, about a quarter were in textiles, but only 27,000 were machinists, which was the largest union of all, and had a major role in working class politics. Among 8.6 million who labored in agriculture (1907), 4,000,000 were female. However women were not union officials, and no one catered to their problems. No woman became a strike leader of note. Adding up the information on rural workers and on women, a tendency may be remarked: where unions were most needed, they were absent.

A liberalization of the associations law (1899) permitted women to join political groups. They no longer had to come to meetings disguised as men! Social democracy now did better than the unions in respect of cultivating women. Of its 1912 membership, 970,000 or 14 percent were female.[48] Yet they did not sit on governing boards and were scarce at national congresses. Clara Zetkin, who built up the women's tabloid *Gleichheit* to a circulation of 125,000, and Rosa Luxemburg, who had a great influence on party theory, gained their positions by force of character, not by grant. The heritage of the centuries was, after all, of male dominance, and the party had quite enough to do to assert itself politically without threatening to deprive proletarians of those helpmates who fed and cared for them after the 11 hour day, 6 days a week. Outwardly the second sex accepted this denigration, and the German feminist movement did not have the drive of the English or American.[49]

Very early Berlin had a women's political commission, and *Vorwärts* carried a particularly full account of 1892 meetings. Berlin 1 (the city was organized by Reichstag districts) stated that women could not even get the floor there.[50] They were often scorned, and always kept from office. Old timer Emma Ihrer remarked: "The equality of women is often recognized in theory, but now there is nothing for us to do." A worse tale came from Berlin 2, where males there were said not even to countenance equality in verbal terms. Berlin 4, a radical center, was a little better, Berlin 6 worse. When Lily Braun joined the movement she was advised, as a person of talent and energy, to devote herself to the men's movement, which she then did.[51] When Luxemburg came to Germany, she likewise scorned the women's sections. Social democracy was a male movement and did not do very well by the women. The seamstresses were allowed to go down in defeat, and only *Gleicheit* promoted the Crimmitschau strike as a way of helping women. Catholic unions stressed what was viewed as women's natural role, despite the evidence that German mothers worked by the millions in field and factory.

A third large group of the disadvantaged who might have profited from unions was that tenth of the population which was not German at all. The Poles, who were usually agricultural laborers, were the largest portion of these. There were also about 2,000,000 Alsatians and Lorrainers who were not regarded, save by themselves, as non-Germans. Danes, Sorbs, and Lithuanians came to an additional near million. Wilhelmine authorities considered all of these, save the Alsace-Lorrainers, to be second class citizens. Under stress of growing tensions, in 1908 a law required that all public meetings had to be held in German. Poles would sometimes gather in silence to make their protest.[52] This tenth of the population would also have profited from more organization. After about 1903 a new activism with many faces came to Germany. In its most innocent form, several million social democratic voters finally had the courage to join unions. Strikes also became more possible. In the mid 1890s there had been years when a stoppage by 16,000 was regarded as prelude to revolution. After 1905 German rulers, captains of industry and even union chiefs had to adjust to the increasing pace of walkouts.

In part employers adjusted by shifting tactics. The lockout now came to be more generally used. For example, in October 1905 several hundred electricians struck major Berlin firms, including Siemens, one of the giants willing to go to any length to block unions. Employers responded by locking out 40,000 men.[53] This was a puzzling situation for locals. At first they were backed by their national offices, and support funds were available to all. The Berlin metal working industries then indicated that they were ready to close the door on 120,000,[54] upon which the unions capitulated, to the discontent of many in the rank and file. The construction industry, breaking with its history, gave indications of worsening relations between master and men before 1914. When one of their national conventions voted to contest the next contract, applause was said to have shaken the building where the contractors were meeting;[55] their statement referred to "taming the arrogance of the unions." In particular they wished to bring to an end talk of reducing the workday to less than 10 hours. They also wanted to be able to fire men at will. The construction unions, among the oldest and best established in the land, with a record of making steady improvements in conditions, disdained to accept, in years of prosperity, such obvious "take-backs." Over 160,000 were then locked out throughout the nation in April 1910, and the central union offices declined to maneuver the men back onto the jobs.

The lockout did not proceed as well for the contractors as they had hoped.

There were many of them, and they had not ordinarily cooperated in the past, as each had reached his own compromise with his men. On this occasion Berlin and Hamburg bosses preferred to settle, and their action gave much impetus to others. By June other employers were signing regional arrangements which had been brought about by Germany's growing number of arbitrators. Here and there the men even managed to crack the 10 hour day. Union officials continued to back those who remained out in the long and costly battle.

A novel sign of prewar tenseness came from the partly working class Berlin suburb of Moabit. Here as elsewhere the price of food was creeping up, and, to protect themselves, 150 coal handlers asked for a pay increase from 43-50 pfennigs an hour.[56] It would have been an ordinary 7 pfennig affair, save that the owner of the firm was Hugo Stinnes. As soon as the men went out he hired strikebreakers. They needed private guards to do their work. That was not enough and police had to accompany the coal wagons. Finally 1,000 gendarmes were put to assisting not very many coal wagons. The entire Berlin force was put on the alert.

Such exaggerated deference to one multimillionaire stirred no little indignation in Moabit. It was not as if police were not often on hand during work stoppages. *Correspondenzblatt* wrote that between 1902 and 1911, the men in uniform appeared at a quarter of all labor conflicts.[57] Statisticians attached the name "strikes" to disputes which took but a day or two, and in other cases only a handful of men might be involved. Such insignificant affairs would hardly bring the men wearing the *Pickelhaube*. Therefore a more realistic figure would put the police not at a quarter, but at half of the strikes. When the police came, the strikers had no special reaction, for so they had been taught by their union and party, and they had no wish for bringing down trouble upon themselves. At Moabit in Fall, 1910, the situation was different, for Stinnes was involved, and there were simply too many police on hand. Stones were thrown, and shots followed. Two workingmen died, and scores of police were roughed up. Urban riots like this were rare since social democracy had obtained control over the working class, and killings usually occurred only in the mine fields.

In automatic and unthinking fashion, *Vorwärts* expressed its anxiety by blaming the outbreak on the unorganized.[58] Actually by 1901 there were few Berlin workingmen who were not attached to some organization, and the strikers were unionized. What appeared to be happening here was that an instinct for fighting was reasserting itself after a generation of social democratic bromides on peace and order. These small signs of rebellion had their similarity to what was happening in German art with the *Blaue Reiter* school, and both these tendencies extended themselves later in the Weimar Republic. In private the emperor raved that legislation to protect strikebreakers was needed,[59] but the Reichstag majority had no taste for new repression. Because of the bloodshed the Moabit strike was, however, lost and coal continued to be hauled at 43 pfennigs. Fourteen men were given sentences totaling 67 months which, given the bloodshed, was less severe than might have been expected.

Hamburg was also heard from in the prewar years. In August 1910 shipbuilders had gone out, seeking a 53 hour week with a 10 percent pay increase. After a two month strike, their union secured them a contract with two pfennigs an hour more and a 56 hour week. This was officially called a victory,[60] though the men may not have thought it such. The vote to accept was a close 1678-1475.[61] Subsequently the men claimed that their bosses were depriving them of some of these gains by altering job rating.[62] If true, yet another more sophisticated union-fighting method was coming into play.

The same shipbuilders grew restive three years later. Their firms offered 4 pfennigs an hour, to be spread out over many months. The men rejected the offer, and their shop stewards were then fired.[63] Against the wishes of their national (machinists) they struck in mid-July. Maintaining as usual that reason must prevail over emotion, [64] Schlicke tried to send them back. (In support of this tactic Winnig was to reason that the machinists' union, not being able to win large battles, had to confine itself to mock struggles, while explaining as little as possible to rank and file.)[65] When the men stayed out, Schlicke denied them support. Here, as on other occasions the national office, having control over money, turned into *de facto* employers of the strikers, with power to hire and to fire. The union heads enjoyed that sense of power but understood its limitations, and when the shipbuilders voted 5662-120 against him, Schlicke gave ground and began making partial payments.

To get the situation in hand, Schlicke called upon the heads of other unions for support. They readily joined him in condemning the walkout. He then called a special machinists' convention, which was to meet on his home soil in Berlin.[66] Here the Hamburg militants moved at once to change the constitution so that the executive would be obliged to back all walkouts.[67] Had this radical measure passed in the country's largest union, it would have had an influence upon the entire working class movement. However, the measure lost by a 3 to 2 margin, half of those present being on Schlicke's payroll. Evidently the majority of the elected delegates did favor stripping executives of the power they had been accumulating in the quiet years.

This initial emotional explosion by the leaderless and poorly organized radicals once out of the way, the majority began to insist on its program. Schlicke spoke to the themes of obedience and discipline, both greatly favored in Wilhelmine society. It was not possible, he declared, to run a large union if each local was to make its own judgements. He sought to have the Hamburg strikers condemned as rebels. They contended in vain that their work situation was worsening, and that a militant response was requisite. Many of the delegates joined in the tense discussion, and the chair permitted them to blow off steam. Then on the second day a cloture vote passed easily, for Schlicke had always had the votes. At the end he summed: was one to obey the law, which meant his office, or not? By now support had dropped away from the men of Hamburg. They lost resoundingly, 125-18.[68] A delegate from the Elbe River city then rose to say that out of solidarity and loyalty, he would endeavor to make the voting palatable at home. The convention as a whole had been a remarkable example of membership manipulation,[69] a craft at which Schlicke was most skilled.

The striking shipbuilders were angered by the report of the delegates. They felt themselves in a strong position, for the economy was prosperous, and there was a long backlog of orders. One after another, in Hamburg meeting, they rose to denounce the "hateful" attacks made by Schlicke and his deputies. Then, like the Ruhr miners, the Hamburg longshoremen, the textile hands of Crimmitschau, and scores of others who had been defeated, they acquiesced. To fight both the capitalists and their organization was beyond their strength. About 1,000 were fired, and the rest had to return without conditions. Thus as late as 1913, in a city with an activist tradition, men were still taking fearful financial and psychological losses when walking off their jobs.

There can be no doubt, however, that more of them were doing so. Between 1900 and 1904 unions paid out an average of 3,337,000 marks a year for strike benefits, in a period including Crimmitschau.[70] In the next 5 years the figure went up to 11,500,000, almost three times as much.[71] To say that men and women were three times as willing to strike after 1905 as before would not be far off the mark.

Union chiefs now felt able to reject social democratic tutelage as never before. The new balance of forces manifested itself on the general strike question. Swept along by the excitement of the revolutionary year of 1905, the party congress had given the approval to a general strike for political ends. This was no very astonishing step, for other European lands were already proceeding to the general strike itself. When Hamburg was about to be deprived of its equal male suffrage, there had even been a half day walkout there (1906). Meeting shortly after the party took its general strike decision, union chiefs knew not whether to laugh or to cry at the monstrous idea; they conferred privately for 5 days, in alarm at the radicalism of 1905. Legien assured them that Bebel had calmed down since backing the majority on the general strike.[72] Von Elm amused them with party press excerpts about the coming revolution; the Hohenzollern state was then about a dozen years from its downfall! Rexhäuser of the printers showed sensitivity to the view, upheld in these pages, that unions were primarily of service to the more prosperous workingmen. As to the mass walkout, he remarked, "give children a knife to play with, and they will cut themselves."[73] His metaphor suggested how the union men identified with the mentality of the patriarchal state. One and all these union chiefs showed contempt for those members who provided them with their daily bread, and spared them the harshness of the labor market.

Then having had it out with each other, they set about making the social democrats reverse their (qualified) 1905 approval of the general strike. Thirteen years after Legien had been roughed up at the Cologne convention, the party bowed to the unions.

Though there was a downturn in radical sentiment, 1906-1907, Germany was not again, in prewar years, as quiet as before 1905. In response to the pressure from ordinary members for some action, social democracy launched its first campaign for a specific, popular goal. This was to substitute a more democratic franchise (still all male) for the existing Prussian arrangement, according to which individuals paying the top third of direct taxes had a third of the electors, those paying the second third of taxes a similar proportion, while the mass of voters were in the third category. In 1903 males in each bracket of Prussian voters numbered:

First	238,845
Second	856,914
Third	6,006,204 [74]

The party liked to speak of this as "the most miserable of all electoral systems."[75] Such statements were a part of the regular exaggeration of the importance of universal suffrage which social democracy practiced. Although an equalization of the franchise would have been a serious psychological blow to the Eastern landowners, in practical terms the working class would only have gained another route for petitions. Nothing was ever said about the upper house, which had a veto power. But Germany was slowly growing more democratic, and the *Junkers* were coming to be hated more, and the party's vocalizing of these sentiments was undoubtedly excellent politics.

Social democracy not only launched its first campaign for a change in Germany, but allowed its followers to go out on the streets - as socialists had been doing in other European countries. The first wave of demonstrations came in 1908 in more liberal Saxony; *Vorwärts* crowed that "the masses have conquered the streets."[76] Tens of thousands were out, orderly, well-dressed and nearly all male. Police confined them to one side of the street. After a few more street marches in 1909, Hamburg led the way the following year, when 100,000 came out against the local three tier franchise.[77] In Frankfurt the demonstrators were set on by the police. *Vorwärts* complained that "they jumped us as colonial troops jump natives."[78] Social democracy responded, in the old free city, with a petite general strike and a demonstration of 60,000.[79] (Here, as elsewhere, it was the division of the streets into permissible and impermissible sides that most often led to skirmishing with the police.) Even the Ruhr had some parades in 1910, but there was no coordination between party groups in one city and another.

Berlin working people also went out. Here, at least, there was old line resistance to the new tactic. *Vorwärts* had greeted the Hamburg parade with the ancient warning: "Do not become provoked," which was a code word for "stay at home."[80] One of the journal's commentators argued that enemies of laboring people were trying to entice them onto the streets, and urged social democracy to hold true its real weapon, which was reason.[81] This view could no longer prevail and, after other cities had acted, Berlin party chiefs decided to go ahead. They went to the police to obtain use of Treptow Park,[82] but were denied. They then cleverly managed, despite the normal high degree of police spying, to assemble 150,000 in the *Tiergarten* before the gendarmes were aware. The rally was a most conservative one, however. Surviving photos show that the comrades did not carry provocative flags or banners, but simply ambled along in dark Sunday suits, usually with proper hat. By contrast with other cities, totals for Berlin demonstrations were well below voting strength, suggesting that party chiefs hesitated to frighten the government with their real numbers.

After 1905 the nature of social democracy was altered in yet another way, for a radical minority now appeared. In the past the party had simply expelled troublemakers, a policy which, in the new atmosphere, could now no longer be carried out. One could not expel the brightest mind in social democracy, Rosa Luxemburg, without causing more trouble than it was worth. She too knew how to hit. As a skilled botanist, she had remarked upon working class leaders:

> There are two types of living organisms, those who possess a backbone and therefore walk, at times even run; the others, they are invertebrates, who either creep or cling...[83]

If Bömelburg, von Elm or Schlicke read her *The General Strike, the Party, and the Unions*, they may well have been pained by the reference. Luxemburg was everything objectionable to them: Polish, Jewish, university trained, female, radical. But there was nothing in the history of the German working class to suggest that radicals might ever dominate save for a passing moment on a single issue.

In July 1911 the German naval vessel *Panther* appeared off French-held Morocco. With a complement of a mere 125, the ship was hardly threatening, yet it sufficed to make the case that Germany wanted more African territory. Despite possessing the world's most formidable army, the Second Empire, having come late to overseas conquests, possessed colonies of almost negligible value. The International Socialist Bureau, a coordinating committee for major working class parties, asked for demonstrations against war. As the party on the defense, the French responded at once, but the Germans held back, for they were notoriously indifferent to international issues.

The party had rather conventional reasons to hold back. As one Executive Board member reasoned, elections were due within a year, and too strong a stand against the Morocco adventure might hurt the party.[84] Elsewhere Hue told a provincial congress that Germany needed colonies; an imperialist line may well have been popular in the male aggressive Ruhr. Eduard Bernstein, however, contended that social democracy could do but little against a threatening war.[85] Radicals put on pressure and by September peace meetings, if not marches, were taking place. That was a breakthrough in the working class movement.

The struggle over Morocco protests prepared the way for the peace meetings of July, 1914, and the effort to end the war in 1917-18. But reining in the forces, and the passions, which propelled the Second Empire towards war was a task beyond the strength of peacelovers. Nearly all Germans felt that their nation did not have a place in the world commensurate with its strength. Faith in the Prussian army was limitless, and the nineteenth century had provided no memory of what conflict might be like. For working class males, there were good reasons to go to war, and Marchwitza, the Ruhr miner born in the East, put them well: daily labor was arduous, monotonous and filled with danger.[86] He would be at it, 6 days a week, until invalidism or death swept him away. Existence in the miners' town was drab, his wife was too fertile, and there was never enough money. These facts of his life made him ready for the quick march on Paris; the Somme and Verdun were not part of his plans. The distant voices of a few thousand advocates of peace would not be sufficient to send such a man back to the cable car.

Thus the strikes of the period after 1905 must be seen against a background of working class activism on a scale far beyond any since the beginning of social democracy in the 1860s.

The summer of 1905 was not a specially favorable one for Ruhr miners. They knew they would receive but little from the Prussian legislature, and the expected wage raises were slow in arriving. Then came the fire at *Borussia*, a mine without an effective ventilation system.[87] On the night of July 10, when there was but a small shift, the men were moving wood to brace tunnels.[88] Someone's petroleum lamp spilled flame onto the wood and a fire erupted. There were the most inadequate protective provisions. Water was unavailable in quantity, and chemical extinguishers belong to the future. The only recourse was to retreat into distant parts of the shaft and there to wait for death. The company had no special means for rescue. After hours of waiting for their fate, 39 miners roasted. Flooding was later necessary to suppress the flames, and the corpses of those who perished in far places were not recovered until 1906.[89] The horror of *Borussia* was well remembered in the Ruhr. The next strike began to grow from these tortured bodies.

In earlier centuries mine fatalities usually came a few at a time. Large scale tragedies have been the fruit of the industrial age's demand for energy. In 1972, following another massive sacrifice of lives *unter Tage*, the New York *Times* provided a table of the century's worst disasters. In 1942 under the Japanese 1542 Chinese miners had perished in Manchuria; there could hardly be a better example of the correspondence between the accident rate and the lack of political influence. A second, at Scofield, Utah (1900) killed 1200, many of them immigrants. Third on the list was the explosion at Courrières, Pas-de-Calais, which occurred just before *Borussia*. The mine was known, *Vorwärts* was to say, for bad air and immense profitability; in that March, 1906 explosion 1200 died. Courrières was a small place, and most of the male population was wiped out. Historians of French strikes indicate that this mass slaughter touched off one of the largest of all strike waves, as French proletarians conquered the 8 hour day.[90]

Back in Germany, a 1907 explosion in the Saar took 148 lives. Just 45 days later in the same region 85 men blew up, the following day 22 more.[91] These losses were moderate compared to what lay just over the horizon. Radbod was known as one of the worst Ruhr mines. The company there was notorious for being interested only in 'getting the coal out' (*Kohlen raus*). Only when inspectors were on hand was there attention to ventilation. Then in 1908 coal was down and so were wages, and that made the men neglect safety more than usual. The explosion came on an early shift; had it taken place but three hours later, the loss would have been over 1,000. As it was, that November 12, 348 miners died. This was the largest casualty list that the Ruhr had ever suffered. Radbod had to be flooded, and it was 4 years before operations could be resumed.

In 1908 Prussia still had one of the world's highest mine fatality rates, but before Radbod no great attention had been paid the problem. The miners now had an opportunity to put their case. They wanted to strike at once, but union officials succeeded once again in restraining them. Instead, as a cathartic, the Old Association held a special convention to bring out the facts on Radbod.[92] There was a national audience, through the press of various parties, for this gathering, where there was much talk of the principle of *Kohlen raus*. Men spoke of how rapidly the complement of miners turned over at this mine with the bad reputation. Old shafts were not closed off, and ventilators did not always function well. Men and inspectors alike who complained found themselves transferred, or relieved of their jobs.[93] So much damaging information was presented that prosecuting attorneys became alarmed. Some miners who had printed accounts of Radbod conditions were jailed,[94] but not one official responsible for any of the fatal conditions suffered imprisonment.

It was the large losses of life in the mines which exercised opinion in both proletariat and bourgeoisie. However the real losses came daily, one here and one there. "In the whole British Empire," wrote Engels in 1844, "there is no occupation in which a man may meet his end in so many diverse ways as in this one."[95] A 1910 Prussian survey of the Hamm district listed 1237 accidents, of which 186 were investigated, including 32 fatalities.[96] (Comparable figures for 1910 in the Dortmund district showed 42 fatalities; clearly neither area had a major disaster).[97] A dozen of Hamm's deaths were due to falls of coal or rock, and 7 more came through collapse of terrain. Two men were killed in dynamiting, four were crushed during transport of coal, one was gassed, one drowned, and one lost his life in a gallery fall. Sometimes death came suddenly, but at other times a mortally injured man could not be rescued and died in agony.

The special Radbod convention heard that of 750,000 German miners, 103,000 had had some serious injury the previous year.[98] For example, Max Lotz described how on the first day he went *unter Tage*, an individual had had his fingernail torn from its socket.[99] An uncle of Johannes Patt had lost a leg;[100] this happened in the 1880s, and since wooden replacements were hard to come by, the poor man had to get about for a time like a three legged animal. If there was not direct damage to the body, there was sickness and old age. A modern Bantu novelist writes of the South African gold mines, at least as dangerous as the Ruhr was, and very much hotter:

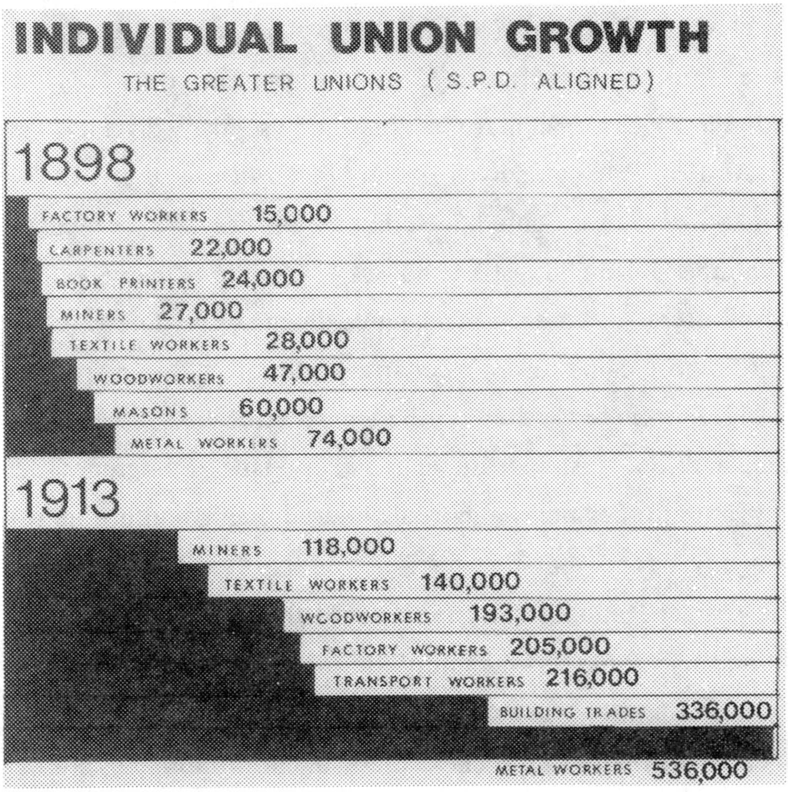
INDIVIDUAL UNION GROWTH
THE GREATER UNIONS (S.P.D. ALIGNED)
1898
FACTORY WORKERS 15,000
CARPENTERS 22,000
BOOK PRINTERS 24,000
MINERS 27,000
TEXTILE WORKERS 28,000
WOODWORKERS 47,000
MASONS 60,000
METAL WORKERS 74,000
1913
MINERS 118,000
TEXTILE WORKERS 140,000
WOODWORKERS 193,000
FACTORY WORKERS 205,000
TRANSPORT WORKERS 216,000
BUILDING TRADES 336,000
METAL WORKERS 536,000

> The mines are no good, Xuma, later on you cough and then you spit blood and you become weak and die. I have seen it many times. Today you are young and you are strong, and tomorrow you are tired and ready to die.[101]

In the last prewar years, the Old Association was still estimating that miners lived 11 fewer years than their forefathers who had been diggers.

Between 1886 and 1909, 172,362 German subjects were killed on the job, and 2,140,798 were injured.[102] Two thirds of these casualties came in industry, and the rest on land. Likely these figures were underestimates; they came to an eighth of the manpower Germany lost in the First World War. Fatal mining injuries passed 1,000 for the first time in 1898, and in 1912 they began to exceed 2,000.[103] No one claimed that German mines were, by act of nature, more dangerous than those in other advanced industrial countries, so it must be safe to claim that half German mining losses were preventable. But while social democrats might be enraged when employers' journals ascribed mine explosions to God,[104] yet they tended only to react when a calamity occurred, and the union did only a bit better, while concentrating primarily upon wages and hours. A likely issue was much neglected, and so men died.

Three hundred men, Walter Rathenau once remarked, held the economic fate of the continent in their hands (none of them the subjects of this volume). Among them were magnates of the Ruhr. Like the Japanese masters of Manchuria in 1912, they had colonial labor at their disposal, for their force was being constantly augmented by *Gastarbeiter*, i.e., Poles from within and without Germany, and lesser numbers of Italians and Dutch. With thousands always waiting to be taken on, the men of the syndicate could well yawn about stories of mining calamities. The failure of the working class to protect its own was to have pathetic wartime effects. When there was not enough to eat, and the experienced had departed for the trenches, the rate of injury rose sharply.[105]

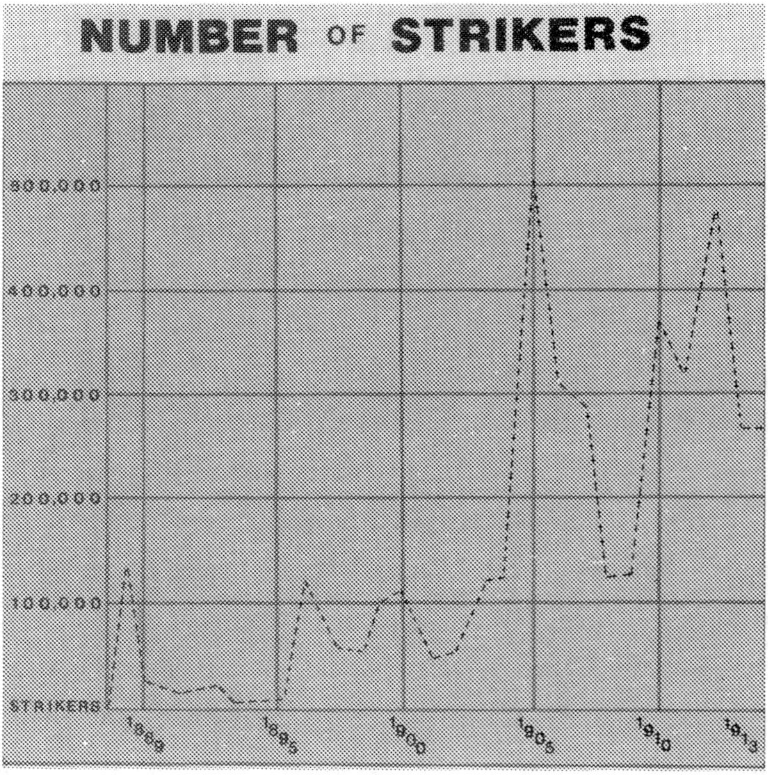
NUMBER OF STRIKERS
400,000
300,000
200,000
100,000
STRIKERS
1889
1895
1900
1905
1910
1913

Ruhr magnates, and others, sought to preserve their power through sponsored unions. They themselves selected the leaders of such groups, popularly known as the "yellows," and financed them as well.[106] Ordinary members had to pledge loyalty to the emperor, to the economic system and, in particular, to their own bosses. The chief activity of these company unions was social. Since the owners maintained that members' wages were all that could be expected , and that work conditions were excellent, such matters did not come under discussion.[107] Despite some small advantages which they offered, and the lack of hazard in joining, class consciousness kept company unions small in the prewar period. They hardly had 100,000 members. "Yellows" occasionally betrayed their *raison d'être*, as when they struck the Krupp docks at Kiel in 1910.[108]

More typical of the post-1905 era was the stirring of the Mansfeld coalies. Unlike the Ruhr, this was a historic area for mining. Hue recorded social struggles here going back to the time of Martin Luther.[109] These diggers tended to be traditionalists, and in the 1890s they had been wont to break up social democratic meetings.[110] However toward 1914 the lignite industry began its massive twentieth century upswing, which continues even today. It may have been this economic success of the companies, and the accompanying modernization which led the brown coal miners to join the mainstream in their trade.

Mansfeld employers demanded loyalty of their men, and company unions were as strong as anywhere. Newspaper tales, printed throughout the land, featured these fine, true, dependable German brown coal miners, so different from the 'reds without a fatherland' of ill repute. At Mansfeld the companies offered low cost homes, and thus acquired a fairly permanent force. So far they followed the precepts of Alfred Krupp. In respect of wages, they did not. "True to the Reich" lignite diggers received about a mark a day less than their counterparts in the Ruhr.[111] The companies here further cut their costs by employing children. The Old Association maintained that one in 20 was under age.[112]

Several times the social democratic union labored to secure a Mansfeld base. Nearly everyone was Protestant, so that was not an issue. The spy system was not as pervasive as in the Saar. These small advantages suggested that there might be a chance. Local events helped. Owners had raised wages to more than 4 marks, but the downturn of 1908 then led them to reduce pay again. This novel roller coaster action suggested to the miners that they might aspire to a higher standard. Already in 1907 preparation for action began as the Old Association put out a special brochure "Mansfeld Miner Awake!" Sachse and Hansmann came to speak for the Old Association in early 1909. Foremen were posted in the street to take the names of those who attended.[113] Sachse told them, in the course of a normal introductory speech, that rashness - he meant a strike - could cost them their jobs, which in Mansfeld meant home and garden as well. If a man was cut off at one pit he was then cut off at all, as was the way in the Saar, but not the Ruhr. The Old Association further warned against a walkout because it was a time of economic downturn.

Both in its political as in its union garb, social democracy was formally honest. Unending charges from the Right notwithstanding, neither party members nor their associations lied, made misstatements, or misrepresentations. In a decade hardly one leader would be caught in a personal misstep.[114] Yet here in Mansfeld, as previously in the Saar in the 1890s, a very hypocritical game was being played with the fates of the inexperienced Mansfeld miners. Believing strongly in the Reichstag, and fearing to adopt extra-parliamentary ways of functioning, it was important to social democratic leaders to expand into areas where they had earlier no footing. Such a one was Mansfeld. They would send a speaker to a previously barred area, an impressive individual of reputation, of prosperous and confidence-inspiring manner, full of ideas and of information and well able to handle himself on a platform. They had dozens such, of course. Like as not it would be a Reichstag deputy, and it would be made clear that he had once been a manual laborer. In his address this individual would stress the inevitable clash of workingmen and capitalists. His listeners, hearing him extol the class struggle, could come to only one reasonable conclusion: that it was time to take up that class struggle with their boss. The great Bebel himself had helped lead the ingenuous Saar miners to the slaughter in just this fashion. Once a strike began, of course, social democracy began to sing quite a different tune.

On October 10, 1909 a Mansfeld meeting voted 500-7 for a walkout.[115] Had it not been so dangerous to commit oneself, the majority might even have been higher! At first the men demanded but one thing, which was recognition of the union. They wanted to end the ignominy of being known as model company men, which they were no longer, if they had ever been. In this rousing moment 8,000 left the pits, though a roughly similar number continued to work. All the villages where miners lived were excited, for such an event had never come their way before. Local authorities were quite anxious and, as a center for imperial patriotism, had excellent ties to Berlin. They had asked for troops, and infantry were soon camped on the streets of Mansfeld. They were not ordinary soldiers, for they came armed with machine guns, a marvel of technology hardly 6 years old. Local inhabitants rode the trams by the encampments just to have a look at this wonder. Sachse later described to the Reichstag what he said were the absurdities brought on by this military occupation of a small town: women on domestic errands had to be escorted past the barricades the soldiers had erected, and men were picked up for appearing to blow smoke into officers' faces.[116] The Minister of War formally denied such incidents had taken place.

Through the later weeks of fall the struggle continued. The low pay, the resentment at the machine guns, the need to keep fighting in order to retain hope of returning to work, all had their share in this campaign. Then, as winter began, the Mansfeld miners drifted back. Their impulsive struggle had been broken. Several hundred were laid off when they came to reclaim their jobs. Yet the long run effects, of little use to those who lost their jobs, were quite favorable. Mansfeld's mentality had been transformed, and it was to become a center of union struggles for higher pay.

Since the 1892 debacle, pay had declined in the Saar, both relatively and absolutely. Corruption prospered as in no other mine field, and workers were as intimidated as *Junker* field hands. Neither unions nor social democrats could make headway. Yet now, a generation after the great defeat, doughty individuals began to reappear. One such was Krämer, who distributed his own leaflet critical of the mine management.[117] He received three months sentence for his pains.

Scenting an issue, social democracy rallied behind the man. A party attorney had the trial shifted out of the area of obvious prejudice. Summoning scores of witnesses, he established that individuals in the Saar feared to talk politics with their neighbors, that spies reported where a workingman drank his beer, and what paper he preferred. A sensation-hunting press, outside the party, and freer than in the past, began speaking of "Saarabies" i.e., conditions so bad that they could only exist in this benighted region. Publicity of this sort was intended to prepare the way for the union drive of the future, but the war intervened. *Vorwärts* speculated in 1913 of a possible strike,[118] but this was not to be. Improvement of the miners' lot was, of course, held back here, as in the Ruhr, by rivalry between social democratic and Catholic unions.

With its great numbers of miners, its Rhineland location, and the tradition of strikes, the Ruhr remained in advance of other fields. The difference in cultural backgrounds was in part overcome. Real politicalization of the valley commenced just after the turn of the century. Solingen and Barmen-Elberfeld, on the fringe of the area, had long been social democratic Reichstag seats, but were not really populated with miners. In 1898 the well-known Schröder, running against young Krupp for the Essen seat, had received only 4429 votes, hardly an indication of intense class feeling.[119] Greater evidence of working class strength came from Dortmund, in the western Ruhr, which had long had a strong party group.[120] Then in 1903 Hue made a breakthrough by taking the Bochum seat. From this point onward the Ruhr began to vote much more consciously for worker candidates. Political and other activity began to increase in every way. Union and party memberships were everywhere up, and so were purchases of newspapers. Open meetings were now held, for instance, on May Day. The Prussian ballot campaign helped stimulate activity, and then in later 1911 the party designated Rhine-Westphalia for special consideration in the following year's elections.[121] That attention was well repaid. In short, the party of 4,000,000 voters, and 2,000,000 newspaper subscribers, the largest political machine in the world, had overcome much of its earlier weakness in the continent's premier industrial center. This was the party of both Alexander Schlicke and of Rosa Luxemburg, and when it housed within its tent persons of such divergent views, there must needs be something which would appeal to the black-faced miners as well.

In 1911 the Old Association had 120,000 dues payers, nearly 30 percent of the Ruhr work force. That was a handsome improvement over 1905, both absolutely and relatively. Had Sachse been asked, he would have also explained that union property was now worth 3,711,000 marks, as against a mere 735,000 in 1905. The situation of the *Gewerkverein* (Cath.) had not improved comparably. Even more than the Old Association, the Catholics were perplexed how to carry on the class struggle yet be moderate. Among themselves they carried on an unending, wasteful haggling over policy, as their recent American historian shows.[122] Social democracy never consumed itself in such a fashion. The august and humane statement of Pope Leo XIII had seemed to point one way: "It is a capital evil to take for granted that one class of society is of itself hostile to the other, as if nature had set rich and poor against each other to fight fiercely in implacable warfare." Yet the miners lived under the tutelage of Stinnes, Kirdorf and the Krupp family, and what they learned in this school made it most difficult to accept such a mild and conciliatory doctrine. In the unions the advantage lay with those who preached hatred of capitalism, rather than with those who rejected that "materialist" preachment, though the predominance of the first belief over the second took some decades to assert itself completely.

In its first years the Works Association had been dominated by Brust, who spoke for class conciliation. Even his closest associates found Brust quarrelsome,[123] and after the Catholics were thrashed by the social democrats in the

1904 mine elections, he gave way to Johann Effert.[124] Fraternal troubles which had long plagued the Catholics now abated, but the union continued to be pulled in opposite directions. Effert apparently yielded to the class conscious side of the dispute when he made this long-remembered rhetorical outburst in 1908:

> ...at the beginning of the [next] period of prosperity in the Ruhr we will put on such a struggle as the world has never seen, even if it throws back the economy of our nation for decades.[125]

Down below, like enough, men talked like this, and Effert had been a miner for 15 years, but it was rare that an officer of a union should permit himself such heated words.

Just when recession was slicing Ruhr wages, the Center Party entered the Berlin cabinet, thereby putting its working class adherents under pressure not to rock the boat by striking. Though Center voters were usually working people and peasants, its Reichstag deputies came from the propertied classes. Thus it took a battle extending over many years before Heinrich Imbusch, longtime leader of the *Gewerkverein* and one of its historians, was considered qualified to run for the Reichstag.[126] Social democratic deputies, on the other hand, save for a few intellectuals who never showed themselves in the coal districts, were all men with gnarled hands who had once submitted to the boss's orders.[127] Thus the *Gewerkverein* had problems both with the Center Party ideology and with the individuals who represented that party.[128]

However the Catholic association had prospered since 1905, going up from 45,000 members to 84,000 (1911). Its property was now worth a million and a half.[129] Its electoral success was not the equal of its statistics. In 1904 contests for those "elders" who helped manage pension funds for miners, the two major union slates received votes roughly in proportion to their respective sizes. Then in 1910, though the Catholics had warmed to the fight against the cartel, they took but 83 posts, while the Old Association garnered 299, a dominating 74 percent.[130] It was a figure such as to revive Catholic fear of being swamped. The argument against materialism was no longer taking hold.

The social democratic miner Schmidt, in his *pro forma* and unilluminating memoirs, did make the remark that in Nazi times the men would chew over the causes of their downfall, the primary one being their earlier disunity.[131] Yet it is difficult to picture either party acting differently. Social democrats, with a membership composed of those working class men who turned their backs on religion as a result of nineteenth century thinking, Catholics who tried to assert the independence of a minority by emphasizing traditional religion, and Poles who were nationalists - how were they to combine when there was little sign from these times that an individual who once adopted an ideology would alter it? One effect of the continual fratricidism was nonetheless beneficial. Between Reichstag elections, and those for mine elders and safety inspectors, and with the unending campaign for more dues-paying members, the political atmosphere in the Ruhr was more intense than in any other major industrial district.[132] Many were educated to politics who might otherwise not have been.

A third of the crew *unter Tage* was now composed of *Gastarbeiter* and 100,000 of these 130,000 were Polish. Principally these men came from western Poland, in the territory between Warsaw and the German border known as Masuria. Here is one of the siren songs by which Slavic peasants were lured from their homeland and away from the sun:

> Masurians! In the Rhineland, surrounded by fields, meadows and woods, there lies, quite like a Masurian village, away from the great establishments of the Westphalian industrial region, a new colony consisting provisionally of over 49

houses and to be increased to about 65. In each house there are four living places, each of which has 3-4 rooms.

Each residence has a good dry cellar, so that fruits and vegetables may be easily preserved. There is also a roomy stall, where one may keep a pig, goat or chickens. Each family has a garden. Rent is four marks a room. But the mine compensates families at one mark per room for keeping roomers. Four men can be put in a room. Each family can earn money from those who stay with them.[133]

Hans Marchwitza was a not untypical migrant from the (German) east. He had been born in a scrawny, sooty, Polish-German village of Upper Silesia where all the families were poor, and wolves even worried the place in winter. Only the nobility had money. Everyone Marchwitza knew was tied to the mines. His father had been born a peasant, but went to the pits to pay off a debt, then stayed on for the better money and to avoid rural life. He had never been injured, but he made up for that with itinerant spells of drunkenness. When he was on one of his sprees all his pay, and everything from the house which was pawnable, went for alcohol. The family would have no bread for days. His foreman once punished him, on his return, with 12 hour shifts.[134]

Marchwitza's mother was a hard-working, loving woman who gave birth to 8 children, 4 of whom survived infancy. She was more rational than her husband, and denied the current belief the Jews were always seeking Christian children for their sacrifices. Her last childbed, coming when she was afflicted with tuberculosis, killed her. The household fell into disorder. When the widower brought home a stepmother who scrubbed everything, put quilts on the beds and flowers in the windows, the children combined to drive her out. They had been appalled by the atmosphere of sex which the old folks had introduced in the narrow quarters.[135]

Initially Marchwitza's family was met in the sleep-and-anger filled hour when miners arise. They had to find and don their moist clothes in the darkness, and then get their feet into hardened boots, while downing bread and coffee substitutes. The original mother soothed them all, while the younger children stirred. Over all watched St. Barbara, patron saint of miners, portrayed *unter Tage* holding the traditional lamp. At school Hans, along with the other children, was regularly beaten by a teacher who made the pupils memorize the names of Prussian victories. This pedagogue was a great admirer of the *Bergmann Stand*, which is to say, miners in their pre-industrial glory. Once young Hans and his friends looked forward to seeing Emperor Wilhelm II pass by; it was to be the greatest event in the history of the miserable village. Children froze by the side of the road for hours, waiting in their bare feet. Plans were changed and the emperor never arrived.[136]

Hans' father was proud when his boy, at age 17, decided to become a miner. The old man touted the greatness of three marks a day, and scorned his son's earlier dream of being a sailor. Now he had to rise at 4 and make the 7 mile trek to the pit, enter the filthy cage and descend into the darkness. His first assigned task was shovelling coal and pushing carts, and his hands were soon blistered. Experienced chaps told him to urinate on them, but nothing really eased the burning. Another problem was that he winced at every noise, whether from seams or supports. Only gradually were his ears to adjust to the various dangers, as men in the front lines came to know the sounds of various artillery. The first day down below he hardly believed he would survive. Sunday following he was in bed the entire day.[137] Soon he saw his first casualty, a neighbor whose head was flattened by a chance fall of coal. The foreman treated him as an animal, and occasionally struck him. The 6 day a week routine soon wore down the spirits of Hans and his young friends, who were not yet men. One of his buddies was crushed by a runaway cart, and another time the father of a comrade was carried out, never to return. Depressed by it all, Hans and his friends skipped a shift, and learned that it was pleasanter to lie in the spring sun than to go to work. They continued to report sick. Since they were obliged as minors, however, to turn over all their pay to their families, they were presently caught. Hans was not only scolded, but thoroughly beaten by his father. It took some hunting before they found another pit.[138]

Young Marchwitza had interests beyond the mines. He met a social democratic agitator, then rare in Upper Silesia. Against this man's advice he had himself tattooed, just as his buddies had, with an image of Wilhelm II. He joined a Polish exercise club, but withdrew when it was suggested to him that the members were "enemies of the Reich." Yet he befriended a little Polish boy who had been taken on at the mine with no questions asked. The lad was not up to the required labor, and was constantly being strapped. Marchwitza tried to spare him, and in gratitude was asked to the boy's home, where he was honored as *pan* or "lord." It turned out the boy was only 11, and he was released.[139]

In their late teens Hans and his friends began keeping company. For most of them sexual activity was very restricted, though one of his sisters had her babies by a non-legal husband.

One day an agent of the Ruhr companies camped out in a dirty hotel in nearby Beuthen. Like millions of other Germans, Hans had read the adventure stories of Karl May. Moving to another coal field might mean some little bit of adventure. The agent saw the miners one at a time. He called Upper

Silesia a "pig pen" compared to the paradise of the West. Hans signed his contract and then told his young lady that he would not return until he had made his fortune! As the special train pulled out of the station some of his friends put flowers in their hats. Their fare had been paid, and there was free *Schnapps*. Also there was surveillance, for drinking was approved, but jumping the train was not.[140]

After the long ride (sitting up), they arrived worn at their "Cape of Good Hope," where they were marched off to be domiciled in a barracks guarded by dogs. The reward for their migration was to be taken on at 4.2 marks, though the first months there were deductions for transportation. The mine was quite as those in Silesia, save that there were so many rats that they had to suspend their lunches from gallery roofs. The first pay went for clothes, so that they could appear weekends as dashing young bloods. Some cash also went to feed the one-armed bandits they discovered in the taverns. Over the years Hans' family periodically applied for a portion of the Ruhr gold, but it was rarely supplied. He was living on a higher standard now, and needed all his earnings.

The 100,000 Poles of the Ruhr had become an established community centered on Herne, Gelsenkirchen and a few other towns.[141] They had their own churches, with good fortune their own priests, and many organizations, but they did not break ties with the homeland. International events were moving more hopefully for them, since it was no longer illusionary to think that the Tsarist government, under which most Poles lived, might fall. Unions in Warsaw, Lodz and Cracow had an intense interest in nationalism, while inside Germany about 40,000 belonged to the Polish trade union (1912),[142] and thousands of other sons of Kosciusko had joined the two larger unions. Among these men belief in the class struggle was likely to run deeper than among Germans, and nationalist issues were felt as well. The Wilhelmine state labored constantly to keep that Polish love of homeland alive by trying to keep out priests from the homeland, by forbidding use of the beloved native tongue in public gatherings, and by other repressive measures.

The Hirsch-Dunckers had also shown a respectable rise in membership since the last strike, and counted now more than 3,000. Each union was growing now, including even the "yellows" (their lists more likely to be full of fakes than others),[143] and the small evangelical associations of working-men.[144]

Such were the organizations of the 400,000 Ruhr miners. They were disunited, pulled this way and that by different ideas and impulses, and were inexperienced in public affairs. Their history suggests that when they engaged in strikes, they tended to lack sufficient determination and persistence to win. Yet now in 1912 they were once again preparing to do battle with the powerful Rhine-Westphalian Coal Syndicate.

When the syndicate was founded in 1892-93, it presided over the production of about 33 million tons of coal. By 1910 that figure had risen to 90 million, out of a national production of roughly 160 million tons. Nearly a quarter of all German coal mined was exported, where it was sold more cheaply than at home, as internal customers financed the efforts of the cartel to take markets from British, Belgians and French.

In its first decades the cartel was ably captained by Emil Kirdorf.[145] It drew strength from having a seemingly permanent leader, as did social democracy. Under Kirdorf crises were regularly overcome, and all the major pits were within the fold. Despite bitter private disputes, the syndicate was ever able to show a united face to the public, to the state, to customers, and to those who produced the coal. The largest single holding was that of the Haniel family, whose owner was a diplomat, and whose mine was in the hands of managers. The Gelsenkirchen, where Kirdorf was in command, was second, producing 8½ million tons compared to Haniel's 9½.[146] Stinnes followed with 8, the Harpener concern mined 7, the once disputed *Hibernia* turned out 5 million, Thyssen 4 and Krupp 3. The Prussian treasury controlled a mere million tons. Strength within the syndicate tended to be in proportion to capital invested in coal and production, save for the giant Krupp interests.

By now those great banks whose risk-taking had done much for the growth of national industry, the *Deutsche Bank*, the *Dresdener Bank*, and the *Diskonto Gesellschaft*, all of them among the mightiest financial houses of the world, had a piece of the Ruhr. Their men served on the boards but, having arrived late among primarily family owned concerns, they usually controlled the pure coal companies, which were of less importance than the vertical giants.[147]

The great Ruhr magnates, those sheiks of yesteryear, continued to have the best of political ties. When less than 200 strikers challenged a Stinnes firm far from the Ruhr, the whole Berlin police force was put on the alert. Aside from the excellent ties to the bureaucracy illustrated in this way, the Ruhr barons could count on friends in Conservative, Free Conservative and National Liberal parties, making a veto of distasteful Reichstag legislation possible. The house of Krupp, once again in strong hands, continued to be close to the royal family, and made payments to high officials as well.[148]

The larger, more powerful, so-called 'vertical' firms dealt in both coal and iron ore, and their derivatives, such as coke. There seemed to be enough coal in Germany to last forever, but the same was not true of iron. The lodes in German Lorraine would run out in few decades, not a satisfactory situation for the masters of the Ruhr mines. Additional iron ore might be secured from France, Spain, Sweden or Morocco, but none of these could be depended upon in time of war, as became apparent in the years 1905-1914.

One solution was close at hand. A line drawn westward from Dortmund and extended 250 kilometers reaches the French coal regions of Pas-de-Calais. Turned southwest to Strasbourg, the same line provides the second side of a triangle. Then, in returning to Dortmund, it encompasses the major mineral resources of Western Europe. Here lay carbon and ferrous ore to supply a major industrial empire for several hundred years. Within this triangle there was ample water, excellent internal transportation, and access to both North Sea and Atlantic. Should a single state other than herself come into possession of this triangle, France would be at once reduced to a second rate state. The controlling power would then be able to press England and Russia hard, while preparing to contest with the United States for mastery of the world. Those most likely to comprehend the significance of this small area, and the opportunity it offered for world dominion, were of course the leaders of the Rhine-Westphalia Coal Syndicate, since they were every day occupied with problems of providing materials for industrial greatness. Their chief business had always been expansion, not coal. They knew how to build their private empires through concentration on the essential, and they were free of the usual businessman's anxieties over profit, loss, and market. Those matters could be cared for by assistants. During the First World War, as has been revealed by writers, and as drew the attention of the world when documented by Fritz Fischer,[149] leaders of heavy industry spoke often and forcefully in favor of German control of this region. It would be difficult therefore to think that they did not have the same desire earlier.

In the 1880s there had been scores of significant Ruhr firms, but in 1913, 82 percent of the miners were employed by a mere 11 companies.[150] Here too was shown that compulsion to dominate which beset the chiefs of the cartel. Social democratic and Catholic union leaders knew the ways of these willful men, but they had trouble finding the determination to oppose and restrain them.

The miners had retired in good order from the 1905 conflict. If some had been laid off temporarily, none had been given a long prison term. Everyone had a job, and the unions had members and cash. At first wages advanced only slowly, then in 1906 came a pay increase of almost 10 percent.[151] Even more encouraging was 1907, for by the fourth quarter a hacker could expect 5 marks a shift. It was the one post-1905 year when there was no hint of a walkout. A heavy industry source boasted that annual pay had gone up from 886 marks (1886) to 1553 (1907).[152]

But in 1908 the bloom was gone. Imbusch has pay declining 4 percent in that year, to a 1494 average.[153] The following year, a poor one, annual wages slid to 1350. The Commission of Seven, left over from the 1905 strike, decided against a new walkout, but did make the gesture, against the vote of the Catholics, of increasing dues for a "war chest" to be used in future conflicts.[154] The cartel delivered a further blow in the unhappy year 1909 by trying to institutionalize the blacklist. Much of German big industry had some way of proscribing the undesirables, indeed lists were said to go back to the 1500s.[155] Those of the coal operators were, however, the most notorious. A typical list was the one brought up to date on June 20, 1908, which carried each designated man by name, date of birth, and firm of last employ.[156] A final column showed the length of time he was to remain jobless. There were

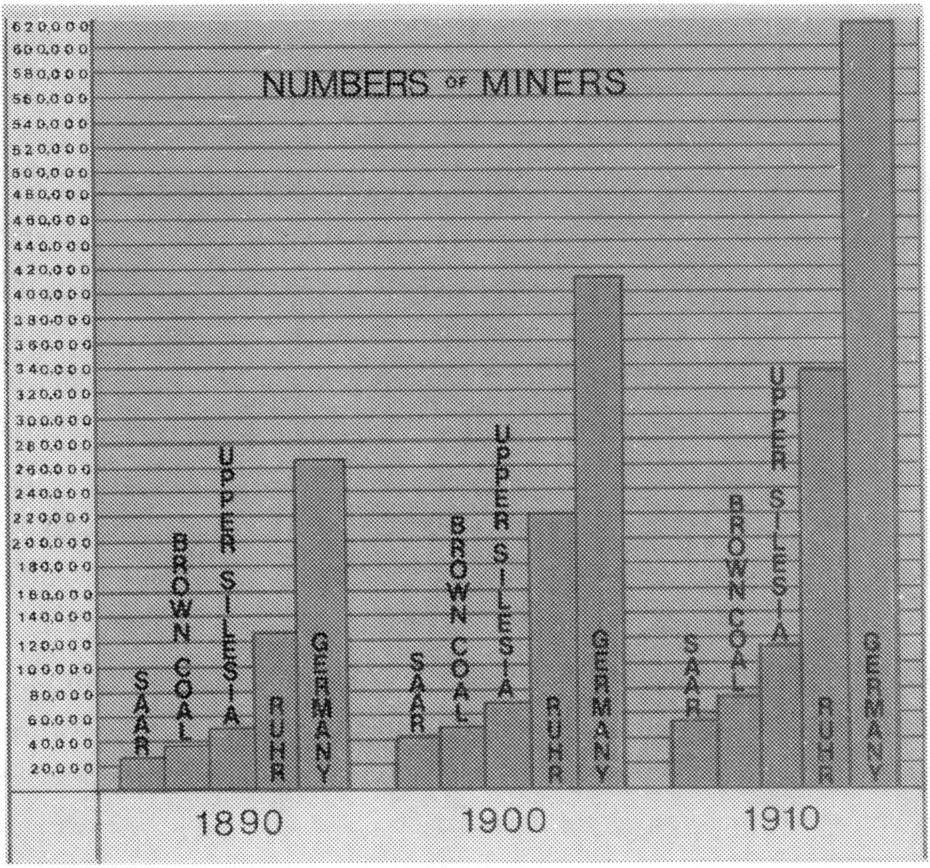

NUMBERS OF MINERS
620,000
600,000
580,000
560,000
540,000
520,000
500,000
480,000
460,000
440,000
420,000
400,000
380,000
360,000
340,000
320,000
300,000
280,000
260,000
240,000
220,000
200,000
180,000
160,000
140,000
120,000
100,000
80,000
60,000
40,000
20,000
SAAR
BROWN COAL
UPPER SILESIA
RUHR
GERMANY
1890
1900
1910

3,800 names on the roster, or a little more than one percent of the Ruhr work force. Unless they were specially in need of hands, the other firms accepted these proscriptions. Suspension was generally for several months. Just like the jailings of pickets for a few days, such private sentencing was not catastrophic. With a little help from family and neighbors, some money from the union perchance, the last supplies from the cellar and some skipped meals, the thing was done.[157] Compared to what happened to Schröder, Sachse, Warken and others in the 1890s, when the men were less feared, losing one's livelihood for a stated three months was not too bad. Unbeknowst to the victim, the time off may have added to longevity. But the blacklist was nonetheless hated with passion.

After the 1905 strike the owners naturally considered placing additional obstacles in the way of its repetition. It was not that they were suffering financial losses, but they felt damaged by the blows the men gave to their absolute authority. They decided to publicize the hurt a man would suffer by rebellion by making the blacklist, long subterranean, a public matter. A man was to be given three months for striking, and two weeks for quitting without notice. As public opinion viewed such matters in Germany, the right of an individual to nourish his family was highly thought of, in fact was well nigh inviolable. Furthermore the bourgeoisie, in the last years before the war, was developing a certain respect for human rights. The coal barons were disliked for their excess quantity of non-royal power, and now there was enough protest about the blacklist to make the cartel hesitate. The announcement was presently made by the coal companies that "workbooks" would be introduced. These records of an individual's employment had long been common. The miners were suspicious. When Marchwitza received his first "workbook," he checked it for surreptitious Braille marks which might have labelled him a militant.[158] The blacklist supplied emotional intensity to the 1912 strike, as *Nullen* had in 1905.

The economy improved in 1910, and shifts were slightly better paid. Imbusch put annual wages at 1,382,[159] a noticeable daily increase of 60 pfennigs over the previous year. There was no new aggravation for the men. Yet *Vorwärts* warned in familiar terms of "catastrophe" to come.

The crucial year, when men were making up their minds, was 1911. Wages were then still going up, and reached a level of 1,446 marks, meaning that industry was thriving, but that pay was not up to 1907. The men were also conscious that the cost of food was now 15 percent higher than in 1907.[160] *Vorwärts* put the ongoing inflationary rate at 5 percent a year. The *Gewerkverein*, ever mindful of what a man required to support his family, maintained that the miners had been cheated of 150,000,000 marks in recent years.

The idea of a walkout was hovering in the air, and in 1911 the Commission of Seven concluded that the men could not be kept in the pits forever.[161] Yet many union officials were running for the Reichstag in early 1912 and it seemed best to them to postpone.

The generational theory of the great mine strikes, as proposed in these pages, can be applied to 1872, 1889, and 1905, but is no longer of any use in explaining 1912. The men were now experienced, trained union members, like their fellows in other European lands. More than half of them had been out at least once. They knew that a walkout did not, as they had so often been told, involve a catastrophe. No state, society, union, or individual suffered irreparably from large scale Ruhr strikes. Thus there was no reason to store up emotional energy for a decade, to forget the wounds of the past, which were light, and to wait for new captains to arise. The baggage of subjection carried by working people over so many centuries was now palpably lessened. Instead there were several hundred thousand regular dues payers who knew what they were doing and who, since they had to, would be willing to go on strike to bring back the standard of living of the blessed fourth quarter of 1907. This was also a season in which German labor was feeling particularly aggressive. The "free" trade unions calculated that in the low year 1908 there were a mere 30 "offensive" strikes, but that in 1909 there were 170. In 1912 there were to be all of 352.[162]

The chiefs of the Ruhr unions, speaking for almost 250,000 organized men, met on February 5, 1912 to formulate strategy. The price of coal was rising, but wages were lagging. "We could no longer eat until our bellies were full,"[163] was miner Schmidt's uncomplicated analysis of why they went out in 1912. There was psychological pressure on the union chiefs, for the giant English unions and also the Belgians were going out soon. In this crucial meeting the Old Association, the Poles and the Hirsch-Duncker settled upon a demand for 15 percent more pay. Their other points were far less important: they wanted another cut in hours, and a final end to extra shifts (though the great majority were by now doing only an actual 8 hours *unter Tage*, as had been fought for in 1889). This light schedule of *desiderata* showed how much had been won over the years despite the formal intransigence of the cartel. How far the men had come was suggested also in a lesser demand that leasers of company homes not be required to take in roomers, which would raise their class position by giving them more privacy while protecting their daughters.

Leading the campaign for the 15 percent were the social democrats. They were not the same men as those of 1905, the year when Sachse had almost

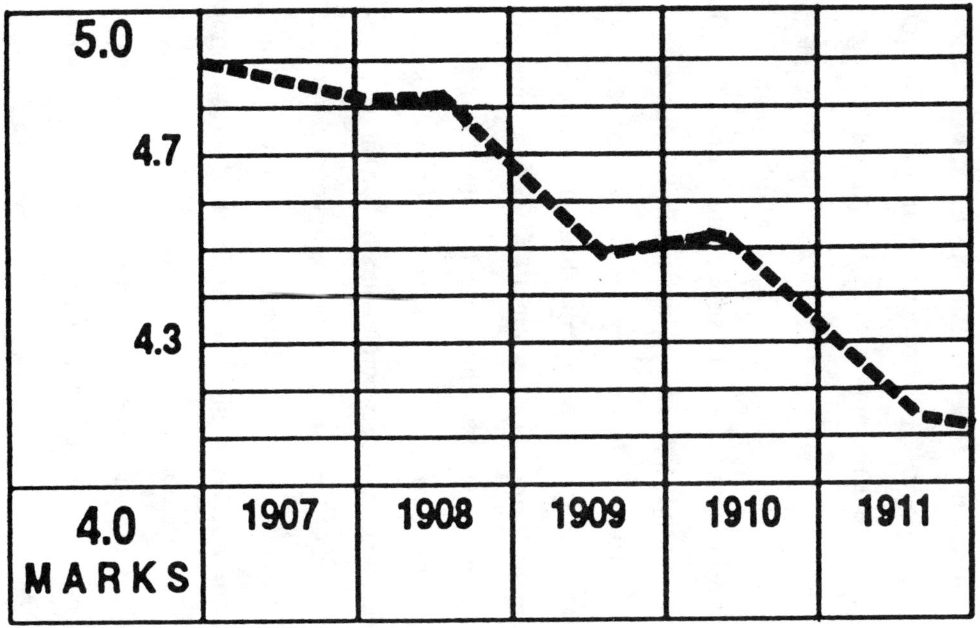

RUHR MINERS' WAGES 1907-1911

been roughed up by a mob of miners. Grudgingly he and his associates conceded the inevitability of class conflict, as maintained in party doctrine since time immemorial. After 1905 the efforts of Old Association officials had gone toward containing militancy rather than blocking it. Such was not the case with the Catholics. They argued that not everything had yet been done for a peaceful settlement. They pointed to the rumor that wages would increase, and they did not wish to harm their association in the meantime. Indeed, since they had a link through the Center Party to the cabinet, they may have had information on that point. They brought up the old argument, much utilized by social democrats, that the miners were not yet well enough organized, that it was not in the interests of the economy "at this time" to strike, and that England would use the occasion to undercut the Second Empire.

In the literature about the 1912 strike England is often cited. The mine owners were to accuse the strikers of having left the pits out of sympathy with their British colleagues;[164] Catholic *Germania* echoed the charge, a ludicrous accusation, yet not untypical of the overheated nationalism of the times.[165] At various moments from 1791 down to 1905, German militants had accepted a lead from abroad, in the sense that when proletarians in other lands were on the move, Germans became aroused as well. Not in the sense that there was ever any significant contact between leaders of two lands, or between rank and file. The only cases of German proletarians in concert with colleagues abroad occurred in the minds of anxiety-ridden conservatives. If anything, German workingmen were more parochial than others, and the summons, "Workers of the world, unite!", was not very well respected in the Second Empire. As for England in 1912, Germans were gaining a heightened consciousness about the empire which controlled a quarter of the world. Even *Vorwärts* joined that chorus in unaccustomed fashion, unwantonly comparing the proletarian standard of living at home with that in the British Isles, to the advantage of the latter.[166]

If the miners had improved their position since 1905, so had the owners. The syndicate had also its usual advantages: finances of the several companies were strong, leadership as well, there was determination and discipline in the ranks, and there were powerful friends in Berlin. The companies had had the sagacity to pile up a 5-6 weeks supply of their product, the better to hold out against a walkout.[167] If, in the prewar decade liberalism was on the march, there was a less numerous but infinitely more potent strengthening of the Right.[168] What aided the magnates yet more was the disarray in working class ranks. That lack of unity had been magnified by the cartel, first with the suggestion of a spring wage rise, followed by a *dementi* in the *Rheinisch-Westfälische Zeitung*. It was this maneuver which lent plausibility to the Catholic position. In the end of ends, the magnates could announce a pay increase in the neighborhood of 8 percent, and this would not harm them financially. They would, of course, grant such an increase when it suited them. That which was to be avoided, however, was a situation in which they would finally 'have to put their feet under the same table' as Sachse, Hue and Moravski (of the Poles). Their circumstances being so strong, the men of the syndicate acted calmly and avoided the provocative declarations which had cost them public support during other strikes.

On the first of March more than 1,000,000 miners, who labored for the multitudinous British companies, left their jobs, part of the massive strike wave which hit England in the immediate prewar years. A visiting reporter for the *Rheinisch-Westfälische Zeitung* marvelled at how placidly the country took the affair.[169] If the Old Association bosses had any last doubts about calling their first major strike, events in England now carried them along. In fact, social democrats could expect to draw advantage from a walkout of just three unions. For should mass enthusiasm bring on a successful stoppage their longtime rival, the *Gewerkverein*, might finally crumble. If things did not go well, they could simply break off the walkout - an action in which they were not without experience - and blame it all on that same *Gewerkverein*. There was nothing to lose. Since the strike was undertaken by leadership in part under compulsion, and in part as a gamble, they did not proceed to those actions which would have been useful preliminaries to a great class struggle. They issued no call to sacrifice and they did not appeal to the German proletariat for funds. Union chiefs had a long history of aversion to asking for sacrifice and for contributions.

At a final meeting the cooperating unions voted 507-74 to go ahead. A breakdown of the 13 percent nay-sayers between social democrats and Poles would be most instructive, but is not available. No rank and file assemblies to confirm this signal from second line leaders were held.[170]

On the occasions of the previous great walkouts, 1889 and 1905, the international scene had been relatively placid. But this time there had been the two Morocco crises, and the Balkan wars were beginning. Internally, class warfare seemed just a shade closer than ever before, as social democracy had begun to unleash its millions into the streets. A *Junker* spokesman had declared that the emperor must always be able to dispatch a lieutenant with 10 men to close the Reichstag. Sachse had not been honest in threatening 1905 strike leaders with troops if they did not end the struggle, but in 1912 the arrival of military, given the changed atmosphere, seemed quite possible.

At several pits miners quit working at the beginning of March. The Old Association sent officials to herd them back, as the men, just as in 1905, showed signs of high spirit. Then finally on March 11, with the Catholics still holding back, and the cartel as undisposed to talk as ever, the miners were called out. The coal owners' statistic for that day, likely an underestimate, was that 120,000 were striking.[171] As before, many of the others were looking over their shoulders to see what their comrades and neighbors were planning, or perhaps getting one last day's pay. More quit on Tuesday, and *Vorwärts* wrote that 250,000 were out.[172] A more accurate total was 182,000. That was well below the figures for 1905, but then most Catholics were going down into the pits.

Divided as they were, the miners were still threatening the German economy. They had the potential of bringing out the whole Ruhr, and then the other fields, as had happened very briefly in 1889. No other trade could have such momentous effect upon the national economy. A contemporary social democrat, analyzing the miners, found them distinct from other proletarians, in many ways an unsurprising judgement.[173] This commentator, Mücke, distinguished two minorities among them: the intellectuals and the alcoholics. The majority, he alleged, though given to emotional extremes, was neither.[174] When sociologist Levenstein polled miners whether they enjoyed their occupation, (not the best question he could have asked),[175] they responded 171-507, i.e., 1 against 3, that they did not. Seventy-one were indifferent. Those who claimed to like their heavy toil did so because of the higher pay.[176] Asked to specify what labor they might prefer, miners from the Ruhr, Saar and Silesia chose as follows:

mining above ground	141
mining	186
rural labor	263
independent labor	274
indifferent	333
highest paid work	343 [177]

Like Mücke, Levenstein claimed to uncover an intellectual minority, consisting of 1 in 5. A larger group, 1 in 5, claimed to read about socialism. These are remarkable figures, testifying both to the enterprise of the individuals and the educational efforts of the working class movement. In German writing of the time the Ruhr figures as a cultural wasteland, but there is evidence of the opposite, though the valley lacked university and orchestra. A tenth of the miners maintained that the movement had turned them into thinking people. A higher proportion, nearly a quarter, believed in a "revolution which would arrive shortly."[178]

As always, many found it difficult to decide in 1912 whether to leave work. Marchwitza and his Silesian friends were then new to the Ruhr and not unionized. They still lived in Willy's barracks, as did also the attack dogs. The first morning of the strike one of their comrades went from bed to bed, announcing gruffly, "Today no one goes to work."[179] The Silesians, however, while not hostile to the walkout, kept their own counsel: "Let these Rhineland-ers settle their own hash." They had come to the Ruhr solely to make money and resented interference. They had breakfast while Willy warned, *á la* John Smith, that he who did not work would not eat.

So far so good, but there was trouble at the gate. Already before dawn there was a crowd which jostled and denounced as "traitors" those heading for the cable cars.[180] Their doubts increased as they descended into the dark with but a small crew. Down below they continued to be hesitant. The overseer was polite, and this unseemly conduct unsettled them almost more than anything else that happened that day. They began to worry whether they would get back to their barracks safely, and it was not reassuring to be told that they would be leaving "with an escort."

When they emerged after their shift, only the police were there. They were instructed to line up in pairs, military fashion, and then they departed at a trot. As they passed through the town there were cries of "bread thieves," and everywhere windows were crowded with hate-filled faces. Stones began to come down off the roofs, and the police fled. They had to make it on their own. By the time they arrived at their base one of them, a natural rebel who had done time and who was now nursing a cut from a stone, had had enough. He refused to eat. Marchwitza followed his example, and so did the others.

When the waking hour came the next morning, Willy did not greet them alone. A foreman was there, and so were police. Thus standing in front of these sleepy recruits were their pay check, their food, and the threat of prison. All these powers, however, addressed them as "gentlemen," making their suspicions rise. The Silesians stayed in bed, saying not a word. After a while, still without their breakfasts as well as their suppers, they went out for fresh air. Circumstances were much against them. Experienced miners always had something to pawn, but they possessed hardly a change of clothes. They had only the vaguest of feeling of solidarity, for Silesia had no such tradition as the Ruhr, but they were much aware of their comrades' wrath. That which bothered them most was the question of food, and through the day they debated how they might get some victuals from Willy's stock. They hesitated for a day and a half, and then they found Willy tossing out uneaten food while they were starving. This was too hard to take. They set upon their tormentor

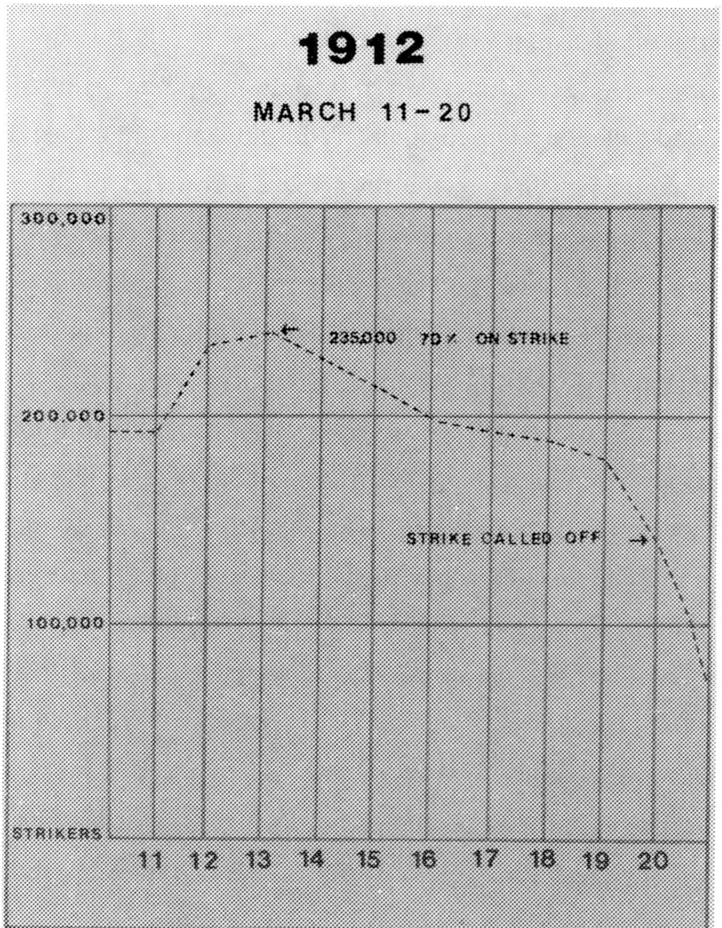
1912
MARCH 11-20
300,000
200,000
100,000
STRIKERS
235,000 70% ON STRIKE
STRIKE CALLED OFF
11
12
13
14
15
16
17
18
19
20

and his canines with fists supplemented by boards. So ended their sojourn in the barracks. Soon they found jobs in construction.

Marchwitza's account tallies with what is known of 1912. Crowds at the gate were large and more insistent than before. The unions had been indoctrinating the valley for 15 years against the use of force, but it was too native to the working class. Incidents were concentrated in the Hamborn area, where not only were stones thrown, but shots fired from houses. Windows were frequently smashed, but there was no Crystal Night.[181] The breaking of a scab's windows could never be spotted by police, and the editor of the *Arbeitgeberzeitung* lamented that there really was no way to protect strikebreakers in their communities.[182]

In the first days of the walkout the Catholic *Gewerkverein* was fighting for its life. Such was its own judgement, and also that of the cartel, which was much interested in its survival.[183] *Germania* wrote how men feared to pull their shifts.[184] Effert spoke militantly, suggesting that he might approve a strike in April, if there were no pay raises by then. Other Catholic writers used the argument that the walkout was nothing but a sympathy strike for the British. Whether any Catholics held back because social democrats had no record of carrying on a mine strike successfully cannot be said.

On Thursday, only three days after the strike began, 5,000 troops took up positions near the mines.[185] It was not bloodshed that had brought them, for there really had not been any. Nor were they needed for security, since extra police and deputized overseers were already on hand in great numbers.[186] In a moment of exceptional candor the *Rheinisch-Westfälische* conceded that no one who had seen the pushing at an ordinary shift change would be alarmed by what was occurring.[187] Rather the 5,000 infantry, complete with machine guns, were there to make clear to the already disunited miners that the Bethmann-Holweg government, unlike that of Bismarck in 1889 or von Bülow in 1905, had come down on the side of the owners.[188] While the strike persisted, miners' meetings were regularly broken up, some streets were blocked off, and blanks were fired on crowds. Yet only two were killed, far fewer than in 1889.

The companies, which had long been prepared, notified the men by postcard late in the week that if they did not return by Saturday, they would be fined 6 shifts' wages, an amount identical with Stinnes' 1905 penalty. On Thursday the total of strikers inched up again. The proportion of strikers varied by area. Sixty percent were out near Bochum, which was religiously mixed, still more around Protestant Dortmund, but only about 30 percent in black Essen.[189] Two fundamental facts had begun to take hold of the miners' minds: that the Catholics were not going to be pulled out of the mines, and that Berlin was putting its weight behind the cartel this time. If there were still miners who believed in taking the peasant's plea to the king, they could observe the answer in the streets of their town. Apparently this was going to be a harder struggle than the previous ones.

On Saturday, when the 6 shift fine took effect, most of the men, loyal union members, continued to hold out. Yet slippage was beginning. If the struggle was to end without agreement, as had always been the case in the past, there were those who did not want to be identified as *Rädelsführer*. Such troublemakers lost an inconvenient three month's wages, had to hunt another mine and, frequently, another house as well. The men began taking their own private surveys of who was going back, and the strike total receded. There was plenty of time on the weekend to consult, and the weekend was decisive. More men were back at work on Monday. Tuesday showed yet another increase in the work force. That night leaders of the striking unions met with their lieutenants. There could be little doubt what they would decide.

Division in the ranks, and the hint of a raise had made the 1912 conflict a very doubtful affair. Nor had Old Association leaders lost the habits of the decades, even centuries. If they had to have a strike, they liked to make their point and then get the men back to work. It might have been more astute to have sent the men back before the fines took effect, but the union may have lacked the strength to do that. There were always the militants to be reckoned with.

That Tuesday night meeting was seemingly dominated by men who worked *unter Tage*. Men who sat at desks were in the minority. The emotions of the workingmen present, and perhaps of all, must have been very considerably exercised. A stenographic account of the debate would certainly add immeasurably to an interpretation of how Wilhelmine workers felt about walking off the job, and about being sent back. The discussion ran well into the night. In the end 349 voted to continue, while 215 wanted to return. The reasonable rule of the unions specified that a strong majority, i.e., three quarters (385 in this case) were necessary to carry on the struggle. Actually the vote against continuing was much more decisive, since if the Catholics were added, only 35 to 40 percent were ready to fight on. No conflict could be sustained with only minority support. The Tuesday night vote confirmed the decisive action of those 35-40,000 waverers who had first gone out late, and then returned early. Men who voted with their feet had also been crucial in 1889, though less so in 1905. Hue remembered that old hands cried when they heard the strike was over in 1912.[190] It would be 7 years, most of them on a sharply declining standard of living, before the shovellers of the black diamond would go out again.

The 1869 law guaranteeing the right to strike to industrial workers meant little to men as strong as the coal magnates. The large number of miners who went back after 9 days had to labor for 6 more before being credited with a pfennig. Yet as in the aftermath of 1889, and of 1905, the brief walkout turned into a fine bargain, as the feudal lords were once again recalled to a sense of their obligations. Historians say that behind the French *ancien regime* lay an unspoken contract permitting the monarch absolute rule over the aristocracy providing they were spared taxation. Here the unwritten agreement was that if the black faces aired their grievances without truly challenging their masters, they would receive the best pay granted Second Empire proletarians. As a version of this demonstration-petition, the 1912 strike served very well indeed. An Old Association brochure designed to win members alleged that Ruhr miners gained 275 marks a year from their 9 day vacation.[191] That sum was roughly 10 times their fine. Another calculation put the profits to miners in tens of millions, once again a deal of which Stinnes or Kirdorf could well have been proud.

Social democrats had this time clearly called the miners out, and thus it could be alleged that the Catholics were "strikebreakers."[192] A ludicrous charge, for the Old Association had always done everything it could to keep the men on the job. Yet those who had not struck this time found it difficult to formulate an effective response. Catholic unionists, fearful of the reaction elsewhere in the church, did maintain, and it may well have been true, that "The union [i.e. the *Gewerkverein*] has been saved."[193] And when the benefits began to flow, they were also among the recipients. Curiously, however, when the next elections for elder were held, the Catholics made significant gains, in reversal of long trends.[194] Actually in the 1912 strike, no union felt free to act, and the reaction of members to this constrained situation might have taken varied forms. In the long run, nevertheless, it is clear that the Catholics lost ground by not going out. Then a year later they passed up the opportunity to organize the Saar where religious circumstances favored, and where there were said to be "conditions which make Stinnes blush" (Hue).[195] When circumstances in the mines seemed to call so loudly for class struggle, it was difficult for an association based on the conciliatory principles of Pope Leo XIII to find its way.

As before, the Rhine-Westphalia Coal Syndicate retired from the fray without harm. Future pay increases, not even promised as yet, would not hurt their profitability, and the *Rheinisch-Westfälische Zeitung* was able to observe that this time public opinion had not sided with the miners, an analysis which was joined in by the trade unions' *Correspondenzblatt*.[196] Legien's journal pointed out that there were now no 12 hour shifts, as in 1889, or *Nullen*, as in 1905, to awaken a bourgeois sense of justice. If miners wanted 15 percent to improve their living, why was that of concern to the middle class? The Ruhr was now generally believed to be well paid, and facts to back this surmise were readily available. Thus the cartel had done very well, for in addition to its political power, it was being better thought of. A more sophisticated approach and the restraining of public arrogance had yielded fine dividends.

The black faces of the Ruhr, nearly 400,000 of them, had done more than any other segment of the German working class to challenge the industrial system - as had other European miners also. They had striven with pertinacity and they had been successful with respect to pay. The level of Silesian wages, normally 30 percent behind the Ruhr, showed what could happen if that question was left entirely to management. A moment's reflection on the remuneration of the unwilling *Gastarbeiter* of 1942-44 might assist in clarifying that matter. In 1889 the Ruhr coalies had led the emperor to harry the Ruhr millionaires.[197] In 1905 they had done much to bring about an upsurge of union membership. Hundreds of thousands of German proletarians had sausage on their tables, and could drink of an evening with their comrades, and might even purchase a second dress for their wives simply because Ruhr coal miners had twice gone out on strike.

The British coalies had stayed out for months in 1844, even taking to tents after being driven from their homes. The next great British coal stoppage (1893) was a direct assault on the national economy, as was the giant walkout of 1912, in which a million participated. No such shattering strikes had ever occurred in the Second Reich. It was as if the men of Dortmund, Bochum and Essen played at class struggle. In the years 1880-1913 the average Ruhr *Kumpel* spent about a day and a third each year in labor disputes. But in the land of the Hohenzollerns the mere shadow of class struggle caused anxiety. That Neurode manager who yawned, "I have seen this sort of thing before," was a rare bird. A fear of disorder was abroad in the land, and that fear was more significant than rational statistical calculations about the occurrence of strikes in determining how often they would break out.

Since in many of their actions, German strikers were not very much different from their counterparts in Austria, England or France, and since they demonstrated on such occasions as Crimmitschau that they would hold out for months, it seems reasonable to conclude that German proletarians were capable of much more resistance than they offered. At the time of the 1889 strike, the miners were simply immature. The Hamburg dock strikers showed real toughness and perseverance. carrying on amid very difficult circumstances. At Crimmitschau sufficient fortitude to win was surely present. The Berlin needlewomen's effort, apparently bothersome to male chiefs, commanded overwhelming support and needed but a few days' assistance to gain a victory more important to strikers' lives than any other in this study. A month more and the Ruhr strikers of 1905 might have humbled the syndicate, with consequences for all subsequent German history. To gain some of these triumphs required sacrifice, but Germans were to prove in the years 1914-1918 how well they could do that.

National history was influenced, especially in the turbulent Weimar years, by the fact the Ruhr miners found it difficult properly to develop their strength. They were the most powerful proletarian influence in the Wilhelmine state, and with unity and leadership they would have been most formidable. Rousseau has written that in a well-ordered society men flock to assemblies - such was not the way of the Ruhr coalies. Rather they were as Schlicke characterized union rank and file: erratic, neglectful of responsibilities, and prone to emotional outbursts. Yet amid the brutishness and peril of their common labor there was born among them a *camaraderie* not unlike that soon to be developed by the men in *Feldgrau*. That fraternal unity, their courage, and the clear consciousness of being exploited, led to the willingness to strike. Had they ever overcome their historic differences and found ways to bring their wills to bear upon their union chiefs, their effect upon German society would have been incalculable.

Former mason August Winnig once insidiously suggested that the much prized discipline of social democracy had brought workingmen next to no direct gains. But a defeat of the Ruhr barons might have turned the Second Empire in the direction of self government. The second and third Ruhr walkouts both occurred during the campaign for a reduction of *Junker* strength in the Prussian parliament. A great union victory might have encouraged all those who were *de facto* second class citizens of the Second Empire to join in the struggle for self-expression, and for a higher standard of living. They would then have been better prepared to reduce the slaughter about to break upon their nation.

Historic circumstances, however, told against the possibility that the miners might do more than they did. Centuries before the industrial age, the Rhineland had been split in its culture, and that division by religion had not only held good into the nineteenth century, but was exacerbated by Bismarck. Then too Germans, especially in Prussia, had been brought up to a very severe discipline, and the industrial revolution had the tendency to consolidate further that devotion to orderliness. It had been a poor world for working people before the machines came, as suggested in this piteous Lennep striker's comment (1850):

> We have appealed to our masters for change of our condition, and have been pushed aside. Then we turned trustfully to the government and begged for help... This too was in vain.[198]

The progress made since such days had been much limited. The national tradition was hostile to popular movements. Unions were formed around the gild idea of social security, and the working class party taught, "Do not become provoked." History had provided the miners with very great potential power, but also with insufficient unity and willpower to capitalize upon their situation. Their weakness conditioned the debility of the working class in Wilhelmine times, and in the fateful and fearful decades to come. They had not gained the strength and the will to call out hundreds of thousands to defend or improve their standard of living or to express their determination on matters of policy as other groups and classes did, and to remain out till victory or defeat. Over the decades they had made progress toward the strike, but they had not come all the way.

NOTES

1. *Corrblatt*, October 1, 1906.

2. *Corrblatt, Statistische Beilage*, 1912, No. 3.

3. Paul Hirschfeld, *Die freien Gewerkschaften in Deutschland: Ihre Verbreitung und Entwicklung, 1896-1906* (Jena: 1906), 17.

4. *Corrblatt, Statistische Beilage*, 1912, No. 6.

5. Ibid., 1913, No. 28.

6. *Vorwärts*, March 25, 1910.

7. On the further development of contracts consult Theodor Cassau, *Die Gewerkschaftsbewegung: Ihre Soziologie und Ihr Kampf* (Halberstadt: 1925), 1880-1896; Siegfried Nestriepke, *Die Gewerkschaftsbewegung*, 3 vols., (Stuttgart: 1920-21), 1, 398-402.

8. For the bookprinters' first contracts there is Wilhelm Kulemann, *Die Gewerkschaftsbewegung: Darstellung der gewerkschaftlichen Organisation der Arbeiter und Arbeitgeber aller Länder* (Jena: 1900), 233ff.; also Karl Zwing, *Soziologie der Gewerkschaftsbewegung* (Jena: 1925), 43-44.

9. *Corrblatt*, February 16, 1913.

10. Hue, *Bergarbeiter*, 2, 550-57.

11. On the yellows: Saul, *Staat, Industrie*, 133ff.

12. *Corrblatt, Statistische Beilage*, 1912, No. 6.

13. Bernhard Adelung, *Vom Buchdrucker in Bremen zum Staatspräsident in Hessen* (Offenbach: 1952), 30-31.

14. Ritter, *Arbeiterbewegung*, 166-69.

15. Ernst Deinhardt, "Das Beamtenelement in den deutschen Gewerkschaften," *SM*, 11 (1905), 1020-21.

16. Kurt Koszyk points to Bebel's wealth in his *Deutsche Presse im 19. Jahrhundert*, pt. 2 (Berlin: 1966), 201.

17.Varain, *Freie Gewerkschaften*, 45.

18. Quoted in Fritz Opel, *Der deutsche Metallarbeiter-Verband während des ersten Weltkriegs und der Revolution* (Hannover and Frankfurt: 1958), 32.

19. Ibid., 31.

20. Idem.

21. Hue has an example. *Bergarbeiter*, 2, 647.

22. Nestriepke, *Gewerkschaftsbewegung*, 1, 398.

23. Otto Hommer, *Die Entwicklung und Tätigkeit des Deutschen Matallarbeiterverbandes: ein Beitrag zum Gewerkschaftsproblem* (Berlin: 1912), 7.

24. Alexander Wende, *Die Konzentrationsbewegung bei den deutschen Gewerkschaften* (Berlin: 1913), 33-34.

25. Around 1900 the unions moved to exclude outside contributions. Nestriepke, *Gewerkschaftsbewegung*, I, 386-87.

26. Hommer, *Entwicklung*, 82.

27. The inability of German unions to handle large strikes successfully was recognized by Cassau, *Die Gewerkschaftwbewegung*, 183-84.

28. Hommer, *Entwicklung*, 7.

29. Hue, *Bergarbeiter*, 2, 739ff.

30. Cole, *Short History*, 245.

31. Kuczynski, *GdL*, 3, 254.

32. The standard of living of Krupp workers is discussed in Richard Ehrenberg and Hugo Racine, *Krupp'sche Arbeiter-Familien*, Jena, 1914.

33. On the condition of landed workers in the East there is Georg Schmidt, *Lohnformen und Arbeiterverhältnisse in der Landwirtschaft*, Berlin, 1913.

34. *Landarbeiter*, 1913, No. 6.

35. Idem.

36. Schmidt, *Lohnformen*, 20.

37. Ibid., 22-23.

38. Franz Rehbein, *Das Leben eines Landarbeiters*, ed., Paul Göhre (Jena: 1911), 15.

39. *Vorwärts*, June 21, 1908.

40. Ludwig Turek, *Ein Proletarier erzählt* (Berlin: 1930), 35.

41. For Vollmar's efforts see Reinhard Jensen, *Georg von Vollmar: eine politische Biographie* (Dusseldorf: 1958), 56-63.

42. Friedrich Engels, "Die Bauernfrage in Frankreich und Deutschland," *DNZ*, 13^1 (1895). 305-06.

43. *Corrblatt*, March 1, 1908.

44. 'I hope you're not one of the bad types that goes on strike' propaganda was regularly used by officers on recruits, as collected by Reinhard Höhn, *Die Armee als Erziehungsschule der Nation: das Ende einer Idee* (Bad Harzburg: 1963), 354.

45. Braun, *Memoiren*, 1, 51.

46. *Corrblatt*, January 26, 1913.

47. Kuczynski, *GdL*, 3, 348.

48. Wilhelm Schröder, *Geschichte der sozialdemokratischen Parteiorganization in Deutschland* (Dresden: 1912), 58.

49. This is certainly the conclusion to be drawn from Evans, *The Feminist Movement in Germany, 1894-1933.*

50. *Vorwärts*, November 2, 1892.

51. Braun wrote of her visit with Wilhelm Liebknecht: "I told him also of my experiences with women." He laughed, good-humored scorn showing in his eyes. 'Shall I really give you

some friendly advice?' said he, "Don't worry about them, if you want to achieve something. They are more backward than the men, and it cannot be otherwise. How are they to understand anything, the poor women? IF, out of their proletarian instinct, they become good female comrades, everything has been done which can be done." Braun, *Memoiren*, 2, 44.

52. Wehler, *Krisenherde*, 236.

53. *Vorwärts*, October 11, 1905.

54. *Chronik*, 222-23.

55. August Winnig, *Der grosse Kampf im deutschen Baugewerbe 1910* (Hamburg: 1910), 96.

56. Saul, *Staat, Industrie*, 306ff.

57. *Corrblatt*, 1912, *Statistische Beilage*, No. 7.

58. *Vorwärts*, October 1, 1910.

59. Saul, *Staat, Industrie*, 311.

60. *Vorwärts*, October 7, 1910.

61. Ibid., October 9, 1910.

62. Ibid., July 14 and 16, 1913 also August Winnig, "Zum Streik auf den Seeschiffwerfen," *DNZ*, 321 (1913-14), 55-59.

63. *Vorwärts*, July 16, 1913.

64. Ibid., July 22, 1910.

65. Winnig, *DNZ*, 32^{1}, 58; also his "Zur Tarifbewegung in Baugewerbe," ibid., 311 (1912-13), 736.

66. *Vorwärts*, July 26, 1913.

67. Ibid., August 9, 1913.

68. Ibid., August 10, 1913.

69. An article by Bernhard Schildbach, "Verfassungsfragen in den Gewerkschaften," *DNZ*, 29^{1}, (1910-11). 327-332, discusses the ability of the union bureaucracies always to prevail in internal conflicts.

70. *Vorwärts*, January 19, 1906.

71. Ibid., June 25, 1911.

72. Legien's remarks were summarized in the protocol of the union chiefs' February meeting. *Vorwärts*, August 11, 1906.

73. Idem.

74. These official figures are reprinted from *Vorwärts*, May 30, 1908.

75. For information on this point, Paul Hirsch, ed., *Unter den elendsten aller Wahlsysteme*, Berlin, 1906.

76. *Vorwärts*, January 13 and 14, 1908.

77. Ibid., May 3, 1910.

78. Ibid., February 16, 1910.

79. Ibid., March 1, 1910.

80. Ibid., January 18, 1906.

81. Ibid., January 21, 1906.

82. *Vorwärts*, March 7, 1910.

83. From Rosa Luxemburg, *Massenstreik, Partei und Gewerkschaft*, 2nd ed., Leipzig, 1919.

84. *Vorwärts*, August 3, 1911.

85. Idem.

86. Marchwitza, *Meine Jugend*, 273ff.

87. Schmidt, *Lang war*, 46-47. He had worked at the *Borussia* pit. *Vorwärts* report came July 1, 1905.

88. Hue, *Bergarbeiter*, 2, 641.

89. There is a detailed discussion of mining accidents in this period in Imbusch, *Arbeitsverhältnis*, 129ff.

90. Shorter and Tilly, *Strikes in France*, 119.

91. Hue, *Bergarbeiter*, 2, 640.

92. *Bergarbeiterschutz Massengräber Radbod*: Protocol of the Mine Workers Association special convention of February 1-3, 1909 (Bochum: 1909), 24.

93. Ibid., 25-27.

94. *Vorwärts*, March 6, 1909 and October 30, 1910, has examples.

95. Engels, *Condition of the Working Class*, 249.

96. *Jahresbericht der Königlichen Preussischen Regierungs und Gewerberäte und Bergbehörde für 1910* (Berlin: 1910), 599.

97. Ibid., 601ff.

98. *Bergarbeiterschutz*, 7.

99. Levenstein, *Aus der Tiefe*, 42.

100. [Johannes Patt] *Ein Bergarbeiter-Schicksal* (Berlin: 1907), 50ff. In this slim volume tragedies greater than those afflicting most miner families are recorded. Of course, it is a document from the eighties.

101. From Peter Abrahms, *Mine Boy*, (New York: Collier Books, 1970), 13.

102. *Vorwärts*, August 11, 1911, takes this count from government figures.

103. Ibid., October 11, 1913.

104. Ibid., August 13, 1912, quotes a mine owners' paper to this effect.

105. The rising injury rate of the war years is noted in *1889-1929: 40 Jahre Bergbau und Bergarbeiterverband: Zur Erinnerung an die Grünndung des deutschen Bergarbeiterverbandes* (Bochum: 1929), 88-89.

106. Mattheier, K., *Die Gelben: Nationale Arbeiter zwischen Wirtschaftsfrieden und Streik*, Düsseldorf, 1974.

107. Mattheir has examples of how the Augsburg MAN firm, also Siemens and Krupp diverted the attention of the workers. Ibid., 65-80.

108. *Vorwärts*, March 16, 1910.

109. Hue, *Bergarbeiter*, 1, 308.

110. *Vorwärts*, June 4, 1891.

111. Hue, *Bergarbeiter*, 2, 681.

112. Suggested in *Mansfelder Bergmann, wache auf!*

113. *RV*, Leg. Per., 2 Sess., Speech of Hermann Sachse, January 18, 1910, 615.

114. *Vorwärts*, February 19, 1905, made plain that City Councilman Antrick, a party member, had to resign his post because of charges of adultery. Such irregularities as his were rare among social democrats.

Where Alex Hall, *Scandal, Sensation and Social Democracy*, (Cambridge, England, 1977) speaks of scandal, the references are to the conduct of others, not to that of party members.

115. Hue, *Bergarbeiter*, 2, 682.

116. *RV*, XII Leg. Per., 2 Sess., speech of Hermann Sachse, January 18, 1910, 615.

117. Hue, *Bergarbeiter*, 2, 630-31.

118. *Vorwärts*, January 22, 1913.

119. For reasons I do not understand, the party never gave Ludwig Schröder that safe seat which, after his many years of devoted service, he surely deserved.

120. On the Dortmund there is Ralf Lütenkirchen, *Der sozialdemokratische Verein für den Reichstagswahlkreis Dortmund-Hörde*, Dortmund, 1970. Unfortunately this volume contains rather little about miners.

121. *Vorwärts*, December 3, 1911.

122. For the Catholic argument check the pamphlet of Heinrich Imbusch, *Ist eine Verschmelzung der Bergarbeiterorganisationen möglich?*, Essen, 1906.

123. *25 Jahre christliche Gewerkschaftsbewegung, 1899-1924 (Festschrift)* (Berlin-Wilmersdorf: 1924), where the biography of Brust powerfully suggests his quarrelsome nature, 123-132.

124. Ibid., 242-46.

125. Quoted in Hue, *Bergarbeiter*, 2, 646; also *Corrblatt*, June 9, 1912.

126. *25 Jahre*, 211.

127. Matthias and Pickart, *Reichstagsfraktion*, 1xi., report that of the 1912 Fraktion 70 percent had been manual laborers.

128. Koch speaks sympathetically, in the Adenauer era, to the difficult position of the Catholic union. *Bergarbeiterbewegung*, 129-134.

129. Hue, *Bergarbeiter*, 2, 737.

130. Koch, *Bergarbeiterbewegung*, 109-10.

131. Schmidt, *Lang war*, 68.

132. Ibid., 67.

133. The leaflet has been reprinted in Fricke, *Ruhrbergarbeiterstreik*, 157-58.

134. The references from Marchwitza's *Meine Jugend* are as follows: wolves in town, 13; father a day laborer, 9; father's drinking, 11, 22, 61-62; punishment by 12 hour shift, 24.

135. Mother's disbelief in anti-Semitism, 30; her character, 32; her death from preventable causes, 63; chasing out the unwanted stepmother, 74.

136. Getting up early, 6ff.; education, 53-54; waiting for Wilhelm II, 36ff.

137. The decision to become a miner, 62; first day at work, 92; sleeping all day Sunday, 95; crushing of neighbor's head, 99; beaten by foreman, 94.

138. The group who skipped work, 105; beaten by father for malingering, 108.

139. The eleven year old miner, 130; meeting the social democrat, 137; the Polish club, 141.

140. Signing up for the Ruhr, with flowery departure and *Schnaps*, 144.

141. On the Poles of the Ruhr see Richard Murphy, "Polnische Bergarbeiter im Ruhrgebiet: Das Beispiel Bottrop." in *Glück auf, Kameraden: Die Bergarbeiter und ihre Organisationen in Deutschland*, Hans Mommsen and Ulrich Borsdorf, eds., (Cologne: 1979), 89-108.

142. Klessmann, *Polnische Bergarbeiter*, 266, counts 135,000 Polish miners in the Ruhr in the years just before World War I.

143. This opinion is disputed by Mattheier, *Die Gelben*, 128-149, but his figures are not meaningful inasmuch as his "members" did not need to go to meetings, nor pay dues, nor believe in the program, nor undertake any action whatsoever which would identify them as members.

144. Saul, *Staat, Industrie*, 168ff.

145. G. Werner, "Die Kapitalskonzentration im Ruhrbergbau," *DNZ*, 31^1 (1912-13), 141.

146. Ibid., 139.

147. Idem.

148. This official was Hermann Lucanus, Chief of the Emperor's Civil Cabinet. Consult Richard Owen, "Military-Industrial Relations: Krupp and the Imperial Navy Office," in Evans, ed., *Society and Politics*, 86, fn. 18.

149. E.g., as reprinted in Bölcke, ed., *Krupp und die Hohenzollern*, 150.

150. *Corrblatt*, May 11, 1913.

151. Hue, *Bergarbeiter*, 2, 667-68.

152. *Die Schwerindustrie*, 306.

153. Imbusch, *Bergarbeiterstreik*, 10.

154. Schmidt, *Lang war*, 66-67.

155. Hue found record of blacklisting in the sixteenth century. *Bergarbeiter*, I, 260. Legien attempted a brief history of the practice. *Koalitionsrecht*, 127-142.

156. *Schwarze Listen*, Essen, 1908.

157. Schmidt, *Lang war*, 64.

158. Marchwitza, *Meine Jugend*, 237.

159. Imbusch, *Arbeitsverhältnis*, 104.

160. Imbusch, *1912*, 15-16.

161. *Corrblatt*, June 9, 1912; Imbusch, *1912*, 14.

162. *Corrblatt*, 1913, *Statistische Beilage*, No. 7.

163. Schmidt, *Lang war*, 76.

164. *Rheinisch-Westfälische Zeitung*, March 11, 1912.

165. *Germania*, March 16, 1912.

166. For instance, *Vorwärts* for July 19, 1908 and July 2, 1912. Such comparisons were not made earlier.

167. Geoffrey Eley, *Reshaping the German Right: Radical Nationalism and Political Change after Bismarck* (New Haven: 1980), ch. 9.

168. *Rheinisch-Westfälische Zeitung*, March 14, 1912.

169. Idem.

170. Imbusch, *1912*, 25.

171. Ibid., 26.

172. *Vorwärts*, March 14, 1912.

173. Herman Mücke, "Einwirkungen der Arbeiterbewegung auf das Gemütsleben der Bergarbeiter," *SM*, IX (1912) 498-99.

174. Ibid., 1380-82.

175. Levenstein, *Arbeiterfrage*, 59.

176. Ibid., 59ff.

177. Ibid., 381-92.

178. Ibid., 298.

179. Marchwitza, *Meine Jugend*, 170.

180. Ibid., 174.

181. *Rheinisch-Westfälische Zeitung*, March 16, 1912.

182. *Arbeitgeber Zeitung*, March 15, 1912 (special issue).

183. *Rheinisch-Westfälische Zeitung*, March 17, 1912.

184. On March 14 the *Leipziger Volkszeitung* reprinted reports from Catholic sources that those who wanted to go to work in the mines were receiving insufficient protection. Such reports were normal in strike times, though they were not usually printed in social democratic journals. *Germania* noted on March 15 that women were even more active than men on the picket lines.

185. *Rheinisch-Westfälische Zeitung*, March 15, 1912.

186. Saul, *Staat, Industrie*, 274.

187. *Rheinisch-Westfälische Zeitung*, March 13, 1912.

188. This is the conclusion to be drawn from Saul, *Staat, Industrie*, 272ff.

189. *Rheinisch-Westfälische Zeitung*, March 13, 1912.

190. Hue, *Bergarbeiter*, 2, 717.

191. Entitled *Mit Herz und Mund für unsern Bund*.

192. This is what *Vorwärts*, said on March 20, 1912. The Old Association's brochure analyzing the strike, *Der Verrat des schwarz-gelben Gewerkverein der Bergarbeiter* (Bochum: 1912), concurred.

193. *Germania*, March 19, 1912.

194. Mattheier, *Die Gelben*, 135.

195. Hue, *Bergarbeiter*, 2, 619.

196. *Corrblatt*, March 2, 1912, conceded that public opinion did not back the miners that year. The *Arbeitgeberzeitung*, April 1, 1912, gloated over the same situation. The miners were no longer poor suppliants, but had become prosperous and active trade unionists, and thus were no longer granted the same amount of sympathy.

197. Kirchoff, *Die staatliche Sozialpolitik*, 56.

198. Klaus Tenfelde and Heinrich Volkmann, eds., *Streik: Zur Geschichte des Arbeitkampfes in Deutschland während der Industrialisierung* (Munich: 1981), 31. This volume, a collection of essays, provides many insights into strikes, but very few into miners.

INDEX